Testimonials

"*Humble Beginnings: A Photographic Memoir*. In many ways, this memoir is a love story! Love of life, family, friends, heritage, and of course, each other. Luzibu and Nsakala poignantly describe a beginning that for some, continues. The path travelled is surgically chronicled through photos and narration that collectively describe a journey that is inspirational, informative, and honest. They have provided a memoir that provokes self-reflection, a desire to strive against fate, and a recognition of the benefits of cherishing those who are important to you. That said, perhaps the most important takeaway for all of us is its challenge to embrace life, persevere, and thank God daily!"
— Dr. Awilda Hamilton, Emeritus Professor of Educational Administration,
Kent State University, Kent, Ohio

"I have known and admired Luzibu Nsakala for several years as a fellow member of University Women of Flagler, an organization that supports women of Flagler County in their pursuit of a post-secondary education. Luzibu is an active member who always avails herself in scholarship fundraising events. This attests to her deep commitment to education. So, I was delighted, but not surprised to learn of her, and her husband, Nsakala's project to create a memoir of their extraordinary and fascinating life. It will be both a legacy to their family and friends and a means of educating and enlightening those who read it."
— Trish Le Net, Retired French teacher in the US, Middle East, and France

"*Humble Beginnings* is a story worth reading. We are so lucky to share friendship with Luzibu and Nsakala. To know them is to feel the charisma of their life's story that is finally revealed in photos for everyone to learn from and be inspired by in our own personal humble lives."
— Mary and Greg Liljedhal, Tariffville, Connecticut

"Humble Beginnings: A Photographic Memoir is a trailblazing and illuminating autobiographical masterpiece. A much needed first of its kind documentation that speaks volumes on behalf of many who came from the continent during that time. This narrative of real lived history of Luzibu and Nsakala, who we were fortunate and indeed blessed to have witnessed since our serendipitous meeting at Penn State University, as fellow graduate students from the continent of Africa some fifty years ago, is exciting. We share a common background of being very poor materially but rich in the culture of hard work, determination, and discipline. This poignant illustrious work should challenge and spur many of us in the diaspora to write our own stories not only for family but also for educational purposes and posterity."
— Dr. Roger and Mrs. Josephine Chiza Gurira, University of Wisconsin, Platteville, Wisconsin

A few examples come to mind:

- The barefooted mile and a half or two to attend our first years of school.

- A shared sixty-kilometer, two-day hike from Luozi to Kibunzi to visit Luzibu and her family and Nsakala's family.

- Luzibu's first journey from Kinshasa to Cedar Rapids, Iowa, which made it possible for her to spend several months with my extended family to learn English.

- My hitchhiking from Iowa City to Nashville to visit Luzibu and Nsakala, then to Spring City, Pennsylvania, to visit Nancy."

—Carroll D. Yoder, Harrisonburg, Virginia

"We have reviewed the book, *Humble Beginnings: A Photographic Memoir.* It demonstrates what we have been telling each other regarding the authors' predisposition to well-meaning kindness to their fellow human beings. They have been building trusting and long-standing friendships throughout their lives. This is illustrated by the ultimate act of trust mentioned in the book: Luzibu and Nsakala agreed in 2012, per our request, to select a house in Palm Coast, Florida, for us to purchase. It was an act of enduring kindness to us, who are thankful and grateful to be in their circles of family and friends."

—Josephine and Edward Lusala, Palm Coast, Florida

"A walk to the front door of the home of Luzibu and Nsakala is a delightful experience. There are flowers of all sizes and shapes, with bursts of color everywhere. You cannot help but smile as you near their entrance. Luzibu and Nsakala are very much like their lovely garden. Both of them are cheerful and provide positive energy when you are in their company. And, like the delicacy of flowers, there is a gentleness in the way they express their friendship. I am proud to have had a very small role in their written and visual history and to be a member of their extended tribe!"

—Francine Smithson, Palm Coast, Florida

HUMBLE BEGINNINGS
A Photographic Memoir

Luzibu Lutete Nsakala
and
Nsakala ya Nsakala, PhD

To My Dear Friends Luzibu and Nsakala
This is for you

From humble beginnings
In a land far away
They came to the USA
Hoping for a better way

So, beginning a new chapter in life
They worked; they studied
And struggled through strife
And many times, along the way
They made new friends with
Whom life-long they would stay

They started their family
And through the years
They continued to prosper
Through laughter and tears

The experiences they had—Oh how many there were!
The homeland they would visit
And to new countries they would go
Even in retirement, travel they chose

And through it all
There always has been
In their minds and hearts
God, Family and Friends

To these two fine people
I dedicate this poem
It just goes to show
No matter how far you roam
Where you settle with family and friends
It is Home

—Louise Delaere, Palm Coast, Florida

Published by Mvibudulu Press, LLC
4 Fariston Place, Palm Coast, FL 32137

Cover Design by Alex Head / Draft Lab

Interior Layout by Alex Head / Draft Lab

Editors: Kirkus Editorial and Keyren Burgess (collaborative editor), Lisa A. Bannick (copyeditor) and Rachel Norfleet (proofreader)

ISBN: 978-1-7354350-0-8

Printed in the United States of America

This memoir is dedicated to Munlemvo Mitchell and Mukiese Nsakala, who occupy, all by themselves, a special compartment in each of their parents' hearts.

Contents

Foreword

Over the last twenty years, I have had a strong and wonderful relationship with Luzibu and Nsakala. Luzibu and Nsakala's son, Mukiese Nsakala, is married to my sister, Karell Rose. My husband and I live in the same neighborhood as the Nsakalas and enjoy getting together for the holidays or various occasions. The story of Luzibu and Nsakala is near and dear to my heart. This is because my parents and my two sisters and I also immigrated to the United States, from Jamaica, when I was five years old. Like the Nsakalas, my family has an immigrant story that is the fulfillment of the American dream.

The Nsakalas are a shining example of God's grace, determination, hard work, and integrity. Therefore, I was delighted to lend a helping hand when Luzibu and Nsakala asked me for advice about writing their manuscript, given that I had previously authored my book, *Long Journey to Freedom*, in 2015.

I am truly humbled by the opportunity to write this book's foreword. This memoir is a work of art and a story about two lives that are well lived! If you had the opportunity to meet the Nsakalas, you would agree with that sentiment.

There are few people who come across our paths who embody such amazing love and acceptance of others as the Nsakalas do. Their life story is a testament to the power of faith, family, and friendship. Additionally, the lives of Luzibu and Nsakala are also a reminder of the necessity and power of gratitude to God for every blessing that we have received, every relationship we have been privileged to have, every opportunity that we have been given.

The life stories of Luzibu and Nsakala began in humble villages in the now Democratic Republic of the Congo. As you will read in the memoir, these villages today still lack electricity, indoor plumbing, running water, paved roads, Wi-Fi drops, and all the amenities that many people in the Western world take for granted. The Nsakalas would later move to the United States, where they would experience both the beauty and the challenges of moving to another country and had to break through many cultural barriers to achieve the life they dreamed of. However, throughout their journey, their faith in God and each other, along with the help of many Good Samaritans, produced a life that is remarkable!

Please read the following pages slowly and reflectively. Think about your own life and the opportunities that are before you. My prayer and hope are that you, like the Nsakalas, will choose to live a life of humility, faith, and love that blesses others and leaves a legacy that will endure in the hearts and lives of others.

—Camille McKenzie, author and lifestyle coach, Palm Coast, Florida

Acknowledgments

Luzibu Nsakala (Luzibu) and Nsakala ya Nsakala (Nsakala) have met many people who have had a significant impact on their lives over the years. It would therefore not be practical to acknowledge every one of them personally. They hereby acknowledge, with gratitude, all those people whose names do not appear on this page but who have made a real difference in their lives in the Democratic Republic of the Congo (DRC), their country of birth; the United States of America (USA), their country of naturalization; and elsewhere in the world. The following individuals are personally acknowledged with affection and gratitude for their impact on Luzibu and Nsakala's lives and/or for helping in the preparation of this memoir:

- Madede Lessa, Luzibu's mother, for being the most positive and important influence in her life. She taught her to be a responsible, independent, loving, and compassionate person. She always encouraged her to be herself and to be true to herself. For all these things and more, Luzibu's mother was her hero.

- Basilwa Mathieu, Luzibu's maternal uncle, an influential spiritual leader of their church, who had the ability to touch many congregants' lives in the community, including Luzibu's.

- Bena Nsakala Ndunga, the first of seven siblings in the family, who perhaps had the greatest impact in the life of Nsakala vis-à-vis financial needs and education, among other things, in the DRC. He and his wife, Batunda Tusevo Esther, were the magnets for the extended family in the DRC. For all these things and more, big brother Bena Nsakala Ndunga was Nsakala's hero.

- Munlemvo Kinsumuna, the third of seven siblings in the family, who became a surrogate mother to the three youngest siblings, including Nsakala, when their mother died in the 1950s.

- Makinutewa Félix, an extended family member, who served/continues to serve as an intermediary regarding financial transactions and family affairs, among other things, between the overseas diaspora and the family in the DRC.

- Carroll D. Yoder, who served in the mid-1960s as a bridge to help Nsakala and Luzibu in their transition from life in the DRC to life in the United States. His family in Wellman, Iowa, served as a host family to Luzibu during her first several months in the United States. To illustrate the closeness of the Yoder and Nsakala families, Luzibu and Nsakala were invited to the Yoder family reunion in Wellman, Iowa, in 2018, as part of the extended family. Carroll received his PhD in French from the University of Iowa and now holds the title of professor emeritus of French at Eastern Mennonite University.

- Diampisa Bena, Nsakala's nephew, who serves as the glue that binds together the family in the United States. Diampisa and his wife, Lukiantima Josée Bena, are the magnets for the extended family in the United States.

- Karell Rose, Luzibu and Nsakala's daughter-in-law, for creating such a special relationship with the whole family that she is, in their hearts, like a daughter.

- Camille McKenzie, author, lifestyle coach, and motivational speaker, for advice on how to put together a manuscript and for writing the foreword section of this memoir. Camille happens to be Karell Rose's sister.

- Norma Rose, who also lives in Palm Coast, Florida, for her invaluable fellowship with Luzibu and Nsakala. Additionally, Norma is the mother of Karell, Camille, and Monique.

- Josephine and Edward Lusala, for thoroughly reviewing this book from the viewpoint of people who were born in villages near Luzibu's and Nsakala's villages in the DRC. Josephine and Edward also live in Palm Coast, Florida. They are extended family members.

- Francine Smithson, for thoroughly reviewing this book manuscript from the viewpoint of a former educator in the state of Michigan's public school system. Francine and Luzibu belonged to the same book club in Palm Coast, Florida. Francine and her husband, Ivor (Jack) Smithson, are good friends of Luzibu and Nsakala.

- Louise Delaere, for thoroughly reviewing this book manuscript from the viewpoint of a former executive administrative assistant of the Palm Coast, Florida, utility company. Louise, Francine Smithson, and Luzibu belonged to the same book club in Palm Coast, Florida. And Louise is also a good friend of Luzibu and Nsakala.

- Extended family members in various villages, towns, and cities in Africa, North America, and Europe, for their enduring love, which makes Luzibu and Nsakala feel special.

- Alex Head of Draft Lab, for his professionalism, integrity, and amiable demeanor throughout the design process of this memior.

Introduction

"A man's heart plans his way, But the LORD directs his steps" (Proverbs 16:9 New King James Version). The idea of writing an autobiography has been on the minds of Luzibu Nsakala (Luzibu) and Nsakala ya Nsakala (Nsakala) for a long time. They have bounced it off some of their friends and family members. Given the journey that Luzibu and Nsakala had taken from the Democratic Republic of the Congo (DRC), their country of birth, to the United States, everyone they talked to seemed to agree that the words "humble beginnings" should be incorporated into their book title.

After much deliberation over an extended period, Luzibu and Nsakala finally decided in early 2018 that they would stop procrastinating and get serious with the book-writing project. They settled on a photographic memoir as the book genre. They further settled on the memoir's audience: family, friends, and other people who might learn a thing or two from their message, conveyed principally through photographs. The English language adage "A picture is worth a thousand words" helped them decide that their memoir should, indeed, be a photographic memoir.

Luzibu and Nsakala spent more than six months going through their numerous photo albums, selecting and digitizing what they thought could be useful and tell a good story in their memoir. They also went through their picture databases in their personal computers and other electronic devices. In the process, they compiled more than four thousand photographs and created collages from some of them. Ultimately, they selected more than 638 photographs and collages, which tell their story, spanning more than five decades.

On Friday, October 19, 2018, they invited Mrs. Camille McKenzie, author, lifestyle coach, and motivational speaker, to their house for advice on how to put together a manuscript. Camille, who happens to be the sister-in-law of the Nsakalas' son, Mukiese Nsakala, came in not only with a ton of ideas of her own but also with written guidelines to writing a book (for example, *Get Your Book Done*, by Christine Kloser). Luzibu and Nsakala went to work, brainstorming potential titles, outlines, front and back covers, internal architecture, et cetera. They talked with family members and friends to refine their thought process. They came up with three tentative titles and a tentative outline.

In the course of conversations with Camille McKenzie; her husband, Chris; and her mother, Norma Rose, while eating dinner at a restaurant in Winter Park, Florida, on Thursday, November 29, 2018, Luzibu and Nsakala brought to the table the topic of their memoir. After some back-and-forth, the group came to a consensus on the book title: *Humble Beginnings: A Photographic Memoir*. This title still stands because it is so appropriate.

Part One of this photographic memoir deals with the lives of the authors and their families, friends, and acquaintances in the pre- and postcolonial Democratic Republic of the Congo (DRC), prior to their immigration, in the 1960s, to the United States. Parts Two, Three, and Four deal with their lives and those of their family, friends, and acquaintances in the United States, where they live today. The authors' story is told in this memoir in a topical chronology with the help of more than 638 photographs/collages.

Now, just imagine what life would be like in a village lacking electricity, indoor plumbing, running water, paved roads, Wi-Fi drops, and all the amenities that many people in the Western world take for granted. Further, imagine a six-, seven-, or eight-year-old child walking two miles barefoot, on hot tropical soil, to attend school. And, when this child returns home, exhausted from the day's activities, he or she needs to do required home chores before getting to do schoolwork under a kerosene lamp. These and many more amazing revelations will be discovered by the reader of this photographic memoir, in relation to the authors' humble beginnings.

Additionally, since the DRC is a French-speaking country, it would be more natural for a Congolese student to consider studying in a French-speaking country (Belgium, France, Guinea, Ivory Coast, Senegal, Switzerland, Luxembourg, etc.) than to go to the United States, where English is the national language. This language barrier notwithstanding, Nsakala immigrated to the United States in 1965 under the sponsorship of the African Scholarship Program of American Universities (ASPAU). And Luzibu would follow him in 1966, shortly after their marriage.

In the United States, both Luzibu and Nsakala worked extra hard and, with God's blessings, were able to overcome language and cultural barriers and achieve advanced academic successes. That is, Nsakala graduated with honors from Fisk University in Nashville, Tennessee, with a BA in chemistry and from Pennsylvania State University with MS and PhD degrees in fuel science. And Luzibu graduated from Morse School of Business with an accounting diploma and from Central Connecticut State University with a BS degree in accounting. They achieved these academic successes while bringing up two children, a daughter, R. Munlemvo, and a son, Mukiese.

Luzibu went on to work for the Travelers Companies, a.k.a. Travelers Insurance, as an accounting technician and for Ames Department Stores and Moore Wallace/RR Donnelly as a staff accountant. Nsakala worked for Combustion Engineering/Asea Brown Boveri/ALSTOM Power as a high-level research and development engineer.

Luzibu and Nsakala retired from their respective jobs in 2010 and moved to their retirement home in Palm Coast, Florida, where they live today. Even in retirement, Luzibu and Nsakala have continued to do much of what they did while working. Examples include:

- Maintenance of a high level of physical activity: they achieve this by working out at a fitness club; walking along streets, trails, and beaches; gardening; playing golf; et cetera.

- Hosting family and friends: they are constantly welcoming family and friends to their home with open hearts and arms.

- Domestic travel: they travel mostly to greater Hartford, Connecticut, where the majority of their family members live, though they also have visited other family members and friends in such places as New Orleans, Louisiana; Newark and Piscataway, New Jersey; Harrisonburg, Virginia; Wellman, Iowa; Melbourne, Florida; and Bloomington/Lexington, Illinois. They also have gone to other places for sightseeing: Key West and Orlando, Florida; Savannah, Georgia; and Charleston, South Carolina.

- International travel: they have gone on four cruises—three ocean and one river—in Europe and North, Central, and South America and many other trips in various countries in Africa and Europe.

- Giving back to the community: they continue to participate in a variety of charitable events through both church and their own initiatives.

Luzibu and Nsakala believe this photographic memoir shows they endeavor to live by such principles as:

- Do unto others as you would have them do unto you, the embodiment of the Golden Rule.

- Treat your family members like your friends and your friends like your family members and always give yourselves fully, do right, love mercy, and walk humbly.

Furthermore, this memoir shows that with hard work, persistence, support from family and friends, and God's grace, one can achieve a high degree of success irrespective of his or her first station in life.

To be sure, Luzibu and Nsakala's journey together for over five decades has been filled with events that have brought tears of both joy and sorrow. While some of the events that brought, for the most part, tears of joy have been duly illustrated in the memoir, some that brought tears of sorrow have not. Here are a couple of examples: (1) Since immigrating to the United States in the 1960s, Luzibu has lost her mom, father, and all her five siblings, and Nsakala has lost his father and four of his six siblings; and (2) Luzibu and Nsakala have had many of their special friends in the Congo and in the United States pass away. In all cases, Luzibu and Nsakala have continued to lean on each other and receive support from family and friends, many of whom are the subjects of this memoir. They depend on God for his grace and strength to overcome the many hurdles that they face in their journey.

Being first-generation immigrants to the United States, who came ashore with nothing but young minds determined to work hard in the pursuit of the American dream, Luzibu and Nsakala find the following quote by Robert F. Kennedy fitting to help anchor this memoir (CitizenPath,

2018): "Our attitude towards immigration reflects our faith in the American ideal. We have always believed it possible for men and women who start at the bottom to rise as far as the talent and energy allow. Neither race nor place of birth should affect their chances."

Part One

Life in the Democratic Republic of the Congo

Luzibu and Nsakala use Chapters 1 and 2 of this memoir to briefly describe the Democratic Republic of the Congo, their country of birth, and to also briefly talk about their lives in the DRC prior to immigrating to the United States of America, their country of naturalization.

1

Democratic Republic
of the Congo

The article "Democratic Republic of the Congo" (Wikipedia[a]) summarizes the history of this country. The DRC, which is in Central Africa, is named after the 2,920-mile (4,699-km) long Congo River, which flows through the entire country. It is a huge country that straddles the equator and extends over two time zones (see the next two maps). The DRC is surrounded by nine different countries, including the Republic of the Congo (also known as Congo-Brazzaville), Central African Republic, South Sudan, Uganda, Rwanda, Burundi, Tanzania, Zambia, and Angola, as shown on the map below. Its capital city of Kinshasa was called Léopoldville in pre- and postcolonial times, until 1971.

From east to west at its widest point, from the Atlantic Ocean to Lake Tanganyika, the DRC is approximately 1,100 miles (1,770 km). And from north to south at its longest point, from the Sudan (now South Sudan) border to the Zambian border, it is approximately 1,200 miles (1,931 km). The total surface area of the DRC is 905,355 square miles (2,344,858 km²) (Wikipedia[a]).

The Democratic Republic of the Congo is the second-largest country in Africa in total surface area and the largest in Sub-Saharan Africa. The DRC is only slightly smaller than the United States' lower forty-eight states, east of the Mississippi River (905,355 mi² vs. 970,014 mi²) (Map[a]); it ranks number eleven in the world (Wikipedia[b]).

The population of the DRC was 81,339,988 in 2017, the fourth largest of fifty-four African countries and seventeenth out of 194 United Nations member countries in the world (Wikipedia[c]).

Consider the sheer magnitude of the Democratic Republic of the Congo in terms of size and population. Consider further that this country is surrounded by nine other countries. Add to these facts that the DRC is one of the richest countries in the world in terms of natural resources (Democratic Republic of Congo's mineral resources); it is blessed with huge deposits of coltan, diamonds, oil, copper, cobalt, gold, uranium, and tin in locations seen on this map. All these ingredients make the DRC an important country in Africa, and, indeed, in the world. Consequently, any major geopolitical events taking place in the DRC would tend to have global implications, as has been the case from precolonial days to today.

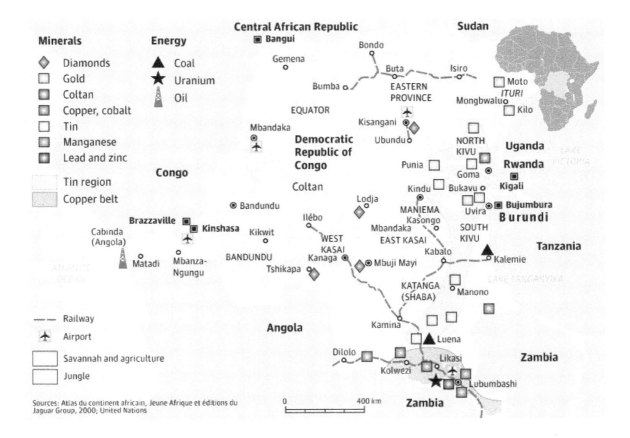

The article "Democratic Republic of the Congo" (Wikipedia[a]) summarizes the history of this country. Information from this and other sources (including Cornevin, 1963; Hochschild, 1998; Meredith, 2005; and other Wikipedia articles) will be used to present a brief summary of the history of the Democratic Republic of the Congo.

The Scramble for Africa, also known as the Partition of Africa, was the occupation, division, and colonization of African territory by European powers between 1881 and 1914. Prior to the onset of the Scramble for Africa, the present-day DRC comprised three kingdoms/empires (Map[b]): a portion of Kongo in the west, Lunda in the center, and Luba in the east, as shown on this map.

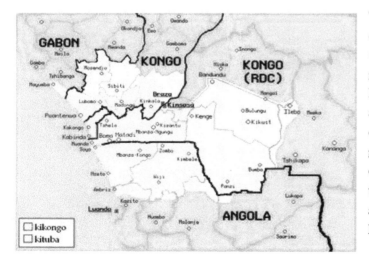

The Kongo Empire stretched over four different present-day African countries (Map[c]): Gabon, the Republic of the Congo (Congo-Brazzaville), the Democratic Republic of the Congo (Congo-Kinshasa), and Angola. The people from the Kingdom of Kongo belonged to a Bantu ethnic group, primarily defined as the speakers of the Kikongo language. The authors of the present memoir, Luzibu and Nsakala, actually belong to the Bakongo tribe. Kikongo is thus their native language.

In the 1870s, a Welsh journalist, Henry Morton Stanley, was the first to carry out the European exploration of the Congo territory under the sponsorship of Belgian king Leopold II. Thirteen European countries (Austria-Hungary, Belgium, Denmark, France, Germany, Italy, the Netherlands, the Ottoman Empire [Turkey], Portugal, Russia, Spain, Sweden-Norway, and the United Kingdom), plus the United States, were represented at the Berlin Conference of 1884–1885 (Wikipedia[d]), organized by Otto von Bismarck, the first chancellor of Germany. It was at this conference that the European powers divided Africa for themselves into various colonies, as shown below (Map[d]), without regard to ethnic/tribal boundaries. The Kingdom of Kongo, described in the preceding paragraph, clearly illustrates this point. That is, both Gabon and Congo-Brazzaville became France's colonies, and Angola became a Portuguese colony. And King Leopold II acquired the rights to the Congo territory (present-day DRC), which he named Congo Free State. King Leopold II used his colonial military unit, Force Publique, to force the local populations into producing rubber. From 1885 to 1908, millions of Congolese died as a result of disease and exploitation. In 1908, Belgium formally annexed the Congo Free State from Leopold II, renaming it Belgian Congo. Belgian Congo would remain a colony of Belgium until June 30, 1960.

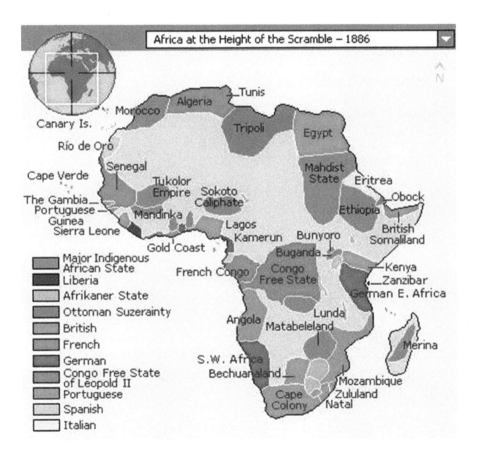

The winds of decolonization swept rapidly through Africa in the mid-1950s (Wikipedia[e]), causing widespread unrest throughout the continent. Africa looked as shown below (Map[e]) during this time frame.

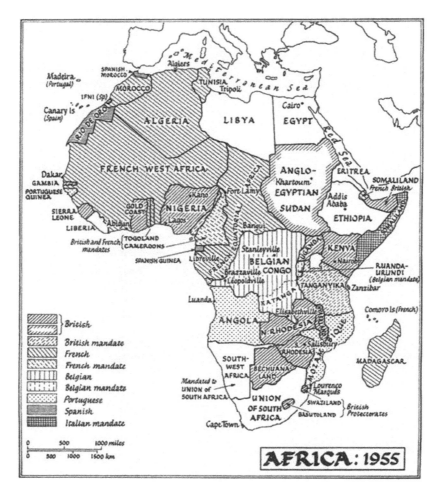

The Congolese political leaders of the day demanded that Belgium immediately grant the Belgian Congo its independence. After the riots of January 1959 in Léopoldville, Belgium convened a Belgo-Congolese Round Table (*Table Ronde Belgo-Congolaise*) in Brussels in January–February and April–May 1960. Some of the key Congolese political leaders at this conference were Joseph Kasa-Vubu, Patrice Lumumba, and Moïse Tshombe. Joseph Mobutu was there as a journalist and Lumumba's secretary. Besides the political leaders, Congolese tribal chiefs from the existing six provinces were also represented at this conference. The Belgian delegation comprised Prime Minister Gaston Eyskens, Vice Prime Minister Albert Lilar, Minister of Belgian Congo and Ruanda Burundi August de Schryver, Defense Minister Arthur Gilson, and Minister for the Civil Service Pierre Harmel.

At the end of the conference, a resolution was adopted to declare the independence of the Congo on June 30, 1960 [The Independence of the Congo (1959–1960)]. At this juncture, the newly independent Congo looked as depicted in the map below. The Congo comprised six provinces (Léopoldville, Équateur, Orientale, Kivu, Kasaï, and Katanga) (Map[f]).

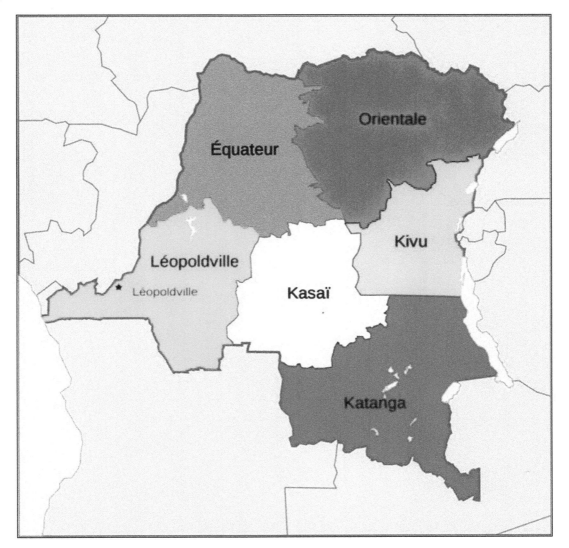

The four most dominant Congolese leaders at independence time are briefly discussed below.

Patrice Lumumba (Wikipedia[f]) was born in Onalua, in the Kasaï Province, on July 25, 1925. In May 1960, his political party, *Le Mouvement National Congolais* (National Congolese Movement), or MNC, won the parliamentary elections. Hence, Patrice Lumumba became first prime minister of the Republic of the Congo on June 30, 1960.

Joseph Kasa-Vubu (Wikipedia[g]) was born in Kuma-Dizi, Mayombe, in the Léopoldville Province in 1915. He was the leader of the political party *Alliance des Bakongo* (Alliance of the Bakongo), or ABAKO. The newly elected parliament elected him as first president of the Republic of the Congo on June 30, 1960.

Moïse Tshombe (Wikipedia[h]) was born in Masumba, in the Katanga Province, on November 10, 1919. He was the leader of the political party *Confédération des Associations Tribales du Katanga* (Confederations of Tribal Associations of Katanga), or CONAKAT. He would lead a secessionist movement soon after the Congolese independence and serve later as prime minister.

Joseph Désiré Mobutu (Wikipedia[i]) was born in Lisala, in the Equateur Province, on October 14, 1930. He was named chief of staff of the first Congolese National Army (*Armée National Congolaise*, or ANC) in June 1960 by Prime Minister Patrice Lumumba. He would eventually overthrow Kasa-Vubu and run the country dictatorially for over three decades.

Shortly after independence, the Force Public mutinied, and on July 11, 1960, Moïse Tshombe led the province of Katanga in a secessionist movement against the new leadership. The Republic of the Congo was thus plunged into crisis. Despite Tshombe's opposition, Lumumba asked the United Nations (UN) to send a peacekeeping force into the Congo in order to stabilize the situation. The UN peacekeeping force started arriving in the Congo on July 15, 1960.

Meanwhile, the more conservative President Kasa-Vubu and the more progressive Prime Minister Lumumba were always in conflict: one desired a central government with moderate powers, while the other insisted on a stronger central government.

On September 5, 1960, President Kasa-Vubu dismissed Patrice Lumumba as prime minister after Lumumba turned to the Soviet Union for assistance in the crisis. A few days later, the army forces loyal to Chief of Staff Joseph Désiré Mobutu arrested Lumumba, and on January 17, 1961, Lumumba was handed over to Katangan authorities, who reportedly murdered him.

In 1963, the UN peacekeeping force succeeded in suppressing Katanga's secessionist movement, thus sending Tshombe into exile in Northern Rhodesia (today's Zambia), then in Spain. In July 1964, Tshombe returned to the Congo to serve as prime minister in the new coalition government. The crisis continued unabated under Tshombe. After being dismissed by President Kasa-Vubu from this position in October 1965, Tshombe again went into exile. He died in Brussels, Belgium, of "heart failure" in 1969.

As political unrest continued under Cyrille Adoula, Tshombe's replacement as prime minister, Mobutu seized power in a bloodless coup d'état on November 24, 1965, deposing Kasa-Vubu and, subsequently, declaring himself head of state. Kasa-Vubu was placed under house arrest but was later allowed to retire to his farm in Mayombe. He died in 1969 in a hospital in Boma after a long illness.

A constitutional referendum after Mobutu's coup of 1965 resulted in the country's official name being changed from Republic of the Congo to Democratic Republic of the Congo. And, in 1971, Mobutu unilaterally changed the name of the country to Republic of Zaïre (*République du Zaïre*).

Mobutu was staunchly opposed to communism. Hence, the United States supported him, believing that his government would effectively counter the spread of communism in Africa. Mobutu took, over a thirty-two-year period, such drastic measures as, but not limited to:

- Establishing a one-party system, with his Popular Mouvement for the Revolution (*Mouvement Populaire de la Révolution*), or MPR, being the official and sole political party in the country;

- Holding periodic sham elections in which he ran unopposed for president;

- Carrying out human rights violations, political repressions, and freedom of the press bans; and

- Ordering all Zaïreans with Christian/Western names to give them up in favor of African names, in the name of "authenticity." He himself changed his name from Joseph Désiré Mobutu to Mobutu Sese Seko. In the same vein, he ordered a change in the names of cities and towns throughout the country. A sampling of these changes is given in this table:

Examples of Name Changes in Zaïre in 1971	
Old Names	**New "Authentic" Names**
Coquilhatville	Mbandaka
Elisabethville	Lubumbashi
Léopoldville	Kinshasa
Luluabourg	Kananga
Stanleyville	Kisangani
Thysville	Mbanza-Ngungu

Mobutu's reforms were deemed "too little, too late" by his political opponents. A coalition of Rwandan and Ugandan armies allied themselves with some opposing Congolese figures, led by Laurent-Désiré Kabila, to form the Alliance of Democratic Forces for the Liberation of Congo-Zaïre (*Alliance des Forces Démocratiques pour la Libération du Congo-Zaïre*), or AFDL (Wikipedia[j]). AFDL launched the first Congolese war in October 1996, which culminated in the overthrow of Mobutu on May 16, 1997. Mobutu fled the country and went into exile in Rabat, Morocco, where he died on September 7, 1997.

On May 17, 1997, AFDL marched into Kinshasa, and Laurent-Désiré Kabila declared himself president and restored the country's name to Democratic Republic of the Congo (*République Démocratique du Congo*), or DRC.

Laurent-Désiré Kabila (Wikipedia[k]) was born in Baudouinville, in the Province of Katanga, on November 27, 1939. He would soon be accused of pursuing Mobutu's policies, characterized by authoritarianism, corruption, human rights abuses, et cetera. By 1998, Kabila's former Ugandan and Rwandan allies had turned against him and backed a new rebellion in the Congo, leading to the second Congolese war. On January 16, 2001, Kabila was shot by his bodyguard and died either on the spot or two days later in a hospital in Harare, Zimbabwe.

On January 26, 2001, his son, Joseph Kabila Kabange, assumed the office of president of the Democratic Republic of the Congo. Joseph Kabila Kabange (Wikipedia[l]) was born in Fizi, in the Kivu Province, on June 4, 1971. Kabila tried to end the ongoing civil war in the Congo by negotiating with various rebellion factions. In 2002, a peace agreement was signed at the Inter-Congolese Dialog in Sun City, South Africa, under the auspices of the government of South Africa. They adopted a 1+4 formula of governing the country. That is, Kabila was maintained as president (1), with four (4) vice presidents [two from the main rebel groups (Jean-Pierre Bemba and Azarias Ruberwa) and two from the civilian and government supporters (Arthur Z'ahidi Ngoma and Abdoulaye Yerodia Ndombasi)]. This nominally ended the second Congolese war.

A constitutional convention by Congolese politicians/leaders culminated in a constitution, which President Joseph Kabila signed on February 18, 2006. Article 70 of this constitution stipulates that the president of the Democratic Republic of the Congo can only serve two consecutive five-year terms. Kabila's political party, People's Party for Reconstruction and Development (*Partie du Peuple pour la Réconstruction et Développement*), or PPRD, formed a coalition with other political parties under the umbrella of presidential majority (*Majorité Présidentielle*), or MP. The MP won the first presidential elections in December 2006 and then again in December 2011.

Under Joseph Kabila, the DRC underwent what was called a *découpage territorial* (territorial

division). That is, the country was subdivided from eleven provinces (implemented under Mobutu) to twenty-six provinces (with the capital city of Kinshasa being one of the provinces) (Map^g).

Administratively, the DRC's provinces are subdivided as follows:

- each province is subdivided into territories;

- each territory is subdivided into *secteurs*;

- each *secteur* is subdivided into *groupements*; and

- each *groupement* is subdivided into villages.

The third presidential election cycle was supposed to take place in December 2016. However, Kabila's government claimed that lack of financial wherewithal and continued political insecurity, particularly in the eastern part of the country, prevented it from holding the elections in 2016. The opposition parties accused the Presidential Majority (*Majorité Présidentielle)* of wanting to maintain Kabila in power, in violation of Article 70 of the constitution. Presidential, national legislative, and national provincial elections were finally held in the Democratic Republic of the Congo on Sunday, December 30, 2018.

Félix Tshisekedi of the Union for the Democracy and Social Progress (*Union pour la Démocratie et le Progrès Social*), or UDPS was declared the winner of the presidential election by the Independent National Electoral Commission (*Commission Electoral Nationale Indépendante*), or CENI, amid protestations by the runner-up, Martin Fayulu, the Roman Catholic Church, and others. Tshisekedi was sworn in as the fifth president of the Congo on Thursday, January 24, 2019, and the power passed peacefully—to the relief of many people—from Joseph Kabila to Félix Tshisekedi (Wikipedia[m]).

Félix Tshisekedi was born in Léopoldville (now Kinshasa, DRC) on June 13, 1963. He became the leader of UDPS in March 2018, following the death of his father, Étienne Tshisekedi, in February of the same year. His UDPS party formed a coalition with political heavyweight Vital Kamerhe of the Union for the Congolese Nation (*Union pour la Nation Congolaise*), or UNC, just prior to the presidential election of December 30, 2018. It was this coalition that CENI declared the winner of this presidential election.

2

Kongo-Central Province

Kongo Central, where the authors of this memoir are from, is one of the twenty-six provinces of the Democratic Republic of the Congo shown on the following map. It is briefly discussed below.

Brief Description of Kongo Central

Kongo Central is located at the southwestern corner of the DRC (see map below, Diyavanga, D., 2018). One of its prominent features is that it is the only province in the country that abuts the Atlantic Ocean, with a coastal line of 23 miles (37 km). The name of Kongo Central comes from the fact that this portion of the land was, from a geographic standpoint, roughly centrally located in the Kingdom of Kongo before the Scramble for Africa. At the time of independence, Kongo Central was part of the Léopoldville province, including the city of Kinshasa. The total surface area of Kongo Central is 20,820 square miles (53,920 km^2), with a population of 5,575,000 inhabitants in 2017 (Wikipedia[n,o]). Kongo Central is today administratively subdivided into ten territories (*territoires*): Kasangulu, Kimvula, Lukula, Luozi, Madimba, Mbanza-Ngungu, Muanda, Seke-Banza, Songololo, and Tshela.

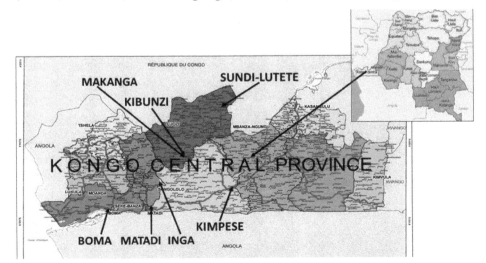

The following information about Kongo Central is noteworthy:

- Matadi, a capital city of about 300,000 inhabitants, is the chief seaport of the Democratic Republic of the Congo. It is located about 92 miles (148 km) from the mouth of the Congo River.

- Boma (Wikipedia[p]) is a port town on the Congo River, about 63 miles (101 km) upstream of the Atlantic Ocean. Boma was the capital city of Congo Free State and Belgian Congo from 1886 to 1926, when the capital was moved to Léopoldville (Kinshasa today).

- Kibunzi and Makanga, nearby villages (neither clearly visible on the map), are the birthplaces of Luzibu and Nsakala, respectively. These villages are located in Luozi Territory.

- Inga is the town where the two hydroelectric dams on the Congo River are located (Wikipedia[q]). Inga is about 87 miles (140 km) southwest of Kinshasa. Additionally, it is about 34 miles (55 km) from Kibunzi. Note the following:

  - Inga I started operations in 1972, with an installed capacity of 351 megawatts (MW);

  - Inga II started operations in 1982, with an installed capacity of 1,424 megawatts; and

  - Inga III is in the planning stages, with a power generation potential of 4,500 megawatts.

- Kimpese is the town where Nsakala graduated from high school at Kimpese School of Pastors and Teachers (*École de Pasteurs et d'Instituteurs Kimpese*). Kimpese is located in Songololo Territory.

- Sundi-Lutete is the village where Luzibu and Nsakala met for the first time while they both participated in an educational program in different capacities at Sundi-Lutete High School. Sundi-Lutete is located in Luozi Territory.

Growing Up in Kibunzi and Makanga-Kibunzi Villages

The first missionary sent by the Swedish Evangelical Church (*Sevenska Missionsförbundet*), or SMF to the Congo, C. J. Engvall, arrived in August 1881. More missionaries would follow and settle in many places: Mukimbungu, Matadi, Diadia, Kingoyi, Kinkenge, Kibunzi, et cetera. To further their mission, they built churches, hospitals, and schools (Palmer and Stenström, 1961).

SMF missionaries built the church shown here in Kibunzi in 1907 (Palmer and Stenström, 1961), with an inscription at the entrance: *"Nzambi ukundanga Mwamu"* ("God dwells here").

They later built a hospital near the church. Even though the hospital was built at the turn of the twentieth century, the photographs in this collage are less than ten years old. The two photographs on the bottom show, from left to right, the maternity ward and a baby delivery bed. This crumbling infrastructure attests to the lack of progress vis-à-vis development.

The missionaries also built a nursing school in Kibunzi in conjunction with the hospital. Shown clockwise are Dr. Elon Mattsson, a Swedish physician standing in front of his class of nursing students; midwives with a baby; and a nurse evaluating a specimen through a microscope (Palmer and Stenström, 1961).

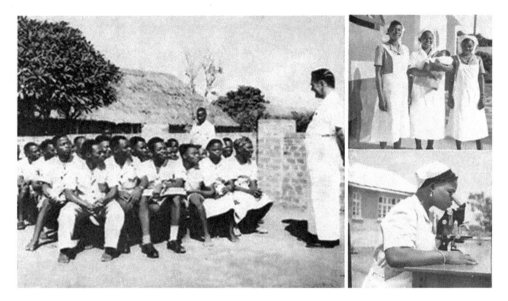

Moreover, the missionaries recruited the native peoples to become pastors (*minvungi*), who would help spread the Good News. This photograph shows some of the *minvungi* (singular, *mvungi*) at a conference circa 1922 (Palmer and Stenström, 1961). The third *mvungi* from the left, sitting in the front row, is Nkambulu Elia, Luzibu's maternal grandfather.

These three pastors were some of the people who were sent to Sweden for further education. They are, from left to right (Palmer and Stenström, 1961):

- Samba Joseph, sent in (1938);

- Kibangu Jeremia, sent in (1928); and

- Basilwa Mathieu, sent in (1953). Pastor Basilwa was Nkambulu Elia's son and Luzibu's maternal uncle.

Kibunzi was one of the SMF churches where Pastor Basilwa served. He is shown in this photograph with some of the laywomen (*minkengi*), who assisted him in the Kibunzi Church. They are, from left to right: Mama Mbumba, Mama Luvovo, Mama Kuyivovila, Mama Madede, and Mama Neli. Quite remarkably, the fourth laywoman from the left is Mama Madede, Nkambulu Elia's daughter, Pastor Basilwa's sister, and Luzibu's mother. The picture that is emerging from this narrative is that Luzibu was born into/grew up in a family that not only welcomed the Swedish missionaries to the Congo but also served the SMF church in various capacities. Administratively, Kibunzi Village is in Kibunzi Groupement, which, in turn, is in Mbanza-Mwembe Secteur. This *secteur* is in Luozi Territoire, which, in turn, is in Kongo Central Province.

As stated previously, Luzibu was born in Kibunzi Village, and Nsakala was born in Makanga, a small village located about 2.5 miles (4 km) south of Kibunzi. Several other villages around Kibunzi hold a special meaning for both Luzibu and Nsakala. Kingoyo, which is about 3 miles (5 km) northeast of Kibunzi Village, is the birthplace of Luzibu's father, Lutete David Duele. Bidi Kindamba, which is about 16 miles (~ 25 km) northeast of Kibunzi, in the Bulu Groupement (see insert, bottom right), is the birthplace of Luzibu's maternal grandfather, Nkambulu Elia. Fwani, which is about 5 miles (8 km) southwest of Kibunzi Village, is the birthplace of Nsakala's mother, Lutayi Rebecca. The other villages highlighted here (Tadi, Ntandu a Nzadi, Ndembolo, and Sundi) are where large concentrations of Luzibu and Nsakala's relatives still live today.

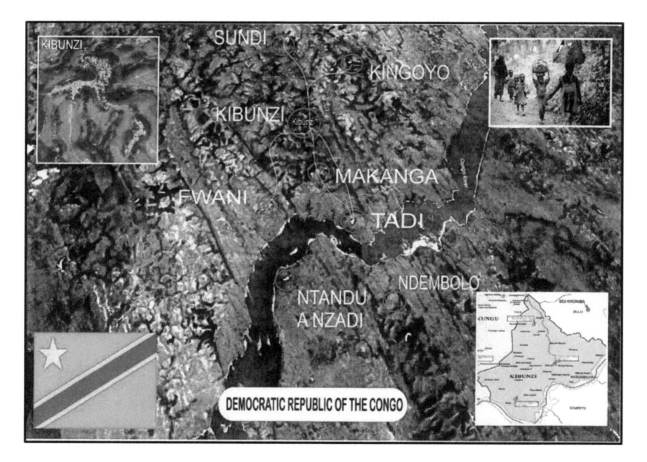

A section of Kibunzi Village is shown in this photograph. Luzibu was born here and lived in this village throughout her childhood. As this photo was taken at the end of 2016, it is safe to assume that Kibunzi still has not undergone any significant developmental improvements.

A section of Makanga Village is shown in this photograph. Nsakala was born here and lived in this village throughout his childhood. This photograph was taken in 1991, and so it is also safe to surmise that this village has not undergone any significant developmental improvements either.

The authors titled this memoir *Humble Beginnings* because Kibunzi, Makanga, and other surrounding villages were impoverished at their births. They were, for example, without electricity, paved roads, and indoor running water. Significantly, the Grand Inga Dam, a hydroelectric facility with a total installed capacity of 1,775 megawatts, in operation since 1982, is located only 34 miles (55 km) downstream of the Congo River; yet these villages are still without electricity today.

Before proceeding with the explanation of Luzibu's family tree, it is important to note a historical development pertaining to peoples' names in the Congo. From the onset of the Congo Free State in 1885, many Congolese were given Christian/Western first names and/or surnames. In 1971, Mobutu Sese Seko decreed, as stated previously, that all Zaïrean citizens had to bear authentic African names. And when President Laurent-Désiré Kabila overthrew Mobutu in 1997, he not only changed the name of the country back to the Democratic Republic of the Congo, but he apparently allowed citizens to revert back to their Christian/Western names if they wished.

Anyway, to comply with Mobutu's decree, Luzibu, then a Zaïrean citizen, replaced her given Western first name, Hélène, with her maiden name, Luzibu, and took her father's last name, Lutete, as a middle name. She thus became Luzibu Lutete Nsakala (and is referred to throughout this memoir as Luzibu).

The explanation of three generations of a typical Bakongo family tree is depicted in the table below. It is used to illustrate Luzibu's three-generation family tree, which includes her plus her siblings, their parents, and their grandparents.

Generation #	English	Kikongo
1	grandparent (grandmother, grandfather)	nkaka/nkoko, yaya (gender neutral)
	grandparents (grandmothers, grandfathers)	zinkaka, bayaya (gender neutral)
2	parent (mother, father)	ngudi evo se (mama, tata)
	parents (mothers, fathers)	zingudi evo mase (bamama, batata)
3	sibling (sister, brother)	mpangi (ya nkento, ya bakala)
	siblings (sisters, brothers)	zimpangi (za bakento, za babakala)

First Generation (Grandparents)

The maternal grandparents, Mina Nsongo and Nkambulu Elia, were from the villages of Kibunzi and Bidi Kindamba, respectively. And the paternal grandparents, Malata Mbumba and Mandanzi Malakosi, were from Kingoyo Village.

Second Generation (Parents)

The parents, Madede Lessa and Lutete David Duele, were from Kibunzi and Kingoyo villages, respectively.

Third Generation (Siblings)

Luzibu is the fourth of six children of Madede Lessa and Lutete David Duele, one girl and five boys. All the siblings were born and grew up in Kibunzi. They are, in descending order of age, Lubombolo lwa Nzambi, Basilwa Mathieu, Mayiza Mvibudulu, Luzibu Lutete, Kiambote Duele, and Lubambuka Malemba.

The figure below shows Luzibu's three-generation family tree. The place of birth of each person in the tree is given in parenthesis.

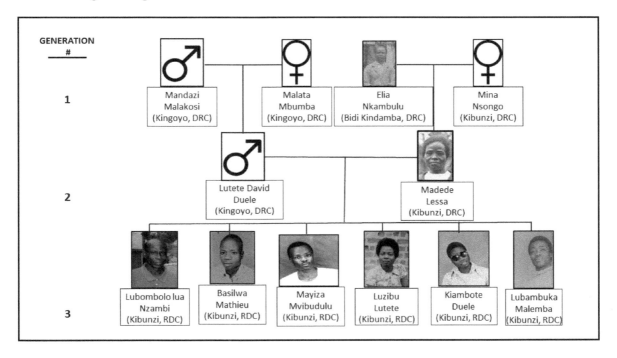

As shown above, in the Bakongo tribe, the children did not necessarily take their father's last name. Instead, they were given their names according to particular circumstances and/or named after elder relatives. An example of a special circumstance is the birth of twins, whereby the first born would necessarily be named *Nsimba* and the second would be named *Nzuzi*. Another example of a special circumstance is when a woman has a difficult pregnancy or delivery. In this case, the baby could be named *Mumpasi* ("with difficulty").

It should be noted that the Bakongo tribe is a matrilineal society, which is a group of people adhering to a kinship system in which ancestral descent is traced through maternal instead of paternal lines. Simplistically, the children of a given family belong to their mother's side of the family.

Many other members of Luzibu's family had a profoundly enriching and indelible impact on her life. Just a few of them are identified below.

Nkambulu Elia was Luzibu's maternal grandfather. He was born in Bidi Kindamba Village, which is about 16 miles (~ 25 km) from Kibunzi, but he resided in Kibunzi his entire life. He was one of the first Congolese natives who welcomed the Swedish missionaries, and so he was one of the first natives trained by missionaries as *minvungi* (pastors). He was a man of faith. His wife, Mina Nsongo, was one of the first native women taught to read and write by the missionaries in order to teach other natives and help spread the Good News.

Basilwa Mathieu, son of Mina Nsongo and Nkambulu Elia, was born in Kibunzi. He was trained as a pastor at EPI Kimpese (*École de Pasteurs et d'Instituteurs Kimpese*—Kimpese's School of Pastors and Teachers). Over the years, he served as a pastor of various Svenska Missionsförbundet (SMF) churches (for example, Kibunzi and Kinkenge). In 1953, he was sent to Sweden by the missionaries for further training and observation of the Swedish culture. Pastor Basilwa was a renowned spiritual leader of the SMF church and the surrounding communities.

Madede Lessa was, like her big brother Basilwa, born in Kibunzi. She was very spiritual, independent, and capable of doing just about anything, including building her own house. She was a strong-willed person, a disciplinarian, but also a kind, loving, caring, and compassionate mother. She inspired many people around her, and she served God faithfully as a deaconess in the Kibunzi church until her death. The refrain of her favorite hymn *"Ku kakwenda si yalanda"* is in the Kikongo hymnal *Nkunga mia Kintwadi* #485, 1963. In English, it is "Where He Leads Me" (*United Methodist Hymnal* #338, 1989). For all these things, and more, Luzibu's mother was her hero.

Matila was born after Madede. She also lived in Kibunzi, next door to her sister Madede. It follows that her children, Luzibu, and Luzibu's siblings all lived together, not as cousins, but rather as brothers and sisters. Like her big sister, Madede, Matila was a very independent woman also. She and her sister were able to do just about anything, including building their own houses.

Having the above strong characters as role models, and all others not mentioned here, makes Luzibu feel grateful and humbled. She will always cherish and treasure the great impact and influence they had on her for they shaped her into the person she is today. The well-known African proverb says, "It takes a village to raise a child."

Nsakala's given Western name at birth (on November 30, 1941) was Albert. To comply with Mobutu's decree of 1971, he became Nsakala ya Nsakala (and is referred to throughout this memoir as Nsakala).

The figure on the next page depicts Nsakala's three-generation family tree, which includes him plus his siblings, their parents, and their grandparents.

First Generation (Grandparents)

The maternal grandparents, Miezi Nsongo and Nsakala Komono, were both from Fwani Village, as shown in an earlier photograph. And the paternal grandparents, Kinsumuna Lessa and Nsakala Lufuku, were from Makanga Village.

Second Generation (Parents)

The parents, Lutayi Rebecca and Metusala Nsakala, were from the villages of Fwani and Makanga, respectively.

Third Generation (Siblings)

Nsakala is the sixth of seven children of Lutayi Rebecca and Metusala Nsakala, three girls and four boys. All the siblings were born and grew up in Makanga. They are, in descending order of age, Bena Nsakala Ndunga, Komono Nsakala, Munlemvo Kinsumuna, Mena Julienne, Dessa Nsakala, Nsakala ya Nsakala, and Swamunu Makomba.

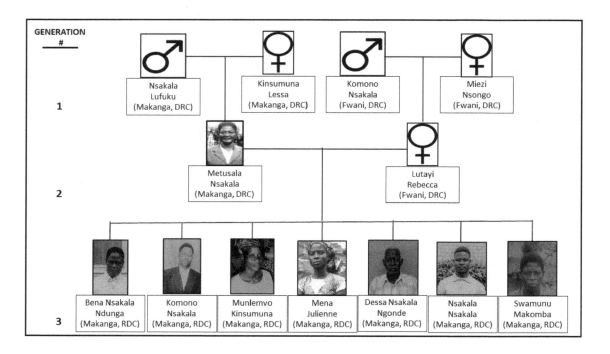

GENERATION #

1

| Nsakala Lufuku (Makanga, DRC) | Kinsumuna Lessa (Makanga, DRC) | Komono Nsakala (Fwani, DRC) | Miezi Nsongo (Fwani, DRC) |

2

| Metusala Nsakala (Makanga, DRC) | Lutayi Rebecca (Fwani, DRC) |

3

| Bena Nsakala Ndunga (Makanga, RDC) | Komono Nsakala (Makanga, RDC) | Munlemvo Kinsumuna (Makanga, RDC) | Mena Julienne (Makanga, RDC) | Dessa Nsakala Ngonde (Makanga, RDC) | Nsakala Nsakala (Makanga, RDC) | Swamunu Makomba (Makanga, RDC) |

Besides his parents, many other family members had a profoundly enriching and indelible influence on Nsakala's life. Just a few of them are identified below.

Lutete Babwa, who was from Fwani Village, was Lutayi Rebecca's younger brother. That is, Lutete Babwa was the Nsakala siblings' maternal uncle (*Ngwa' Nkazi*). It follows that, according to the Bakongo tribe's matrilineal customs, he was a very important and influential person in their lives. For example, living with their family in Makanga was as seamless as living with Uncle Lutete Babwa's family in Fwani. Lutayi Rebecca's and Lutete Babwa's children lived together as brothers and sisters, as the term "cousin" actually does not exist in the Kikongo vocabulary. Virtually all important decisions pertaining to Lutayi Rebecca and Nsakala Metusala's children, such as marriage, had to receive Uncle Lutete Babwa's official permission or stamp of approval.

Munlemvo Kinsumuna was the third child and eldest girl in the family. Hence, when their mother, Lutayi Rebecca, died in the early 1950s, Munlemvo became both a big sister and surrogate mother to the three youngest children of the family (Dessa, Nsakala, and Swamunu). And big sister Munlemvo successfully fulfilled both functions.

Pictured here is Bena Nsakala Ndunga, the eldest child of Lutayi Rebecca and Metusala Nsakala, with his wife, Batunda Tusevo Esther. By the time Lutayi Rebecca died, this couple was already living in Léopoldville, where Bena was working for the national postal services. Bena and his wife, whom everybody affectionately still calls Mama Kota (Elder Mother) today, also looked after the interests of Nsakala's older brother, Dessa, and younger sister, Swamunu. In fact, Swamunu went to Léopoldville to live with them after the death of Lutayi. And both Dessa and Nsakala would vacation in Léopoldville during some summer months throughout their primary school education. Perhaps more significantly, this couple took charge of all the financial needs of Dessa and Nsakala vis-à-vis their education and well-being.

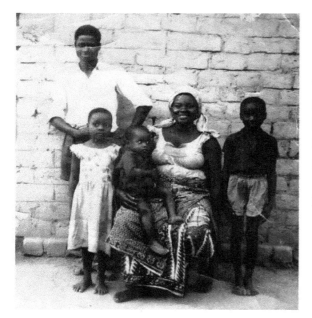

This photograph, for example, shows a young Nsakala vacationing in Léopoldville with Mama Kota Batunda, plus her first three children with Bena: from left to right, Binga Suzanne, Bena Diampisa, and Bena Joseph.

For all these things, and more, big brother Bena Nsakala Ndunga was Nsakala's hero.

Pictured here is Komono Nsakala, the family's second-born sibling, with his wife, Bankadila Esther; their firstborn, Lutayi Rebecca; and Bankadila's younger sister in Léopoldville. Komono was an accomplished auto mechanic who became a successful leader in the Congolese national public transportation system. In fact, when the Belgian leader King Baudouin went for an official visit to the Belgian Congo in 1955, and again in 1960 to celebrate the Congolese independence, he was chauffeured around by Komono. Soon after the country's independence, Komono would spend several months in Brussels, Belgium, to further his education in the field of public transportation. The Komono family also was helpful in defraying Nsakala's high school education expenses. And whenever Nsakala spent his vacation time from Kimpese High School in Léopoldville, he would always stay at their house.

Pictured here is Dessa Nsakala Ngonde, the family's fifth-born sibling, with his wife, Nkenda Pauline. Dessa studied nursing at the Nursing School of Kibunzi. He, too, moved to Léopoldville in the very early 1960s, where he still practices nursing today. This family also helped defray Nsakala's high school education expenses.

Nsakala benefited tremendously from these strong role models in his life. They, along with many other people not identified here, shaped Nsakala into who he is today. It would indeed be hard to imagine who Nsakala would have been without these characters.

Just how did the people in these various villages survive economically? Luzibu and Nsakala are glad you asked! Well, they survived under a largely subsistence-based economy. That is, to provide for their basic needs, they relied on fishing, hunting, and farming. The practices of fishing and farming are illustrated below.

Fishing

Makanga is slightly less than 1 mile (1.6 km) from the Congo River. Hence, fishing is a given for many male adults and some boys in the village. Shown here, for example, is a canoe (*nlungu*), with two fishermen (Image[a]), one of whom is casting a fishing net (*konde*) into the water while the other is steering the canoe with a paddle (*nkafi*).

The routine when Nsakala was growing up was for the fishing crew to go to the Congo River on a Sunday afternoon and fish until the following Saturday morning. The fish caught during the week would be smoked for safe preservation, and the fish caught during the night of Friday to Saturday would be taken to the market in Kibunzi, along with the smoked fish, on Saturday morning. The children, especially, were excited to go to the market to sell their catches and earn some money: money that would occasionally allow them to buy kerosene for their lamps, bread, sugar, salt, soap, clothing, and other basic needs.

Farming

Cultivating the fields to plant a variety of tropical fruits and vegetables was/ still is virtually everybody's business in a village. Shown here (Image[b]), for example, are men, women, and children working in a field, each with a hoe (*nsengo*). Machetes (*bitanzi*) are also used, especially to initially clear a terrain being prepared for a farm. It is an important survival skill to learn.

The following three photographs show some of the tropical fruits and vegetables typically harvested by people in Congolese villages.

This montage shows harvested peanuts (*zinguba*) and zinsafu/plums (*mimbozi*) and bananas (*bitiba*) still hanging on the tree (Image[c,d]).

This collage shows mangoes (*bimanga*), avocados (*mavoka*), and papayas (*bimandi*) still hanging on the trees (Image[e,f]).

This collage shows a cassava plant (*nti'a yaka*), a cassava root (*yaka*), and a cornstalk (*nti'a sangu*) bearing a corn ear (*sangu*) (Image[g,h]). The cassava plant is perhaps one of the most versatile tropical agricultural products in that the whole plant is useful: its leaves can be cooked and eaten as one would do with, say, spinach; its root can be peeled and eaten raw or cooked; it also can be soaked, dried, and then pulverized to produce cassava flour, which can then be cooked as one would cook grits (*fufu*). Also, the root can be left in the water until soft, then mashed to make a soft dough, which is wrapped in banana leaves and then boiled, with the final product being called *kwanga*. The root is also used to make tapioca pudding and starch. Finally, the stem itself can be used to start a new plant. Is that not amazing? Cassava is clearly a staple food.

The important point to make is that the equatorial weather offers abundant fruits, vegetables, roots, et cetera, some of which grow on their own. What Luzibu and Nsakala remember vividly is that as children growing up in their villages, they did not go to bed hungry for lack of food.

Primary and High School Education

Have you ever imagined what life is like in a village that lacks electricity, running water, paved roads, school buses, indoor plumbing, and all the amenities people in the Western world tend to take for granted? Imagine such hardships as the ones listed below for young school children:

- Fixing your own breakfast and lunch to take along to school in Zinga-Mboma, which is located halfway between Kibunzi and Kingoyo;

- Walking about two miles, barefoot, on hot, humid tropical soil to attend classes because you want to learn;

- Returning home in the late afternoon, exhausted from the day's activities, and having chores yet to be done (for example, fetching the water from a creek and the wood from a nearby forest to facilitate the preparation of the evening meal); and then

- With the aid of a kerosene lamp, doing your homework before going to bed.

These are some of the challenges that children growing up in an impoverished village face daily regarding education.

Aside from the day-to-day challenges of attending school, Luzibu and Nsakala were deeply immersed in the culture of their local churches. For example, one of the rites of passage in the SMF church was for people to publicly confess their sins during a service, take a catechism class, and be water baptized, as shown in this photograph (Palmer and Stenström, 1961). The special biblical reading on the baptism day was "Therefore go and make disciples of all nations, baptizing them in the name of the Father and of the Son and of the Holy Spirit" (Matthew 28:19 New International Version). In Kikongo: *"Luenda luavanga makanda mamonsono mabantu nlonguki miami, lubabotika mu nkumbu a Se ye Mwana ye Mpeve yanlongo" (Matai 28:19).*

In the fall of 1962, Luzibu would accept Christ and take a catechism class from and be water baptized by her uncle, Pastor Basilwa, with the help of other Svenska Missionsförbundet (SMF) Kibunzi clergy members.

Luzibu worked hard to overcome the hardships of village living and continue her education beyond primary school. She attended an all-girl three-year post–primary school that prepared young girls for self-sufficiency. This school (see collage below, Palmer and Stenström, 1961) was called Kibunzi Home Economics School (*École Ménagère Kibunzi*). This school was open to girls graduating from all SMF-run primary schools throughout the Kongo Central Province who so desired and met the academic qualifications. These students were trained and qualified to teach kindergarten children. So students graduating from this school had a host of options in life: they were qualified to teach kindergarten children. Alternatively, they could complete the remaining three years of high school elsewhere.

For Nsakala, attending primary school was a bit more complicated than it was for Luzibu. Makanga is located approximately 4 miles (~ 6 km) from Zinga-Mboma. Hence, it was not possible to commute to and from school daily. The only available option was to board in Zinga-Mboma on school days. The boarding school lodgings offered no beds and no cafeteria. Therefore, the children slept on mats and cooked their own meals. Given these facts, children from Makanga did not start school until they were seven, eight, or maybe nine years old. On weekends, the children went back home briefly to visit with their parents and to get the food supply for the following week.

The above-mentioned and other hardships did not deter Nsakala from going to school faithfully and without relenting. Shown in this photograph is a fifth-grade class (1955–1956) taught by a teacher (*maître,* in French) named Mpanzu. The first child on the left in the front row is Basilwa Mathieu, Luzibu's second-born sibling, and the first child on the right in that same row is Nsakala. Basilwa and Nsakala were good friends throughout their primary school years.

Nsakala accepted Christ in the fall of 1956 and took the catechism class from and was water baptized by Pastor Basilwa with the help of other SMF Kibunzi clergy members in December that year.

The sixth and seventh grades of the primary school were located in Kibunzi rather than Zinga-Mboma. This photograph shows Nsakala graduating from the primary school in Kibunzi in June or July 1958. The suit he wore was a reward that Nsakala received from his brother Bena not only for doing so well throughout his primary school education but also for passing the test to attend a prestigious and highly competitive high school in Kimpese.

Nsakala started his high school education at EPI Kimpese (*École de Pasteurs et d'Instituteurs Kimpese*—Kimpese School of Pastors and Teachers) in September 1958. This high school was run by a consortium of protestant missionary churches in the Congo, namely:

- The American Baptist Foreign Missionary Society (ABFMS);

- The British Missionary Society (BMS);

- The Church Mission Association (CMA, British); and

- Svenska Missionförbundet (SMF, Swedish).

Kimpese is a town along the railroad that links the port city of Matadi to the capital city of Léopoldville (Kinshasa today), in the Songololo Province. Shown here is the EPI Kimpese's school chapel on the right (Palmer and Stenström, 1961). Students were required to line up promptly at 6:00 a.m. for prayers before the start of classes. The chapel was also used for church services on weekends and special occasions. Shown on the left is a series of student dormitories. EPI Kimpese was a boarding school without electricity, running water, indoor plumbing, or cafeterias. Hence, the students had to fend for themselves in relation to their alimentary and other needs.

A sampling of the activities Nsakala participated in during his six-year tenure at EPI Kimpese is given below.

In the left-hand photograph, Nsakala is with his classmates at EPI Kimpese; he is the fifth student from the left in the front row. And he is with his friends Freddie Makokele and Jean Luvamba-nu, shown in the top right and bottom right photographs, respectively.

Soccer was virtually every student's pastime at EPI Kimpese. Near the campus was a spring-water-fed pond at the bottom of the Bangu mountain chain, where students would go on some weekends to swim and relax. Nsakala is the second student from the left in the top right photograph and fourth from the left in the bottom right photograph.

Throughout his high school years, Nsakala was active with the Christian youth movement. Here, he is shown standing in the middle of the back row at Kikwit Airport, Bandundu, at the beginning of the summer of 1963. The group was en route from Léopoldville (Kinshasa today) to Luluabourg (Kananga today). At Luluabourg, the group attended a national Christian youth movement conference, sponsored by the Protestant's Church of Christ in the Congo (*Eglise du Christ au Congo*).

In July 1964, Nsakala graduated from EPI Kimpese high school with *the Plus Grand Fruit* honors, which literally means "the Greatest Fruit." As it was possible for more than one student to earn such honors, Nsakala thinks that it simply meant that he graduated either on top or near the top of his class, though he was chosen by the school faculty to deliver the "traditional" goodbye speech at the graduation ceremony. By God's grace and blessings, this milestone helped in opening the doors of opportunities for Nsakala. Importantly, as he studied pedagogy at EPI Kimpese, Nsakala was qualified to teach in a primary school and/or a high school's *Cycle d'Orientation* (the first two years of high school).

With the independence of the Congo in June 1960 came the independence of various churches in the nation. This meant that the American and European missionaries had to relinquish operational powers of even the churches to the Congolese leaders. Svenska Missionsförbundet (SMF), for example, became Evangelical Church Mamianga-Matadi

(*Eglise Evangélique Manianga-Matadi*, or EEMM) (Palmer and Stenström, 1961). Luvambanu Jean and Nsakala (see Teaching Activities below) were assigned by Mr. Tukeba André, the general inspector (*Inspecteur Général*) of EEMM's primary and secondary schools, to teach students in the *Cycle d'Orientation* of Sundi-Lutete High School during the 1964–1965 academic year. Sundi-Lutete is in the northeast corner of Luozi territory.

How Luzibu and Nsakala Met

Nsakala and Luvambanu were also assigned by Mr. Tukeba André to help teach a three-week refresher course (*Cours de Perfectionnement*) in August at Sundi-Lutete High School. This refresher course was being offered to the EEMM's primary school teachers. Unbeknownst to Nsakala, Luzibu had signed up for this refresher course.

It follows that Luzibu and Nsakala found themselves in each other's path for the first time. Well! Have you ever felt an instant connection with someone you just met, leaving you totally confused? Is that love at first sight? Is it possible? Luzibu and Nsakala felt, in their own ways, a magnetic force the moment they met for the very first time. Strangely, each one felt that the other one was meant to be in her/his life forever. Isn't it amazing how a person who was once a stranger can suddenly, without warning, mean the whole world to you?

Conversations between them revealed that they were from the villages of Kibunzi and Makanga, respectively, which were only 4 kilometers apart. It also became clear that Nsakala had been a good friend of Basilwa Mathieu, Luzibu's brother, throughout their primary school years and that a good many members of Luzibu's and Nsakala's families knew each other. Luzibu and Nsakala continued their conversations every day for three weeks. They were becoming more and more attracted to one another. Hence, on the morning of the last refresher-course day, on Saturday, August 22, 1964, Nsakala popped the question: "Would you consider marrying me?" Luzibu would eventually say yes, and the rest is history. With God's grace, it has been a journey together of fifty-three happy years and counting!

Teaching Activities

In September 1964, Luzibu was assigned to teach a class of kindergarten children in Zinga-Mboma. She taught at this school for two academic years, 1964–1965 and 1965–1966. In the below left photograph, Luzibu is shown with the Kibunzi primary school system's director and some other teachers. She is third from the left in the front row, and Director Jacques Manko is third from the left in the back row.

The other two photographs in the collage show two of Luzibu's brothers, who were in the field of education. In the top photograph, Mvibudulu Mayiza is pictured with his students at a Kibunzi primary school. Kiambote Duele is shown with his class at a Matadi primary school.

This collage shows various poses of Luzibu from 1963 through 1966, when she was a student at École Ménagère Kibunzi and teaching in Zinga-Mboma. Yes, youth comes only once in a lifetime!

44

Nsakala's teaching activities at Sundi-Lutete for the academic year 1964–1965 also started in September 1964. He is shown in this photograph with his friend Luvambanu Jean, with whom he had graduated from EPI Kimpese, and Kitutu, Sundi-Lutete Mission's chief auto mechanic and chauffeur. Luvambanu's and Nsakala's assignments entailed teaching mathematics, science, and technology, plus physical education, to the high school students in their first two years, which, as mentioned earlier, were called *Cycle d'Orientation*.

The other teachers at Sundi-Lutete were missionaries from Belgium, Sweden, and the United States. Some of these teachers are shown in the next three photographs. This collage shows, on the right, Jean Beugels from Belgium. The left-hand photograph shows Sigbrit Josefsson from Sweden. Mrs. Josefsson was at Sundi-Lutete with her husband, Calle, and their two young children (not shown). Sven Nordling, also from Sweden (not shown), was the high school director.

This collage shows Nsakala with one of the classes that he taught; he is the one wearing a jacket (left-hand photograph). The top right photograph features students standing in front of a school building. The bottom right photograph shows Birgit, a Swedish teacher, standing behind her students in the classroom.

Shown in this photograph is Carroll David Yoder. He was teaching at Sundi-Lutete High School under the auspices of the Mennonite Central Committee's Teachers Abroad Program (TAP). Early in 1965, Carroll urged Nsakala to apply for a scholarship from a US program that was offering them to recent Congolese high school graduates.

The program was called African Scholarship Program for American Universities (ASPAU). ASPAU was under the umbrella of the United States Agency for International Development (US AID). In fact, Carroll took it upon himself to obtain the application forms from the US consulate in Léopoldville (Kinshasa today) and hand them to Nsakala.

Nsakala immediately filled out the application forms and sent them off to the consulate. He was invited to take a comprehensive examination in May 1965. At the end of the examination, the chairman of the committee told Nsakala that he should return to the American consulate in July to hear the results of the examination.

Nsakala is shown here with the teachers from other EEMM high schools in the spring of 1965 in Luozi, which was, at the time, the headquarters of EEMM. The teachers were correcting the tests of all EEMM students who were graduating from primary schools and seeking to be admitted to various affiliated high schools. Nsakala had composed the mathematics test and so was responsible for selecting, based on established criteria, the students who passed it.

Starting in September 1964, after Luzibu and Nsakala were on the same page in relation to their burning desire to be married to each other, it was necessary to inform appropriate people on both sides of the family and seek approval. Remember the matrilineal thing mentioned earlier? Well, Nsakala's maternal uncle Lutete Babwa and Luzibu's maternal uncle Basilwa Mathieu had to and did approve of the engagement. Subsequently, early in 1965, the families from both sides got together to make the engagement official. This ceremony is called *Kanga lupangu* (engagement party).

This photograph was taken in a professional photographer's studio in Léopoldville (Kinshasa today) in July 1965.

Luzibu and Nsakala are shown in the photograph on the left with nieces Ndimbani Damienne and Gertrude, Luzibu's cousin Mantombulua Sophie's daughters. Both of them were constant chaperones of Luzibu and Nsakala. The photograph on the right shows Luzibu, Damienne, Gertrude, Thérèse (Luzibu's cousin), plus three of Bena Nsakala Ndunga's daughters.

Immigration to the United States

In July 1965, Nsakala found out at the American consulate in Léopoldville that he was one of nine students who were selected from the entire country to study in the United States under the auspices of the US Agency for International Development's African Scholarship Program for American Universities (US AID's ASPAU) program.

With the support of the American consulate personnel, all nine of the ASPAU students garnered the appropriate documents (passports, judicial and medical clearances, student visas, laissez-passer, et cetera.) for immigration to the United States. On Wednesday, August 18, 1965, they embarked on a Belgian cargo ship at the port city of Matadi for a twenty-three-day trip to the United States via Lobito and Luanda in Angola and the Cape Verde Islands to pick up cargo and/or passengers. They disembarked in New York City on Friday, September 10, 1965.

In December 1965, while Nsakala was visiting Carroll Yoder's family in Wellman, Iowa, Carroll offered to sponsor Luzibu's immigration to the United States through the Mennonite Central Committee (MCC).

In July 1966, Luzibu and Nsakala were married by proxy in Kibunzi Village, in accordance with the Bakongo tribe's customs. That is, for example, Nsakala's side of the family was required to pay a dowry (*nkanka*) to Luzibu's family during the marriage celebration, which typically lasted from Friday to Sunday of the chosen weekend. The dowry consisted of monetary and materials goods, whose total cost was quite small, though necessary, in accordance with the Bakongo tribe's customs. This photograph shows a typical gift—though not required—brought to the future household by the bride. The two baked clay pots (*minkudu*), united by a string of beads, symbolize a union between the bride and groom and both families.

To the above gift, Luzibu added this pillowcase, with inscriptions cross-stitched by herself: *"Sans toi je meurs"* (Without you I die).

Soon after the wedding ceremony in Kibunzi in July 1966, Luzibu moved to Léopoldville, where she stayed with Bena Nsakala Ndunga's family while awaiting immigration to the United States. Rollin R. Rheinheimer, who was the regional director of the Menno Travel Service (MCC's travel agency), assisted Luzibu in obtaining all required traveling documents at the request of Carroll Yoder. Luzibu flew from Maya-Maya Airport in Brazzaville, Republic of the Congo, ultimately landing in Cedar Rapids, Iowa, on September 9, 1966, where Carroll and Nsakala were waiting for her.

Part Two

Life in the United States of America—Educational and Employment Activities

3

Nsakala's Arrival in the United States of America: Cultural Hurdles

Arrival in New York City

The Belgian cargo ship, which had originated in Matadi, Republic of the Congo, on Wednesday, August 18, 1965, arrived in New York City (NYC) early on the morning of Friday, September 10, 1965. All nine Congolese students were warmly welcomed at the arrival pier by Ms. Lyons and other representatives from the US Agency for International Development's African Scholarship Program of American Universities (US AID's ASPAU). They were taken to the Hotel Tudor (Image[i]) on East Forty-Second Street, near the United Nations Plaza, where they would stay for two nights.

The NYC skyline was awesome, nothing like anything that Nsakala had ever seen before. Three iconic structures particularly captivated Nsakala's hungry young mind:

- The Statue of Liberty (Image[j]), not only for its imposing size, but also for the indomitable "Land of Liberty" symbol that it represents.

- The Empire State Building (Image[k]) , for its towering over and domination of the skyline of Manhattan Island; and

- The United Nations Building (Image[l]), flanked by its member nations' flags, fluttering in the air as if to say, "This place is your place, irrespective of where you are coming from."

Ms. Lyons spent the next day, Saturday, orienting the students about the three-pronged ASPU program and helping them shop with the stipend money she had given to each one of them for such things as toiletries and cold-weather clothing. The three-pronged approach of the ASPAU program entailed:

1. Attending a three-month intensive course in the English language and American culture at the School for International Training (SIT) in Brattleboro, Vermont.

2. Living with a host family somewhere in the United States for several weeks to experience firsthand life in an American family setting; and

3. Attending one's assigned American college or university, where everything was taught in the English language.

This photograph shows Nsakala with one of the other eight students, Lomena Sébastien, standing outside, perhaps near the Tudor Hotel, on Sunday morning, September 12, 1965, shortly before they were sent off, via a Greyhound bus, to Brattleboro, Vermont.

Study of the English Language and American Culture in Brattleboro, Vermont

The Greyhound bus carrying the ASPAU students left NYC in the midmorning on Sunday, September 12, 1965, arriving in Brattleboro, Vermont, in early evening. A welcoming party of school representatives warmly greeted them, then took them to the campus of the International School for Training (SIT). There were several ASPAU students from other non-English-speaking African countries at the SIT, along with Americans studying foreign languages in preparation for their deployment abroad, et cetera. This school, run by Director John Wallace at the time, was a tremendous environment in terms of interactive cultural setting. It was, in effect, a microcosm of the United Nations.

The ASPAU program, which, for the Congolese students, started on Monday, September 13, 1965, ran until Friday, December 17, 1965. The program was extremely intense. Typical activities included but were not limited to:

- English language classes, which ran from about 8:00 a.m. to 5:00 p.m., with appropriate breaks in between. Bene M'Poko, another Congolese ASPAU student, and Nsakala are shown here in the front row of the language lab with the teacher, Mr. John, as he was called, standing in the back;

- Planned interactions with all kinds of people, such as high school and college students, business and bank managers, law enforcement agents, et cetera;

- Participation in sports, including soccer, roller-skating, Frisbee throwing, et cetera; and

- Attendance at some cultural events, such as the Big E in West Springfield, Massachusetts; a college football game in Hanover, New Hampshire; and the New York World's Fair in New York City.

Nsakala is shown in this photograph with, from left to right, Lomena Sébastien, Ousmane Kane (from West Africa), and Bene M'Poko. A SIT staff member took them to her home in Burlington, Vermont.

Knowing in September 1965 that they would be in college or university in January or February of the following year gave each student more than enough incentive to work hard, particularly on the mastery of the English language. That said, there was plenty of "burning the midnight oil" for the majority of the ASPAU students. There were, nonetheless, some moments of fun and levity. Here are a few such humorous moments Nsakala experienced while attending the School for International Training:

- On one Saturday afternoon, ASPAU students had an outing to Hanover, New Hampshire, to watch Dartmouth College play football against another college. Virtually everyone had tears of laughter, as there was no understanding of how a player could be hit and thrown to the ground whether or not he had the ball. Some students even went as far as equating what was happening on the gridiron to "plain and simple savagery."

- On another weekend, the outing was planned to the Eastern States Exposition (or Big E) in West Springfield, Massachusetts. At lunchtime, one of the school staff invited some of the students to try hot dogs. Nsakala shot back, in all seriousness, "In my country, we do not eat dogs, hot or cold!"

- On yet another weekend, the outing was to New York City, where the students:

  - visited the NYC World's Fair;

  - toured the United Nations headquarters

  - went to the top of the Empire State Building; and

  - *watched a movie, Zorba the Greek, at the Radio City Music Hall.*

Some additional happenings/major events:

- A headline on November 24, 1965, concerned a bloodless coup d'état carried out in the Congo by then Lieutenant Général Joseph Mobutu against President Joseph Kasa-Vubu.

- Beatlemania was all over the country on a daily basis. One couldn't turn on the black-and-white TV without seeing the four young Brits—John Lennon, Paul McCartney, George Harrison, and Ringo Starr—on a stage or turn on the radio without hearing "I Want to Hold Your Hand."

- New England's kaleidoscopic of fall foliage was simply mesmerizing.

- The first snowfall, accompanied by an Arctic blast, was both exciting and awful.

Anyhow, Friday, December 17, 1965, arrived, and it was time to say goodbye to one another. Following a brief graduation ceremony, run by school director John Wallace, each ASPAU student was sent off to a host family, where he or she would experience firsthand life in an American family setting until the time came to start college/university life. Nsakala, who had been assigned by ASPAU to attend Fisk University in Nashville, Tennessee, was sent off to live with the Levine family in Bedford, New York. Two other African students, whose names and nationalities Nsakala does not recall, were on the same Greyhound bus, which dropped them off somewhere near Bedford in the early evening. Everybody's host family was at the Greyhound bus depot, eagerly awaiting their arrival.

Living with a Host Family in Bedford, New York

Nsakala's host family, shown in this photograph, from left to right—Mrs. Hope Levine; Dr. Benjamin Levine; and children Hope, Ken, and Faith—was not new at hosting foreign students at their home in Bedford. Hence, they knew how to ease the anxiety of a young African person. They did so by treating Nsakala as if he were one of their family members. The youngest child, Faith, fourteen years old at the time, became a de facto English language instructor to Nsakala. Dr. Levine, a prominent dentist in New York City, would occasionally take Nsakala with him to work. Mrs. Levine—perhaps a philanthropist—would take Nsakala to many fundraising/charitable events in Bedford, Mount Kisco, and other locations. Ken would, at times, invite Nsakala to his dormitory at Columbia University to see how university students lived. And Hope would occasionally invite Nsakala to some of her high school classes, where Nsakala would be given the opportunity to say something about himself, the Congo, and his aspirations.

The Levines also got together with the other two host families in the area. This photograph depicts one of those occasions. Featured here are, from left to right: Hope Levine; an African student, perhaps from Morocco; Faith Levine; Ken Levine; Nsakala; and another student from West Africa.

Nsakala's experience with the Levine family was tremendously enriching. He learned something new virtually every day. That is why it was hard for him to ask the Levines for permission to visit his friend, Carroll D. Yoder, in Wellman, Iowa. Carroll had just returned from his Mennonite Central Committee's (MCC's) Teachers Abroad Program (TAP) assignment in the Congo. The Levines were understandably concerned, given Nsakala's newness to the United States, but said, "Permission granted." Hence, Nsakala spent the last few days in December 1965, and the first two weeks in January 1966, with the Yoder family in Wellman, Iowa.

During this time, Carroll and Nsakala visited Carroll's friends at the University of Kansas in Lawrence, and at the University of Minnesota in Minneapolis-Saint Paul. Nsakala had fun, though he constantly complained about the snow and cold weather. It was during this time that Carroll agreed to sponsor Luzibu, Nsakala's fiancée, who was still in the Congo, to come to the United States. Carroll's parents, Carrie and Lester Yoder, agreed to host Luzibu upon her arrival in the United States. Finally, the Mennonite Central Committee officials in Léopoldville agreed to help Luzibu obtain the necessary travel documents to the United States and to pay for all the expenses, including the airline ticket. Carroll would give them the money upfront, and Nsakala would reimburse Carroll in due course.

Two weeks after Nsakala returned to Bedford, New York, he took a Greyhound bus from New York City to Nashville, Tennessee, where he would start his college life with a major in chemistry at Fisk University at the beginning of February 1966.

4

Nsakala's Life in Nashville, Tennessee

The Test of College Life at Fisk University

Nsakala was met at the Nashville Greyhound bus depot by Dr. Nelson Fuson, Fisk University's international students' adviser. Dr. Fuson was waiting because a Fisk University alumnus living in the Bedford, New York, area had given the university Nsakala's arrival schedule. The following day, Nsakala spent all day taking placement tests at the Fisk University campus. He qualified to take second-semester classes across the board. The following are some of the challenges that Nsakala faced:

- For the very first time in his young life, Nsakala was in a strange university setting, where he knew nobody;

- The English-language barrier was real, primarily because of limitations to understanding its subtleties and verb conjugation exceptions, exacerbated by the limitations of his vocabulary; and

- Starting college during second semester meant taking, for example, General Chemistry 112, English 22, and Western Civilization 12 without the benefit of having taken the corresponding first-semester classes.

Science, math, and physics required real, hard work but came easily to Nsakala. The social studies—political science, English, Western civilization, music, arts, et cetera—on the other hand, were hard nuts to crack for Nsakala. It goes without saying that fundamental to success in academia is possessing a good command of the language, something Nsakala was lacking. Nevertheless, he was determined to succeed by working extra hard relentlessly, day in and day out.

By midterm, Nsakala was beginning to get accustomed to the university life; he was scoring well in quizzes and midterm examinations across the board. So he started to relax a bit and occasionally meet people, both American and international students. One of the Fisk University students who became a friend of his was Orson W. Steward from Forrest City, Arkansas. In the photograph above, Nsakala is in the middle of the first row, and Orson is third from the left in the back row. Nsakala and Orson spent the 1966 Easter break with Orson's family in Forrest City. Nsakala also met some students from Africa and other countries who were studying at Fisk University, Vanderbilt University, Meharry Medical College, Scarritt College, et cetera.

Shown in this photograph are Sheline and her fiancé, Alain de Fontenay. Nsakala did not know where Sheline was going to school and/or what she was doing in Nashville. On the other hand, Alain de Fontenay was a graduate student in economics at Vanderbilt University. Nsakala became friends with Alain since he was French, meaning they could speak in French together. On some weekends, they would hang out, usually with other international students. One day, Sheline, Alain, and Nsakala went to a fast food restaurant near Vanderbilt University for lunch. In contravention of the Civil Rights Act of 1964, the restaurant refused to serve them because, they were told, the restaurant did not serve mixed couples. Yes, Nashville was still openly racially segregated; blacks and whites lived predominantly in different sections of the city. And they, for the most part, did not go to, for example, the same churches, and their children did not go to the same schools. In other words, blacks and whites were separate but not equal. These events left Nsakala disillusioned and bewildered.

All things considered, the spring semester of 1966 was a resounding academic success for Nsakala at Fisk University, as he was able to maintain better than a B average. After taking the first summer-school session, Nsakala headed to Wellman, Iowa, to spend the balance of the summer with the Yoder family and to welcome Luzibu, who was arriving from the Congo at the beginning of September.

5

Luzibu's Arrival in the United States of America: Cultural Hurdles

Living with a Host Family in Wellman, Iowa

Soon after the wedding ceremony in Kibunzi in July 1966, Luzibu moved to Léopoldville, where she stayed with Bena Nsakala Ndunga's family while waiting to immigrate to the United States.

The week before Luzibu's first airplane ride was very exciting and stressful. She spent sleepless nights with many thoughts racing through her mind: traveling to an unknown world, where she didn't know the culture, the language, or many people. She pondered how she would make the airplane connections in New York City without speaking the English language. Would she safely get to her destination? All these questions made the knots in Luzibu's stomach tighten. It all became a reality on Thursday, September 8, 1966, because on that date, Luzibu flew out of Maya-Maya Airport in Brazzaville in Congo-Brazzaville on KLM Airlines to JFK International Airport in New York City, via Amsterdam, the Netherlands.

As the airplane approached JFK International Airport, Luzibu felt her heart palpitate erratically with the fear of getting lost. The airplane landed, and the passengers proceeded to exit to their destinations or to make their connections. Luzibu sat down, petrified, because she didn't speak English. She plucked up her courage, got her travel documents out, approached one of the flight attendants, and asked, in French, if there was anyone who spoke French so that she could explain her situation. She needed to make connections at JFK and O'Hare Airport in Chicago for a final destination of Cedar Rapids, Iowa. A few minutes later, a gentleman came, and Luzibu showed him her travel documents. The gentleman told the flight attendants to ensure she made all the connections.

From JFK, she took another flight to O'Hare Airport in Chicago, Illinois, and then she finally made her connection to a smaller airplane to her destination. Luzibu was pleasantly surprised and relieved by the excellent help she received from the flight attendants throughout the trip. She made all her connections without a major hitch. Thanks be to God, there were/always are people with good hearts.

After about twenty hours of seemingly endless airplane rides, Luzibu arrived at the Cedar Rapids airport late at night on Friday, September 9, 1966, exhausted and confused. As she walked down the ramp, her legs trembled greatly with fear, and she glanced over at the arrival waiting lounge, where she noticed that Nsakala and Carroll were waiting for her. Luzibu felt a sense of relief. Then, with Carroll at the wheel, it was on to a Wellman, Iowa, farm. The host family was excited to meet Luzibu that evening; a cake and ice cream were served in her honor and in honor of the newlywed couple, Helen and Wilbur Yoder. Luzibu thought that ice cream was just too cold for her taste buds.

The next morning, at the break of dawn, Luzibu was awakened by crowing roosters, baaing lambs and goats, and mooing cows. She thought, *What?* These were some of the sounds she had heard back home in her village. Was she dreaming? Did she not get to the United States?

Now, recall that Luzibu came from a family of five brothers. What was peculiar about her host family was that there were also five brothers in the family. This photograph shows Mrs. Carrie Yoder and Mr. Lester Yoder (seated), and, from left to right, children Galen, Marcus, Wilbur, Carroll, and Milford. The Yoder family was not new at hosting foreign students at their home in Wellman, though Luzibu thought that she was the first girl they hosted. That being the case, Mrs. Yoder took it upon herself to make Luzibu feel comfortable, and a relationship between them began to develop. Luzibu's host family accepted and accommodated her as if she were one of their own.

Lester Yoder was a farmer who owned a mixed-crop and dairy farm with many types of livestock, including pigs, sheep, chickens, and cows. Two of the children, Marcus and Milford, ran the dairy part of the farm, among other things. Also, they grew crops such as corn, soybeans, and hay. Luzibu did not participate in milking the cows, but she participated in some of the many tasks the women on a farm performed—feeding the chickens, collecting the eggs, tending the garden, and preserving the crops from the garden through canning and freezing. She also participated in baking and quilting. Despite the language barrier, the host family went out of their way to make Luzibu feel at ease. The whole family was very kind, caring, loving, accommodating, and understanding.

Luzibu remembers vividly that a few days after her arrival, Mrs. Yoder was in the kitchen, giving her instructions to set the table for dinner. Luzibu stood there bewildered, listening to what Mrs. Yoder was saying. But all she could hear was "blah, blah, blah." Mrs. Yoder quickly realized that Luzibu did not understand a single word. Then Mrs. Yoder took a plate, showed it to Luzibu and said, "This is a plate, a spoon, a fork, a knife," and so on. That was one of Luzibu's first English lessons, and she began to learn English and practice speaking. Luzibu's experience with the Yoder family was very beneficial. She was learning to adapt to new places and situations and learning the American culture firsthand. Luzibu stayed with her host family for several months, and they became her family away from her motherland. She continues to keep in contact with the members of her host family and will always be thankful for their kindness in opening their home and their hearts to her.

Here, Luzibu and Nsakala are on the steps outside the backdoor, shelling beans just a few days after her arrival.

Shown here is Luzibu carrying the egg baskets on her head and in her hand, en route to the house from the chicken coop. This action so terrified Lester Yoder that it caused him to panic and almost gave him a heart attack. For good measure, he feared that the eggs would fall to the ground and all be damaged.

Here, Luzibu and Nsakala are with Milford at Great Grandma Barbara Yoder's, right after church service on a Sunday morning.

Luzibu Joins Nsakala in Nashville, Tennessee

In January 1967, Luzibu was ready to join Nsakala in Nashville. Nsakala had come to Wellman so they could travel together. Shown in this photograph are Luzibu and Nsakala opening the gifts that the Yoder family had given them to start their new life together.

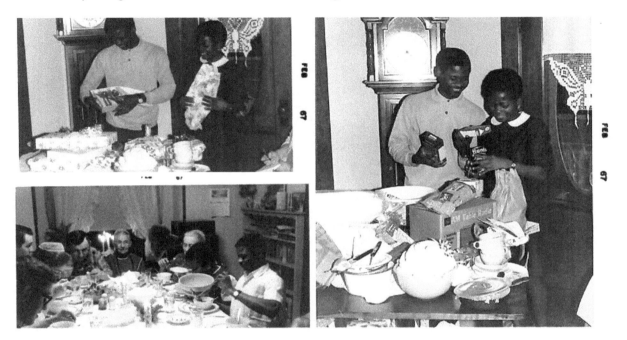

6

Life in Nashville, Tennessee

Financial Challenges

Luzibu and Nsakala arrived in Nashville by Greyhound bus in early February 1967 to a small apartment Nsakala had rented on Jefferson Street near Fisk University. A Jamaican fellow, John Daley, who had stayed in the apartment during the Christmas vacation, moved out. Luzibu and Nsakala found themselves with a bank account with only nine dollars in it. Luckily, the following day, Nsakala received his monthly stipend check from the ASPAU office through Fisk University. To supplement their rather low income, Luzibu started to babysit. In the top left photograph, she is with two toddlers: a baby girl, Fungai Chikosi, and a baby boy, Kotsanai Chikosi. They were children of a Meharry Medical School of Dentistry student from Rhodesia (Zimbabwe today), Chakanyuka Chikosi, and his wife, Winnie Chikosi. The other two people in the collage are obvious.

Luzibu and Nsakala started meeting other international students in Nashville through the International Students Association. Shown in this photograph is Nsakala with Lionel Gwadua from Cameroon.

Fisk University, being a historically black university, welcomed many famous speakers to address the issues of the day (civil rights, the Vietnam War, etc.). Shown in the photograph below, in the middle of the front row, is Miriam Makeba, then a political exile from South Africa, with the mostly African diaspora in Nashville in the spring of 1967. Nsakala and Luzibu are second and third from the left. In this photograph are students from such countries as Ghana, Kenya, Liberia, Malawi, Morocco, Mozambique, Nigeria, Tanzania, and Zimbabwe. It was taken at Fisk University following Makeba's talk about South Africa's apartheid system.

Welcoming Their First Bundle of Joy

The Nsakalas' first bundle of joy, a baby girl, Rose Marie Munlemvo Nsakala (Lemvo), was born at Meharry Medical Hospital in Nashville, Tennessee, on Wednesday, June 14, 1967. As Lemvo was born via a Caesarian section, she and her mom stayed at the hospital for ten days. This photograph was taken four days after her birth. Luzibu and Nsakala named their lovely daughter Munlemvo after Nsakala's big sister, who had taken care of him and his baby sister Swamunu after their mother died in Makanga in the early 1950s. Also, *Munlemvo* means "grace" in the Kikongo language. Therefore, this was appropriate, since Lemvo was born via a Caesarian procedure. As Luzibu did not have a family nearby, a Rhodesian (Zimbabwean today) lady, Winnie Chikosi, a registered nurse at Meharry Medical Hospital, was helpful in baby-caring matters. Another source of helpful advice was Mrs. Petit, who lived near Vanderbilt University with her husband, Tom, and their two young children. Dr. and Mrs. Petit belonged to an organization sponsored by the faith community of Nashville. Through this organization, they were the Nsakalas' host family.

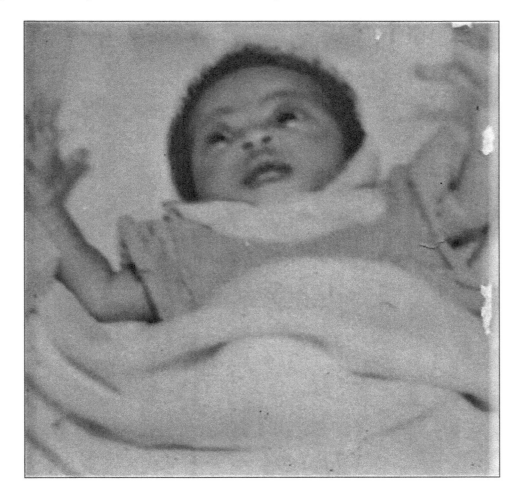

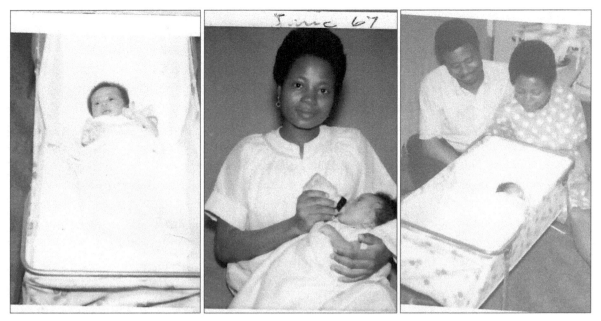

This collage shows Lemvo lying in her bassinet, being fed by her mom, and being admired by her visibly proud parents.

Here, Luzibu and Nsakala are with Sheline and Alain de Fontenay in August 1967. The four of them got together often on weekends.

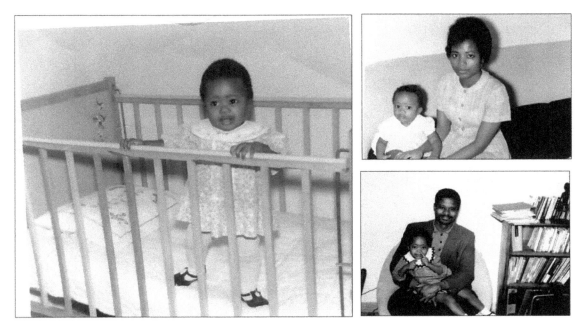

Here, Lemvo is trying to impress her parents with her standing skills. And she is pictured with Mom and Dad.

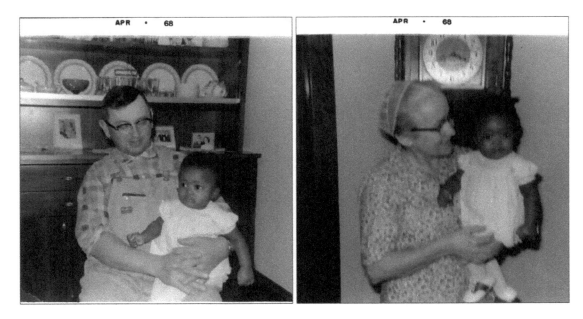

Lemvo, Luzibu, and Nsakala spent their Easter 1968 break with the Yoders in Wellman, Iowa. Here, Grandpa Lester and Grandma Carrie are proudly holding their "adopted" granddaughter.

75

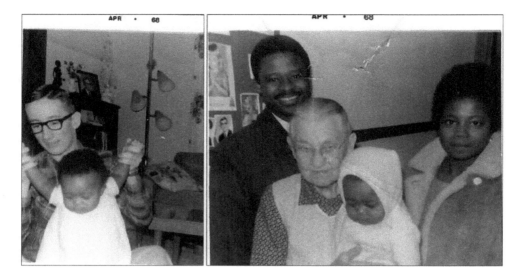

Not to be outdone, Galen Yoder is having fun with his "niece" Lemvo. And Great-Grandma Barbara Yoder, Grandpa Lester Yoder's mother, is enjoying the company of "great-granddaughter" Lemvo, Luzibu, and Nsakala, and vice versa.

Back in Nashville, from left to right, are Kotsanai Chikosi, Lemvo Nsakala, and Fungai Chikosi. Luzibu was babysitting the Chikosi children to get a few dollars to help supplement Nsakala's stipend from ASPAU.

Another source of income was Nsakala's various work activities:

- During the academic year, at Fisk University in the French language laboratory and the business office; and

- During summertime, in between summer school classes, as a chemistry lab assistant in the morning and as a bagger at a local supermarket.

In the above left photograph, Lemvo and Luzibu are with some Congolese folks in Nashville. Bitema Jean, third from the left, was in the United States for a few-months course in public health under the sponsorship of the Presbyterian Church in the Congo. The rest are Rémy Tshihamba, his wife Ruth, and their three children. Rémy was a student at Scarritt College. The photograph on the right features Lemvo, Luzibu, and the Tshihamba family, plus Lionel Gwadua from Cameroon and an unidentified fellow behind Luzibu and Ruth.

First Family Car Purchase

Around the spring of 1968, Luzibu and Nsakala made their first major investment with the purchase of a used VW Beetle for $350. A local bank reluctantly financed $300 for a twelve-month term. The car was insured through State Farm Insurance Company. Luzibu and Nsakala still insure their vehicles through State Farm today.

Educational Achievement

On June 2, 1969, Nsakala graduated cum laude from Fisk University in Nashville, Tennessee, with a four-year bachelor's degree in chemistry.

This collage shows the graduation exercise on the right and some of Luzibu and Nsakala's friends on the left. The left-hand photograph features Lemvo (in front) and the Tshihamba children. Also pictured are—in the back, from left to right—Lionel Gwandua from Cameroon, Luzibu, Nsakala, and Ruth Tshihamba from the Congo.

By graduation time, Nsakala had been admitted to all the graduate schools he had applied to, including Pennsylvania State University (Penn State); the University of Iowa; Howard University; and Worcester Polytechnic Institute, in Worcester, Massachusetts. Penn State offered the best financial package, vis-à-vis, particularly, graduate assistance. Hence, Luzibu and Nsakala selected Penn State.

7

Life at Pennsylvania State University, University Park, Pennsylvania

Cultural and Financial Challenges

At the beginning of September 1969, Lemvo, Luzibu, and Nsakala arrived at Pennsylvania State University, University Park, which is within the boundaries of State College, Pennsylvania. One of the first shockers was that there was no housing available for them, as a married couple with a child, on the university campus. Finding an affordable apartment became a big challenge. They would, for instance, call someone at a certain apartment complex to go see a unit advertised as being available. When they showed up, they would be told that the apartment had been rented out in the past few minutes. This was clearly in contravention of the Civil Rights Act of 1964. While discriminatory practices were out in the open in Nashville, it appeared that they were subtly alive in State College.

That said, they had to stay temporarily at an unaffordable executive house on Waupelani Drive in State College while waiting for campus housing to become available. Finally, there was an opening at Eastview Terrace, a collection of buildings that used to serve as military barracks. Their apartment was not ideal because it only had one bedroom. As a result, it, too, was a temporary home while they waited for availability in the Graduate Circle housing complex. The often-windswept Happy Valley weather was another challenge. It snowed a lot, and it was very cold. This photograph depicts one snowy day during the 1969–1970 winter season.

In June 1970, Lemvo, Luzibu, and Nsakala attended the wedding of Nancy Meyers and Carroll D. Yoder in Spring City, Pennsylvania (see photograph below). It should be recalled that Carroll Yoder taught at Sundi-Lutete High School in the Democratic Republic of the Congo with Nsakala during the 1964–1965 academic year.

In about September 1970, the Nsakalas finally moved into an apartment at the married graduate students' housing complex, called Graduate Circle (as mentioned above). In September 1970, they visited Nsakala's host family in Bedford, New York. These photographs show Mrs. Hope Levine with Lemvo, Luzibu, and Nsakala.

At Penn State, Luzibu and Nsakala found themselves facing financial challenges. As a holder of a J-2 visa, Luzibu was not permitted to work. Hence, she forcefully made her case to Mrs. Ardeth Frisby, Penn State's international students' adviser, to get her working permit papers. Mrs. Frisby, perhaps annoyed by Luzibu's relentless persistence and decision to remain in the office with her daughter until she was granted permission to work, successfully petitioned the Immigration and Naturalization Service to grant Luzibu a special permit to work. Furthermore, Luzibu also insisted that Mrs. Frisby help her find a job on the campus. Luzibu worked at Waring Dining Hall during the fall and spring terms and with the campus maintenance crew during summer terms. Besides working on the campus—and without the benefit of the three months of intensive English classes that Nsakala had taken—Luzibu took adult evening classes in English as a second language. She also took classes in sewing. Furthermore, she and Nsakala rented a garden lot from the university to grow vegetables to supplement their food needs.

And now, on to another wedding, this one also in Pennsylvania. At Penn State, Luzibu and Nsakala were active with the International Students' Organization's affairs. In the top left photograph are Tom Mukake and his wife from Cameroon, and on the bottom left is James Ashu, also from Cameroon. Along with Luzibu and Nsakala, they were some of the attendees of the wedding ceremony on the Penn State campus of Angelus Owili-Eger from Uganda and Michelle from Philadelphia, Pennsylvania.

This collage shows the international diaspora getting together around the spring of 1972 at Penn State. People from different nations prepared their favorite dishes to share.

This photograph shows Lemvo, Luzibu, and Nsakala with Ruth and Rémy Tshihamba, plus their three children, who were visiting from Washington, DC, at the beginning of the summer of 1972; it also shows Nancy and Eric Yoder and Nancy's mother, who, with Carroll Yoder, were visiting from Harrisonburg, Virginia.

In the middle of a closeted Jim Crow environment, there were plenty of kind and loving people. Having a soft heart in a cruel world is courage, not weakness. As an example of this philosophy, Luzibu's coworkers at Penn State's Waring Dining Hall gave her a baby shower shortly before the birth of their second bundle of joy.

Welcoming Their Second Bundle of Joy

From the beginning of Luzibu's pregnancy, her obstetrician-gynecologist had determined that she would have to deliver her baby via Caesarian section. As September 1, 1972, was the target due date, Luzibu had to check into the Mount Nittany Health Center in State College on August 31, 1972. This photograph shows Lemvo and Nsakala taking Luzibu to the hospital.

On Friday, September 1, 1972, Luzibu delivered a healthy baby boy via Caesarian section. He came out screaming and ready to conquer the world, according to one of the delivery room nurses. This photograph shows the baby at four days old. The happy and proud parents named him Mukiese Nsakala. *Mukiese* means "with happiness" in the Kikongo language.

After seven days in the hospital, both Mukiese and Luzibu were released. In the left-hand photograph, they are being wheeled down by a nurse with, from left, Roger Gurira and his daughter Shingai, Lemvo, and Nsakala, surrounding them.

This collage shows the Nsakalas and their friends arriving from the hospital to their Graduate Circle apartment. The photograph on the left features Josephine Gurira holding Mukiese and Luzibu and Lemvo holding a gift for the baby. The top right photograph shows Emmanuel Mundi with the Guriras, Lemvo, and Luzibu. The Gurira and Nsakala families are shown together in the lower right photograph.

At home, Mukiese is being fed by his mother and admired effusively by the whole family.

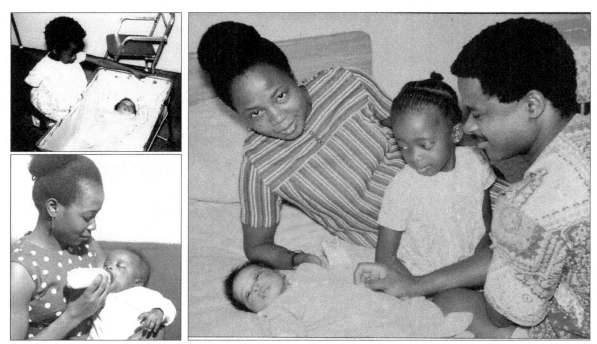

Family Activities

The family is celebrating Mukiese's first birthday on September 1, 1973.

In 1974, the Nsakala family spent part of their summer vacation in Wellman, Iowa, with the Yoder family. Grandma Carrie Yoder is flanked by Lemvo and Mukiese. After the Nsakala family returned to Penn State, Lemvo used this photograph in her first-grade show-and-tell time to introduce her "Grandma Carrie."

The Yoder family was that special to the Nsakala family! During their many visits to Wellman, the Nsakala children enjoyed spending time with some of the local children of their own ages. In this photograph, Lemvo is hanging out with Sheila, Shari, and Shaun Yoder, all related to Carrie and Lester Yoder.

This photograph features Lemvo's second-grade class (1974–1975) in State College, Pennsylvania.

This 1975 collage shows a variety of people. In the top left photograph, Luzibu and Nsakala are shown with a Congolese couple, Bwela and Mavumisa Kiantandu, visiting from Virginia. Bob Ulshaefer, a graduate student at Penn State, is shown with his brother during a visit with his family in Mahanoy City, Pennsylvania, in the bottom left photograph. The photograph on the right shows some students from the African diaspora, with the exception of Bob Stewart from Massachusetts. Bob had recently returned from Zaïre, where he had served in the Peace Corps. He was visiting his friend Bob Ulshaefer at Penn State.

This collage of photos from 1975 shows the Nsakala family on the top right, with Gwandua Lionel from Cameroon. Lionel was at Fisk University in Nashville and at Penn State University; he was like a little brother to Nsakala. The rest of the photographs in the collage feature those two special African families: the Oumas from Kenya and the Guriras from Zimbabwe.

This other 1975 collage shows, on the top right, Luzibu, Lemvo, and Mukiese posing beside the family's second car, a brand-new Datsun 710. The top left photograph shows Lemvo and Mukiese with the Ouma children (Adhiambo and Akinyi, third and fourth from the left). The Ouma and Nsakala families were enjoying themselves at an amusement park near Penn State University.

Ultimate Educational Achievements

Educational achievement is one of the most important factors of a student's academic journey. Nsakala graduated twice from Penn State University. The first graduation was when he received a master's degree in the fuel science section of the material sciences department in June 1973. The second was for a PhD from the same department in November 1976.

This collage shows Nsakala in a PhD cap and gown and his joyful family during the graduation ceremony.

Following a successful defense of his PhD thesis in September, Nsakala was hired by Professor Philip L. Walker, his thesis co-adviser (the other adviser was Professor Robert H. Essenhigh), as a postdoctoral scholar. This job entailed, principally:

- supervising the research and development (R & D) work of some PhD candidates in fuel science; and

- continuing his own R & D work in coal pyrolysis/devolatilization/combustion processes.

During his postdoctoral scholar tenure, Nsakala made a technical presentation of his PhD-based work at the 1977 meeting of the American Chemical Society Division of Fuel Chemistry in New Orleans, Louisiana. And, in 1977, he also coauthored, with professors Philip L. Walker and Robert H. Essenhigh, a technical paper based on his PhD work in the journal *Combustion Science and Technology*, Volume 16. Additionally, in 1978, two of his technical papers coauthored with others were published in volume 57 of the journal *Fuel*. Nsakala's educational journey would not have been possible without the support of his wife, Luzibu Nsakala, and family, and many other people. Nsakala is thankful for this support and the encouragement and inspiration to follow his dreams. More importantly, he thanks God for all His grace and blessings.

The collage below shows Lemvo celebrating her eighth birthday (left-hand photograph) and an earlier birthday (lower right photo). The top right photograph shows the Nsakala family with a special friend of theirs, Jerry Jessop of Bellefonte, Pennsylvania. Jerry was Luzibu's mentor when they both worked at the cafeteria in Penn State's Waring Dining Hall.

Occasionally, Luzibu and Nsakala got together with their fellow Penn Staters to relax. Here, they are enjoying themselves at the Phyrst bar in State College with the Ohmines from Japan, the Gootzaits from the United States, and Angelos Kokkinos from Greece.

In the fall of 1977, Nsakala accepted a job offer from Combustion Engineering, Inc., as it was then called, in Windsor, Connecticut, effective December 5, 1977. His initial title with this boiler solutions/ original equipment manufacturer was senior research and development engineer.

8

Life in Greater Hartford, Connecticut

The Nsakala family spent thirty-two and three-quarters years in greater Hartford, Connecticut, which made organizing the information in Chapter 8 by topics very challenging. Hence, the authors chose to arrange it by decades.

First Decade

The following highlights/major events took place during the Nsakalas' first decade in greater Hartford, which extended from 1977 to 1986:

- Transition from the academic world of Penn State University to the business workforce in greater Hartford in 1977;

- Purchase of the first family house in West Hartford in 1980;

- Luzibu's graduation from Morse School of Business in 1980;

- Family visit to Zaïre in 1981;

- Arrival of Nsakala's nephew Diampisa Bena from Zaïre in 1984;

- Lemvo's graduation from Conard High School in West Hartford in 1985; and

- Diampisa Bena's graduation from Hartford Community College in 1986.

Some of these and other events are highlighted photographically in the following pages.

In the November 1977 time frame, the Nsakala family flew from the airport in Black Moshannon, Pennsylvania, to greater Hartford to find an apartment in which to live. Based primarily on the good reputation of the West Hartford public school system, they rented an apartment there, on Kane Street. This collage shows Lemvo and Mukiese riding their bicycles, walking to school, and, of course, learning some of the essential life skills by doing their chores in the apartment.

Here are more glimpses of life in 1978. The left-hand photograph shows Mukiese playing with a friend inside the apartment; the top right photograph shows Satome Ohmine with Luzibu, Lemvo, Mukiese, and the Gurira children; and the bottom right photograph shows Luzibu, Lemvo, and Mukiese with Josephine Gurira and her children. Satome and her husband, Shigeto, were living in the same apartment complex that the Nsakalas were living in, and the Gurira family was visiting from Grinnell, Iowa.

Children's birthdays were always a big occasion in the Nsakala household. In the photos below, the family can be seen celebrating Mukiese's sixth birthday.

In the summer of 1979, the Nsakala family visited with the Levine family in Bedford, New York. The Levines were Nsakala's host family in 1965, right after he completed his English training in Brattleboro, Vermont. Here, Lemvo, Mukiese, and Nsakala are enjoying a swim in the Levines' swimming pool; Lemvo and Mukiese are walking the host family dog; Mrs. Hope Levine and Luzibu are watching the swimmers; and the Nsakala family is posing for a snapshot.

In the photograph below, Lemvo is playing flute with her friend Theresa Frank and others during a 1979 Sedgwick Middle School winter concert.

Here, the Nsakalas are spending quality time together at various Connecticut amusement venues: Ocean Beach in New London, Farmington Reservoir in West Hartford, and the Elizabeth Park Rose Garden in Hartford.

Agnes and John Cogoli, shown with Lemvo, Mukiese, and Luzibu in the two photographs on the right, were friends of the Nsakala family. John and Nsakala were fellow graduate students in fuel science at Penn State. After earning his MS degrees in fuel science and education at Penn State, John and his wife, Agnes, returned to greater Hartford, where he was a mathematics teacher in one of the local public school systems. John and Agnes, who also lived in West Hartford, joined the Nsakala family to watch Lemvo march in the 1979 Memorial Day Parade with the Sedgwick Middle School band (left and top right photographs). The Cogolis and Nsakalas also visited Yale University's Peabody Museum of Natural History together in the fall of 1979 (bottom right photograph).

Pictured below are Lemvo and Mukiese showing off their favorite stuffed animals, which they called Teddy Bear and Canaan Koala Bear, respectively, and their pet cockatiel named Koko.

Below, Lemvo is celebrating her eleventh or twelfth birthday with her middle school friends Dinah Creco and Theresa Frank.

In 1980, the Nsakala family achieved yet another major milestone in their lives. That is, realizing the American dream, they bought their first house on Hollywood Avenue in West Hartford, into which they moved at the end of October. The photographs in the collage show some of what it takes to be homeowners, for example:

- Shoveling the snow in winter,

- Raking the leaves in the fall, and

- Painting the house.

Family history is very important to an individual. By knowing where one comes from, one can have a better perspective on one's life. Having a better understanding of one's family background allows one to appreciate the things that he or she would normally take for granted. Keeping this in mind, Luzibu and Nsakala decided to take their family on a one-month vacation to Zaïre in 1981 to let Lemvo and Mukiese experience firsthand the culture of their parents and meet their parents' relatives. This collage shows, on the left, Luzibu, Lemvo, and Mukiese at Brussels Airport, en route to Zaïre, in June 1981. The photographs on the right show Lemvo with first cousin Diampisa Bena and Mukiese playing with neighborhood children in Kinshasa.

This collage shows Nsakala's relatives in Makanga Village and Kinshasa. In the photograph on the top right, Nsakala and first cousin Nsakala Lusolamo are kneeling in the front row. Standing in the back row are, from left to right, Uncle Lutete Babwa, a cousin from the village of Tadi, Bena Nsakala Ndunga, and another cousin from Tadi. The bottom right photograph shows some of Nsakala's siblings: sisters Swamunu Makomba (holding a baby), Mena Julienne in Makanga, and brother Bena Nsakala Ndunga. The left-hand photograph shows Ngizulu Simon, the family chief in Kinshasa.

Shown in this collage are more of the relatives from Nsakala's side of the family. On the top left are, from left to right, Nsakala's sister Munlemvo Luvisa and two sisters-in-law, Nkenda Pauline and Batunda Tusevo Esther (who, as mentioned earlier, is affectionately referred to as Mama Kota). The bottom left photograph shows Mama Kota with, from left to right, her niece Claudine Makinutewa and children Bena Jeannette, Bena Nzuzi, Bena Ali, and Bena Ndaya. The right-hand photograph shows, from left to right, Bena Bernadette, Lemvo Nsakala, and Bena Constance.

Back at home in the United States, Luzibu and Nsakala always supported their children's interests in their educational endeavors and their extracurricular activities as well. Here, for instance, the whole family is on the grounds of King Philip Middle School in West Hartford on a Saturday morning in 1981, helping Mukiese launch a rocket that he built from a kit with Dad's help. Was this foreshadowing the creation of a future engineer? Stay tuned!

The Guriras and the Oumas are the two families from the Nsakalas' Pennsylvania State University days (see Chapter 7) with whom they still keep in touch today. These two collages are cases in point. In 1983, the Gurira family decided to move from Grinnell, Iowa, where Roger and Josephine were a chemistry professor and librarian at Grinnell College, respectively, to Harare, Zimbabwe, their homeland. Before making this move, the Gurira family drove more than 1,200 miles to greater Hartford to say goodbye to the Nsakala family. This collage shows, on the left, Nsakala, Luzibu, Roger, and Josephine enjoying a stroll on the beach at Ocean Beach, New London, Connecticut. The other two photographs show both families standing in front of the Nsakala home in West Hartford.

After a few days together in West Hartford, both the Gurira and Nsakala families drove to Piscataway, New Jersey, for the three Penn State families' reunion, where the Guriras would say goodbye to the Ouma family. The photograph on the left shows Henry and Nsakala in the front row and Grace, Roger, Josephine, and Luzibu sitting in the back row in the living room of the Oumas' home. The photograph on the right shows the Gurira family standing in front of the Oumas' home. Yes, the ties between the Gurira, Ouma, and Nsakala families are still today virtually equivalent to actual family ties. Yes, indeed, true friends are like family.

Speaking of family ties, since 1978, Luzibu and Nsakala had attempted to invite Diampisa Bena to join them in the United States to continue his higher education studies. This effort finally came to fruition on Friday, February 7, 1984. This collage shows Diampisa arriving at John F. Kennedy International Airport in New York City, where he was welcomed by Luzibu and Nsakala. It was a major event in the lives of the Nsakalas, as it represented

the addition of a fifth member to the family. Diampisa is the third child of Bena Nsakala Ndunga (Nsakala's eldest sibling) and Mama Kota Batunda Tusevo Esther (see Family Tree: Two Generations of Nsakala and His Siblings in the appendix).

On Saturday, February 8, 1984, the family took Diampisa on a tour of greater Hartford. In this collage, Diampisa is standing in front of the Connecticut State Capitol, and the rest of the jubilant family is shown with him in downtown Hartford.

On Sunday, February 9, 1984, the Nsakalas took Diampisa to Northampton, Massachusetts, where he would study English as a second language (ESL) at the New England Language Institute until August 1984. After the successful completion of his ESL study, Diampisa enrolled at Hartford Community College. Having many nieces and nephews in Zaïre meant that Luzibu and Nsakala were already an aunt and an uncle. Nevertheless, Diampisa calling them Auntie Luzibu and Uncle Nsakala popularized these attributes among family, in greater Hartford and beyond.

This set of photographs from 1984 identifies some Combustion Engineering, Inc. (C-E) employees who made a big difference in Nsakala's life during the early years of his career at C-E. The top photograph shows Richard (Dick) Borio, who hired Nsakala and was his first manager in fuel technology at the Kreisinger Development Laboratory (KDL), in Windsor, Connecticut. Sitting around a table in the foreground of the lower photograph are, from left to right, Gary J. Goetz, Nsakala's first supervisor in fuel technology; Gary's wife, Christine Goetz; Luzibu; and JoEllen Allen, the fuel technology department's secretary.

Another major milestone was reached by the Nsakala family in 1985. It pertained to the graduation of their daughter Lemvo from Conard High School in West Hartford. The next three collages depict Lemvo's graduation ceremony and the party thrown by the family on her behalf. This collage shows Lemvo posing for a photograph in front of their home in West Hartford, then she is performing in the school band with others during the ceremony. Lemvo actually played flute with the school band throughout her high school career in concerts, in Memorial Day marches, at charitable events, et cetera.

The photograph on the left shows the proud family sitting in the audience at the Bushnell Amphitheater in Hartford during the graduation ceremony. The top right photograph shows Bwela Kiantandu, Diampisa Bena, Luzibu, and Lemvo. And the bottom right photograph shows Lemvo with her classmate friends during her graduation party at home in West Hartford. It is noteworthy that

Bwela Kiantandu and her son Matondo Kiantandu (next to the last from the left in the left-hand photograph) were staying with the Nsakala family while Bwela's husband, Dr. Mavumisa Kiantandu, was working in Kenya for the Institute for Biblical Languages & Translation. It is also noteworthy that, to the joy of the family, by Lemvo's graduation from Conard High School, she had already been admitted to the University of Connecticut in Storrs for the fall of 1985 to study business administration.

The collage below shows some of the guests at Lemvo's graduation party. The left-hand photograph shows Neela and Ramesh Patel (Nsakala's coworker at C-E). The top right photograph shows Agnes and John Cogoli with their son John-Mark. And the bottom right picture shows the Nsakalas' immediate neighbors, the Podrebartz family, on the left and the Carlson family on the right. The Cogolis were friends of the Nsakala family.

Another major milestone was achieved by the Nsakala family in 1986. It pertained to the graduation of Diampisa from Hartford Community College. This collage shows the proud family members at his graduation ceremony. The way forward for Diampisa was, to the satisfaction of the family, to attend Central Connecticut State University to study biology.

In the summer of 1986, the family drove to Wellman, Iowa, to visit with the Yoder family. It was Diampisa's first approximately 1,100-mile trip by car. It afforded him the opportunity to appreciate the vastness of the United States. The top left photograph in this collage shows Mukiese with some Wellman-area children. The bottom left photograph shows Luzibu and Lemvo proudly posing with Grandma Carrie Yoder. The top right photograph shows Lemvo with Renée Yoder, Grandma Carrie's granddaughter. And the bottom right photograph shows Mukiese, Diampisa, and Nsakala playing soccer in the backyard of the Yoder family home.

Second Decade

The Nsakala family's second decade in greater Hartford, which extended from 1987 to 1996, was full of major, transformative events. Some of them are listed below.

- Lukiantima Josée Bena's arrival from Zaïre in 1987;

- Luzibu and Nsakala becoming US citizens in 1988;

- The birth of grandniece Luann Bena in 1989;

- Three family graduations in 1990: Mukiese from Conard High School, Lemvo from the University of Connecticut, and Luzibu from Central Connecticut University;

- Luzibu and Nsakala's trip to Zaïre in 1991;

- Luzibu and Nsakala's trip to Sydney, Australia, in 1992;

- Bena Nsakala Ndunga's four-month visit from Zaïre to the United States, Lemvo and Jay's wedding, and grandnephew Brian Bena's birth in 1993;

- The acquisition of Combustion Engineering by Asea Brown Boveri, which opened the door for Nsakala to work in Switzerland intermittently, starting in 1994;

- Mukiese's graduation from Rutgers University in 1995; and

- Luzibu, Mukiese, and Nsakala's move from West Hartford to South Windsor in 1996.

Some of these and other events are highlighted photographically in the collages presented on the following pages.

On Saturday, November 7, 1987, the extended Nsakala family was delighted to be joined by another member, Kitomba Lukiantima Josée Bena, from Zaïre. This collage shows Josée arriving at John F. Kennedy International Airport in New York City, where she was welcomed by her husband, Diampisa Bena (left-hand photograph), and Luzibu and Nsakala (top and bottom right photographs).

It is perhaps noteworthy that the Nsakala family's hospitality continued, and still continues, to know no bounds. In the two top photographs from 1988, the Nsakala family is posing in front of their home in West Hartford with the Nzima family (Ayicha, Antoine, André, and Mae), who were visiting from Pine Hill, New Jersey. The bottom left photograph features Nsakala and Luzibu with Dr. and Mrs. Kiantandu (from left to right, Bwela and Mavumisa). Both Bwela and Mavumisa were from villages near Kibunzi in the Democratic Republic of the Congo (DRC). The Nsakala family hosted Bwela and son Matondo (second from left in the lower right photograph) while Mavumisa was working in Kenya with the Institute for Biblical Languages & Translation. The lower right photograph also features the Kiantandu family, Diampisa Bena, Lemvo, Mukiese, Luzibu, and Joseph Kunzika (far right). Joseph Kunzika is an Angolan citizen who grew up in the DRC.

The Swedish Evangelical Church (*Sevenska Missionsförbundet,* or SMF) founded the Kibunzi Mission (*Vula dia Kibunzi*) in 1888. So, in 1988, the church, at the time called Evangelical Community of Zaïre (*Cummunauté Évangélique du Zaïre*, or CEZ), celebrated the centennial of the Kibunzi Mission. The church building, which was completed in 1907, looked in 1988 as shown in the top right photograph of this collage. The lower right photograph shows a presumably Swedish missionary shaking hands with Madede Lessa, Luzibu's mother, during the centennial celebration. Madede was one of the senior deaconesses featured at the event.

Madede Lessa's prayer during this celebration, transcribed by Dr. Kiantandu Mavumisa, is shown below. Luzibu and Nsakala's translation of the prayer from Kikongo to English is shown on the next page.

```
          Lusambulu lwa mama Madede lukasambila mu kia sabala kia
1 okoba mvu 1988 ku lukutakanu lwa nkembo a 100 mvu kia vula dia
Kibunzi.

          Tata, Se dieto mu kayengele ;
          I ngeye wa sema biabio !
          Tata, Se dieto.
          Tu kutondele mu nlemvo aku usikilanga
          Ntangu i kayimani
          I ngeye, tata wafila ntumwa
          zaku zatuka ku nsi ya Ntama
          mu kutulonga mambu maku ;
          Mambu maku i minsiku mitufweti tumama
          mpasi vo twakala Banlongo.
          I mambu maku makutulonganga vumi ye yenge biaku.
          Mfumu Nzambi ,
          Nkie mpila matondo mfweti vutula kwa ngeye
          Mu mona ndonga ya mpila yayi
          Mu diambu dia nlemvo aku
          tumweni diaka zintumwa zaku
          zafilwa mu nsi yayi
          mu samuna mambu maku
          I bau bamweswa mpasi zazingi mu nsi yayi
          Mu diambu dia samuna  Nsamu aku.
          Tata Se dieto mu kayengele,
          Tutondele mu babonsono
          Bameni sala mu vula dia Kibunzi
          Tutondele mu ntumwa zaku ziwafila
          Tata, Se dieto mu kayengele ;
          Tukutondele mu 100 mvu za Kibunzi
          Bwabu, zola kwaku kwa mwangane mwamo
          Bwabu mbebe ya mwangisa
          Mambu maku mu nsi eto
          I yeto
          Matondo Tata Se dieto Nzambi
          Mu diambu dia nlendo kiaku
          Mfumu makayi kalunga
          Watambudila nsamu wa mbote
          Walongwa mu nsi yayi
          Nzambi Se dieto,
          Nga bwe tulenda visila mavanga maku e ?
          Nga bwe tulenda toma ku ki-
          yakula kwa ngeye ?
          Mfumu Nzambi
          Utusadila beto babo mu yinza diaku
          Bika twavanga mavolele
          Bika twatina mayubelanga.
          Mfumu Yisu
          Utulemvukila mu momo
          Matwalembane vanga
          Mpeve ya Nlongo utusadisa
          Tulombele bo mu  nkumbwa Yisu Mvulusi eto
          Amen :
```

Née 1911–1995

Mama Madede.

This prayer lasted about 45 minutes and was the Highlight of the celebration. she is a Prophetess.

Madede Lessa's Prayer on October 1, 1988, During the Centennial Celebration of Kibunzi Mission[1]

Our Father in the highest

It's you who created everything

Father, our Father

We thank you for everything that you do for us at all times

It's you who sent to us your Servants from afar to teach us your word

Your word constitutes the laws that we need to obey in order to be Saints

It's the word that teaches us your respect and peace

Father God

How can I thank you for the huge crowd at this celebration?

By your grace, we now see again here your Servants

who were sent to this country to preach the word?

They are the ones who were given a hard time in this country for preaching your word

Our Father in the highest

We thank you for all who have served in Kibunzi

We thank you for the Servants that you sent to us

Our Father in the highest

We thank you for the one hundred years (of Missionaries) in Kibunzi

Now, your love is spread all over the place

Now, the responsibility to spread your word is ours

Thanks, our Father God, for your power

A good many people accepted the Good news

Preached in this country

Our Father God

How can we understand your word?

How can we give ourselves to you?

Our Father God

Use all of us in your pastures

May your will be done

Lead us not into temptations

Lord Jesus

Forgive us our transgressions

May the Holy Spirit be with us

We ask all these things in the name of Jesus Christ

Amen

---

1   Kikongo version written by Dr. Kiantandu Mavumisa. Translated to English by Luzibu and Nsakala.

Back to the immediate family matters: Mukiese played peewee football in West Harford when he was in the third grade in 1980. His parents were dissatisfied with the behavior of the coaching staff. Consequently, they decided that Mukiese would not continue to play football the following season. Obviously, Mukiese was not happy with this decision, though he realized that it was pretty much final. To his credit, Mukiese did not strenuously object. Instead, he negotiated a deal with his parents to allow him to play football starting with his freshman year (1986–1987) at Conard High School.

Fast-forward to the beginning of the summer of 1986. Mukiese, Matondo, and other neighborhood children were riding their bicycles around the tri-city (West Hartford-Newington-Hartford) corner. Mukiese took a spill and broke his right wrist. He was immediately taken to the orthopedic department at Hartford Hospital, where they put a cast on his arm, as shown in this collage. After the cast was removed from Mukiese's arm, the orthopedist declared Mukiese healed. At this point, the parents privately asked the doctor to forbid Mukiese to play football, at least during his freshman year at Conard. To the embarrassment of his parents, the doctor flatly rejected their request and said that Mukiese was ready to play any sport and that there was nothing to worry about. Hence, Mukiese went on to be a football superstar throughout his high school years at Conard. And this anecdote became an internal family joke for a long time.

In 1989, the extended Nsakala family welcomed their first third-generation child when Lukian-tima (a.k.a. Josée) and Diampisa Bena welcomed their baby girl, Luann Bena, on Sunday, March 12, 1989, at the New Britain Hospital, New Britain, Connecticut. The proud parents are shown in the top right photograph holding baby Luann. In the lower right photograph, mother and child are surrounded by an unidentified lady, Dad, and Auntie Luzibu.

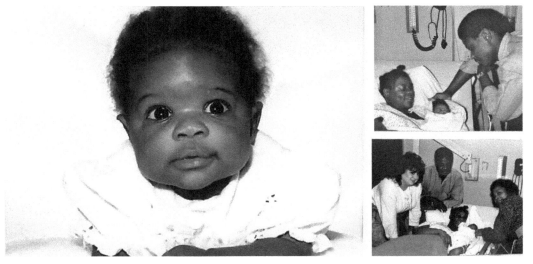

Here, mother Josée, cousin Lemvo, Auntie Luzibu, and Uncle Nsakala are showering baby Luann with unconditional love.

Below, Luann is shown with cousins Lemvo and Mukiese and being fed by Lemvo.

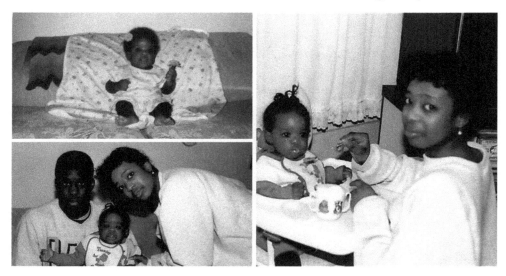

In the spring of 1989, Nsakala and his colleague at Combustion Engineering Ramesh Patel attended a technical conference on fossil fuels combustion in San Francisco, California. Nsakala was presenting some of the results of their research and development work regarding fluidized bed combustion technology. The left-hand photograph in the collage below shows Nsakala standing on the San Francisco side of the Golden Gate Bridge. In the top right photograph, Ramesh and Nsakala are standing near the bridge overlooking San Francisco. Finally, Nsakala is seen standing in front of the Coit Tower in San Francisco.

In the spring of 1989, Nsakala took Mukiese and two of his Conard High School friends (Brian Cagney and Kevin Digby) to Penn State to visit (see collage below). The top left photograph shows, from left to right, Brian Cagney, Kevin Digby, and Mukiese. The bottom left photograph shows Nsakala with Brian and Kevin. The top right photograph shows the three lads posing in front of Beaver Football Stadium. The Nittany Lions ice creamery is a popular attraction, and the group did not fail to sample some of the yummy ice cream produced there.

The Mubagwa and Nsakala families met in greater Hartford around 1988. Dr. Kanigula Mubagwa (a.k.a. Kani) received his MD degree from the University of Kinshasa, Zaïre, and his PhD in physiology from Leuven University in Leuven, Belgium. From Leuven, the Mubagwa family moved to Harare, Zimbabwe, in 1985, where Kani did postdoctoral work at the University of Zimbabwe. From Harare, the family moved to Farmington, Connecticut, in 1988, where Kani continued postdoctoral work in physiology at the University of Connecticut Health Center until 1991. The Mubagwa and Nsakala families forged an enduring relationship, which would continue beyond 1991, when the Mubagwa family moved back to Leuven, Belgium. During their more or less two years together in greater Hartford, the two families got together many times at the Nsakalas' home in West Hartford and at the Mubagwa's apartment in Farmington.

These two collages below illustrate some of their times together.

The first collage shows Fortuna Mubagwa, Lemvo, and Luzibu in African outfits and Kani and Fortuna at the dinner table in West Hartford with Luzibu, Nsakala, and others.

The right-hand photographs in this collage show the Mubagwa children Nsuli and Linda (from left to right) in the top photograph and Ndamuso and Akonkwa (from left to right) in the bottom photograph, picnicking in West Hartford. And the left-hand photograph again shows Fortuna, Luzibu, and Lemvo, with the Mubagwas' family friend.

The visits from friends didn't stop there. In 1990, the Gbadebo family visited the Nsakalas in West Hartford from Ellicott City, Maryland. Standing in the back row, from left to right, are Moni, Obisesan (Obi), Evonne, and Peju; Kemi is in the front row. The Gbadebo family is also shown in the right-hand photographs taken earlier, in 1986, when they still lived in the greater Hartford area. Obi is originally from Nigeria, and Evonne is an African American.

As stated before, Mukiese was involved in athletics throughout his tenure at Conard High School. This collage depicts some of the activities he was involved in during the 1989–1990 academic year, including football, basketball, and the long jump. Mukiese excelled in all these activities.

Luzibu's artistic creativity is one of her God-given gifts that she puts to good use. Here, Luzibu is shown with some of her creations at a fair in Enfield, Connecticut. She often creates these dolls, principally to raise funds for charitable causes.

After graduating from Morse School of Business in 1980, Luzibu went on to work for Travelers Insurance in Hartford, Connecticut, as an accounting technician. But Luzibu's eagerness to learn more did not stop there. She was ambitious and driven by her desire to achieve a college degree. Over the next seven years, Luzibu would accumulate enough college credits from the University of Connecticut, West Hartford Campus; the University of Hartford; and Central Connecticut State University (CCSU) to fulfill the typical requirements of the first academic year. In 1987, she matriculated at CCSU full time after resigning from her job at Travelers. She went on and majored in accounting and successfully gained her bachelor's degree. The previous collage shows Luzibu with family during her graduation ceremony at CCSU in June 1990. Soon after graduation from CCSU, Luzibu would start working at Ames Department Stores Inc. in Rocky Hill, Connecticut, as a corporate staff accountant.

Lemvo is shown here graduating from the University of Connecticut, also in June 1990, with a BS in business administration. The family is proudly sitting in the stands of the on-campus football stadium during the graduation ceremony and posing for a snapshot afterward. Lemvo was later hired permanently by ADVO Corporation in Windsor, where she had been working on a part-time basis.

The trifecta of 1990 culminated in Mukiese's graduation from Conard High School. This collage shows Mukiese posing in front of the family home in West Hartford alone and with his high school buddy Russell Romano. The whole family is sitting in the audience at the Bushnell Amphitheater in Hartford during the graduation ceremony. Finally, Mukiese is posing in front of the cake during his graduation party at home.

A lot has to be said about Luzibu's ambition, as she graduated from the university at the same time as her children: one from a university and the other one from high school. She seized the opportunity to get her BS to fulfill her dream/goal. The United States provides the opportunity for success to anyone from any background. Consequently, one should jump at the opportunity whenever it knocks at his or her door.

Luzibu and Nsakala decided to make a three-week visit to the Republic of Zaïre in June and July 1991, after several family members passed away. During this stay, they spent one week in Kinshasa, one week in the Makanga and Kibunzi villages, and then one more week in Kinshasa before returning to the United States. In Kinshasa, they stayed with the Bena family in Kindongolosi, Camp Christ Roi.

This collage features Luzibu sitting with some of the relatives on her side of the family in the backyard of the Benas' Kindongolosi residence: with paternal uncle Kalabi in the left-hand photograph; with brother Lubombolo lwa Nzambi and his wife, Matondo, in the top right photograph; and with other relatives in the lower right photograph.

In the left-hand photograph of this collage, Luzibu is using a mortar and pestle (*Su ye Muisu*) to grind cassava leaves while Nsakala's sister Munlemvo and sister-in-law Nkenda Pauline are looking on. In the top right photograph, Luzibu is manually doing the laundry, and in the lower right photograph, she is decanting the ground cassava leaves into a bowl while Mama Kota Batunda and others are looking on.

Many of the houses even in Kinshasa lack the basic modern amenities, which make such easy tasks as washing clothing and grinding cassava leaves very time consuming and laborious to do. During this first week in Kinshasa, the extended family gathered at Kindongolosi to make a few decisions: for example:

- The expenses incurred by the family in Kinshasa during the passing of Komono Nsakala would need to be defrayed. Luzibu and Nsakala paid off all outstanding debts; and

- Family Chief Ngizulu Simon and Bena Nsakala Ndunga would accompany Luzibu and Nsakala to Makanga, Kibunzi, and other villages. Lubombolo lwa Nzambi would go by truck from Kinshasa to Kibunzi, carrying various gifts for the family, particularly in Makanga, Kibunzi, Ntandu a Nzadi, and Kingoyo.

So, after one week in Kinshasa, Ngizulu, Bena, Nsakala, and Luzibu went by a commercial truck to Kimpese, which is located along the railway between Kinshasa and Matadi, where they would spend one night at the home of Kitomba kia Lwamazi and family before flying to Kibunzi. The lower left photograph of this collage shows the Kitomba family the night before the foursome (see the other two photographs) flew to Kibunzi. For the reader's information, Kitomba kia Lwamazi and Mama Lusavuvu Luzolo Bungiena are the parents of Kitomba Josée Bena, Diampisa Bena's wife, whom the Nsakala family affectionately calls ya Josée. The other two photographs show Luzibu and Nsakala with Bena and Ngizulu shortly before taking off from the airfield in Kimpese to Kibunzi.

In Kibunzi, Luzibu is shown having a heart-to-heart talk with her mom, Madede Lessa, in the backyard of her house. In the top right photograph, Luzibu and her mom are standing in front of Madede's house with some other relatives. The bottom right photograph shows other relatives of Luzibu and Nsakala, sitting under a mango tree in the backyard of Madede's house.

The left-hand photograph in the collage below shows the two sisters in the front row (Madede Lessa and Matila) and Luzibu and her brother Mvibudulu Mayiza in the back row. The bottom right photograph shows Mayiza with other fellows in their Kibunzi neighborhood.

The collage below shows a number of people in Makanga Village. The left-hand photograph shows Nsakala's younger sister Swamunu Makomba with seven of her ten children, and the other two photographs show some village people, most of whom are relatives of Nsakala. At the far right in the top right photograph is his uncle Lutete Babwa, who came to Makanga from his village of Fwani specifically to visit with Luzibu and Nsakala. Nsakala Lusolamo, Nsakala's first cousin, is second from the left in the lower right photograph.

Shown in this collage are photographs depicting Ngizulu (in the blue shirt), Nsakala, and more people from Makanga and other villages. The lower right photograph depicts some members of the extended family who came from Kizeka Village (Mabengi Nsansa, Nsakala's cousin, and her two sons) to Makanga to visit with them.

Back from the villages to Kinshasa, Luzibu and Nsakala continued to visit with relatives and friends in various parts of the area. Here, Luzibu, Nsakala, and Bena are with Dr. Nsiangani Kimpiatu (driving) at N'Sele, on the outskirts of Kinshasa.

In the top left photograph of this collage, Nsakala is shown with, from left to right, cousin Nsakala Muke and brothers Bena Nsakala Ndunga and Dessa Nsakala. The bottom left photograph shows, from left to right, Dessa Nsakala; his wife, Nkenda Makonko Pauline; and the family of their firstborn son Metusala Nsakala. The right photograph shows Dessa Nsakala, on the far left, with extended family, standing in front of his family home. Luzibu is standing on the far right of the photograph.

In July 1992, Nsakala attended the Twenty-Fourth International Symposium on Combustion at the University of Sydney in Australia. This symposium was attended by a who's who on the world stage of combustion science and technology. While Nsakala attended various sessions of the conference, Luzibu, who had accompanied him, participated in the spouses' program activities.

This collage shows, in the left-hand photograph, Luzibu and Nsakala standing in front of the famous Sydney Opera House. The top right photograph shows them standing in front of the statue depicting British convicts transported to Australia. The bottom right photograph shows Luzibu at a local petting zoo.

And the next collage shows Luzibu and Nsakala doing some sightseeing in downtown Sydney and enjoying a peaceful dinner.

The following section provides further evidence that Luzibu and Nsakala's hospitality knows no bounds. In July 1991, Luzibu and Nsakala met Barbro Nyqvist, a Swedish SMF missionary in Kibunzi, where she and her daughter Nzuzi had lived for a long time. After her retirement, she and Nzuzi returned to Sweden. In August 1993, Luzibu and Nsakala hosted them while they visited the United States for a weeklong stay at their home in West Hartford, Connecticut. The collage below shows them at the Nsakala family home with Luzibu and other people from the African diaspora.

Over the course of a conversation, it was discovered that Nzuzi and Nsakala were blood relatives. Here is how: A nurse, Barbro (top left photograph), delivered Nzuzi (bottom left photograph) and her twin sister, Nsimba, at the Kibunzi hospital. Nsimba was stillborn, and the mother of the twins died during childbirth. To make a long story short, Barbro adopted Nzuzi from her father, Nkenda Lutete (bottom right photograph). It turns out that Nkenda's father was Lutete Babwa (top right photograph), Nsakala's maternal uncle, described further above. It's amazing how things happen!

In the collage below, Barbro, Nzuzi, Luzibu, and Nsakala are enjoying visits at the Mystic Aquarium in Mystic, Connecticut (left and bottom right) and New York City (top right).

In late August 1993, Nsakala's brother Bena Nsakala Ndunga traveled from Zaïre to the United States to participate in Lemvo and Jay's wedding ceremony in September. In the collage below, Bena poses with Luzibu, Nsakala, Diampisa (his son), and Luann and Lukiantima Josée Bena upon his arrival at the John F. Kennedy International Airport in New York City.

Saturday, September 25, 1993, was quite a momentous and joyful day for the extended Nsakala family. Family and friends came from Zaïre and all over the United States to celebrate the wedding of Munlemvo Nsakala (Lemvo) to James Anderson Mitchell Jr. (Jay), originally of Wantage, New Jersey.

The left-hand photograph of the collage shows Lemvo at the altar of Asylum Avenue Baptist Church in Hartford, Connecticut, where the wedding took place. The top right photograph shows the façade of the church. And the photograph on the bottom right shows Lemvo, Jay, Pastor Doug Donnelly (the officiating officer), and Jonathan Mitchell, Jay's brother and best man in the wedding. The following photograph shows the members of the wedding party:

- First row: James Thorpe, André Jett, Luann Bena, Josh Hale, Brittany Joiner, Steve Shepard, and George Sailor;

- Second row: Cheryl Thorpe, Josée Bena, Janet Joiner, Jean Merrill, Trish MacDonnell, and Michell Walsh; and

- Top row: Rod Smith, Mukiese Nsakala, Kevin Joiner, Jay Mitchell, Lemvo Mitchell, Jonathan Mitchell, Rodney Whitmore, and Greg McGriff.

This collage features Jean Merrill attending to Lemvo in West Hartford (left), and Lemvo and Jay with their immediate family members.

In this collage, James Anderson Mitchell Sr., Jay's father, escorts Lemvo's mom, Luzibu, and Jay's mom, Alberta, to the altar to light the unity candle; Mukiese escorts Josée Bena to the altar; and Dad is proudly walking his daughter to the church altar.

The next collage shows Lemvo and Jay with her parents in the left-hand photograph. In the top right photograph are Alberta and Jim Mitchell, Jay's parents, and paternal grandmother, Jermima Mitchell Butler. The bottom right photograph shows Mukiese, Lemvo's brother; Luzibu and Nsakala, Lemvo's parents; and Lemvo's paternal uncle, Bena Nsakala Ndunga.

Right after the wedding ceremony, some of the wedding attendees gather up in front of the church. It's unmistakable that everyone is all smiles. What a joyous day!

The collage below shows Lemvo and Jay standing under a chandelier at the Holiday Inn in downtown Hartford, where the wedding reception was held, then cutting their wedding cake. The top right photograph features some wedding attendees:

- Sitting in the front row, from left to right, Carolyn Yoder, Bwela Kiantandu, Grace Ouma, and Henry Ouma; and

- Standing in the back row, from left to right, Lester Yoder, Shem Okombo (Henry Ouma's brother, visiting from Kenya), Bena Nsakala Ndunga, and Diampisa Bena.

The left-hand photograph in this collage shows Dad and daughter opening the dance floor with a famous Congolese rumba, *"Afrique Mokili Mobimba."* In the top right photograph, Bena Nsakala Ndunga is blessing his niece in accordance with the Bakongo tribe's traditions. He is essentially saying, "May God bless you, and if you should step on a stump, it shall break up into pieces" (*"Nzambi ka kusakumuna, wadiata sinza kitoluka"*). He followed up with the traditional order, "Jump, jump, jump!" (*"Dumuka, dumuka, dumuka!"*) The bottom right photograph shows Nancy and Carroll Yoder sitting at their table during the reception.

Here, the photographer from Empire Photo & Video demonstrates his photoshopping skills by showing Dad and daughter dancing side by side. Others in the photograph are Janet and Kevin Joiner on the left and Jean Merrill and Johnathan Mitchell on the right.

Another happy event occurred not too long after Lemvo and Jay's wedding. That was the birth on Monday, November 1, 1993, of a baby boy, Brian Bena, at a Hartford hospital. This collage shows that Brian is all smiles in his crib in his family's apartment in New Britain, Connecticut. It also shows him with his mom, Josée, and dad, Diampisa.

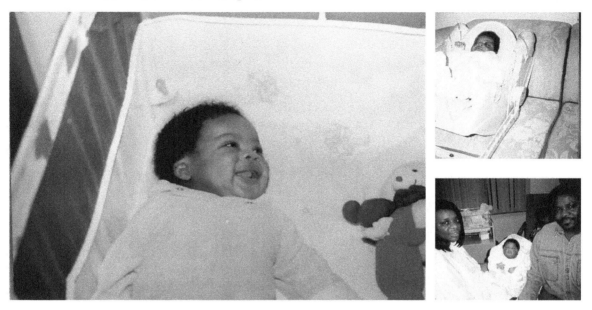

The next collage shows Brian opening his first birthday gifts, big sister Luann proudly clutching him, and Auntie Luzibu holding him.

And this collage shows some members of the extended family holding Brian: Lemvo in the left-hand photograph and Khadidiatou Niang and Mukiese in the top and bottom right photographs, respectively.

The Switzerland-headquartered Asea Brown Boveri (ABB) acquired Combustion Engineering, Inc. (C-E) in November 1989. Soon thereafter, ABB's Corporate Research Center, based in Baden (CRC Baden), sought the expertise of ex-C-E engineers in coal utilization processes. Nsakala was selected to help out the engineers in the CRC Baden commission their pressurized pulverized-coal combustion system. CRC Baden, which is located in Baden's suburb of Dättwil, is shown in the left-hand photograph; and, in the photograph on the right, Nsakala is shown with one of the engineers he worked with to successfully commission the combustion test facility in February 1994.

In October 1994, Nsakala presented a technical paper at the Pacific Rim International Conference on Environmental Control of Combustion Processes in Maui, Hawaii, with several ABB engineers. Luzibu went along to enjoy the warm weather, among other things, that Hawaii offered. In this collage, Luzibu and Nsakala can be seen in their hotel room and about to enjoy an aerial adventure tour of Maui Island from local company Hawaii Helicopters.

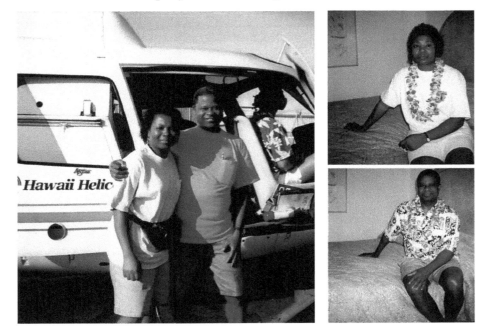

In the left-hand photograph in the following collage, Luzibu and Nsakala are standing under the Banyan tree in Lahaina. In the top right photograph, Nsakala, Luzibu, and David Thornock (an ABB colleague of Nsakala) are enjoying lunch at a restaurant in Lahaina. And in the lower right photograph, David Thornock, John Marion (another ABB colleague), Arun Mehta (an employee of the Electric Power Research Institute in Palo Alto, California), and Nsakala and Luzibu are pictured in front of a Maui sugar-processing factory.

The photographs in this collage show Luzibu and Nsakala peacefully enjoying themselves at various nature venues on the island of Maui.

Another milestone was achieved in the Nsakala family in June 1995. It concerned Mukiese graduating from Rutgers University in Piscataway, New Jersey, with a bachelor's degree in electrical engineering. He is shown in this collage, in cap and gown, with his parents and other family members (Lemvo and Jay Mitchell and Diampisa, Brian, Luann, and Josée Bena).

Mukiese poses in the right-hand photograph with Henry Ouma (a.k.a. Uncle Ouma), who lived with his family on the edges of the Rutgers' Bush Campus in Piscataway. The Oumas' home was Mukiese's second home while he was away from West Hartford throughout his years at Rutgers. The top left photograph depicts Mukiese with other family members' names above, plus the Mathos family (Mike, Tony, Mathosette, Nick, and Odette). The Mathos family traveled from nearby Newark, New Jersey, to be at Mukiese's graduation ceremony. Odette and Mike Mathos were originally from Angola but lived in the Congo at one point.

The left-hand photograph shows Mukiese and his friend Russell Romero from Conard High School. In the lower right photograph, Mukiese poses with the Mathos family. Throughout his career as a student at Rutgers, Mukiese worked in the control systems engineering department at Pratt and Whitney in East Hartford, Connecticut, during his vacations. During his senior year at Rutgers, Mukiese secured a permanent position at Pratt and Whitney. Consequently, Mukiese's family was, at this moment, celebrating both his successful completion of electrical engineering studies at Rutgers University and his securing a permanent job at Pratt and Whitney.

As a result of his help in the successful commissioning of the pressurized coal combustion system at CRC Baden in 1994, Nsakala became a de facto member of the CRC's aerodynamics and thermodynamics department. He would be asked to go to Baden, sometimes on short notice, to help with issues pertaining, principally, to pulverized coal combustion. In this 1995 collage, for example, Nsakala is shown in the left-hand photograph with Dr. Peter Janson and his wife. Peter Janson was a supervisor in the aerodynamics and thermodynamics department.

The two right-hand photographs show Nsakala and Nsakala with Luzibu in downtown Baden.

Starting in March 1996, Nsakala was assigned to work on a specialized project for an extended period (six months to one year) at the fuels combustion systems business unit in Baden with other ABB scientists and engineers from all over the world. Additionally, Nsakala worked, as usual, in the aerodynamics and thermodynamics department at CRC Baden in Dättwil. This time, ABB rented an apartment for Nsakala near the CRC office. The apartment belonged to Dora and Werner Schott. The apartment was part of the Schott's residence, as shown in the top left photograph below. In June 1996, Luzibu went to Baden/Dättwil for a one-week visit. Here, she and Dora are fixing a cookout dinner for the family. The lower left photograph shows Nsakala, Dora, and Werner during a sightseeing outing somewhere near Dättwil, Switzerland.

The collage below shows the Schott children, Gabriela (on the left) and Pia, playing outdoors and Nsakala and the Schott family at their vacation campgrounds on the banks of Lake Ägeri in southern Switzerland. The Schotts and the Nsakalas would form an enduring friendship, which goes on strongly today.

At the Corporate Research Center Baden, Nsakala got to know Dr. Jürgen Bittner, who was working contemporaneously on mercury measurements/control from municipal waste incinerators. This collage shows Jürgen; his wife, Monika; Luzibu; and Nsakala sightseeing in the Swiss Alps.

During his six-month stay in Switzerland, Nsakala traveled to Belgium by train to visit with family and friends. His friend Dr. Kanigula Mubagwa (Kani) lived in Kumtich with his wife, Fortuna, and their four children. In the left-hand photograph, Kani is with Dr. Sanginga Nteranya of Ibadan University in Nigeria, and Nsakala on the banks of the Maastricht River in Maastricht, Netherlands. Nsakala also visited with his niece Claudine Makinutewa and her family, who, at the time, lived in Wavre. The two photographs on the right show Claudine and her husband, Bambi Zolani Ndunga, with their children, Jonathan and Allégresse Bambi.

The Belgian trip afforded Nsakala the opportunity to interact with family, friends, and many others of the Zaïrean diaspora living there.

At the end of September 1996, Nsakala returned to the United States, having fulfilled what he had been sent to Baden/Dättwil to accomplish. Luzibu and Nsakala immediately resumed their search for a home elsewhere in greater Hartford. They found one in South Windsor. A&A Movers relocated them from their home in West Hartford to South Windsor (left- and right-hand photographs, respectively) in December 1996. Simultaneously, Josée and Diampisa Bena and their two children moved from a New Britain apartment to the Nsakalas' West Hartford home on a rent-to-buy basis. The Benas would purchase this house in June 2001, and it's where they live today.

Third Decade, Plus

The Nsakala family's third decade, plus, in greater Hartford, which extended from 1997 to 2010, was also full of transformative events. Some of these events are listed below.

- The births of grandson James A. Mitchell III and grandniece Constance (Kosi) Bena in 1997;
- A five-month visit to the United States by three members of the extended family—Bena Nsakala Ndunga, Lubombolo lua Nzambi, and Kitomba kia Lwamazi—from the Democratic Republic of the Congo (ex-Zaïre) in 1998;
- Luzibu and Nsakala's European trip (Switzerland, Belgium, and France) in 2000;
- Granddaughter Zola Mitchell's birth and Karell and Mukiese's wedding in 2001;
- Granddaughter Jianna Mitchell's birth in 2002;
- The building of Luzibu and Nsakala's Palm Coast, Florida, home in 2004;
- The arrival of nephew Dieyatondulua Lutete from the Democratic Republic of the Congo and the birth of grandson Nkailu Nsakala in 2007;
- The election of the first African American, Barack Obama, as forty-fourth US president in 2008;
- The birth of granddaughter Nailah Nsakala in 2009; and
- The retirement of Luzibu and Nsakala from their respective jobs in 2010.

These and other events are highlighted in the photographs and collages presented on the following pages.

The collage below shows, clockwise, Josée Bena with Khadidiatou Niang and Khadidiatou and Lamine Niang with their son, Mohammed. In the bottom photographs, Khadidiatou is holding Mohammed while Josée looks on, and Kitomba Luvevo Noël, Diampisa, and Lamine are enjoying their camaraderie together. The Niangs, who are originally from Senegal, live in Windsor, Connecticut, and Kitomba is Josée's brother. The Niangs and the Benas have known each other since the 1980s.

On September 2, 1997, Luzibu and Nsakala were bursting with joy when their first grandchild, baby boy James Anderson Mitchell III (J3), was born in Hartford Hospital to his proud parents, R. Munlemvo (Lemvo) and James Anderson Mitchell Jr. (Jay). The photograph on the left was taken at the hospital. The other two show his smiling father and mother cuddling him and putting him into his bed, respectively.

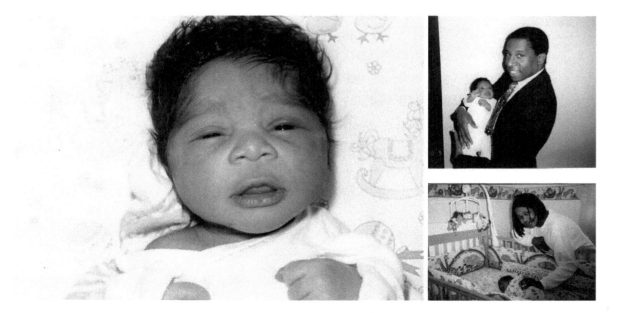

The next collage depicts J3 with his parents, grandmothers (Luzibu Nsakala and Alberta Mitchell), and grandfathers (James Anderson Mitchell Sr. and Nsakala ya Nsakala). All are rejoicing and giving thanks to God Almighty for His blessings and this precious gift.

The left-hand photograph of this collage shows Josée Bena holding J3 while visiting him and Lemvo in the hospital. The top right photograph shows J3 with his parents, grandfather Nsakala, and Liliann Nzuzi, a member of the extended family visiting from New York City. Last but not least, J3 is with his smiling maternal uncle Mukiese Nsakala in his East Hartford apartment. With the birth of J3, Luzibu became *Yaya* ("grandparent" in Kikongo), and Nsakala became *Nkaka/Nkoko* (also "grandparent").

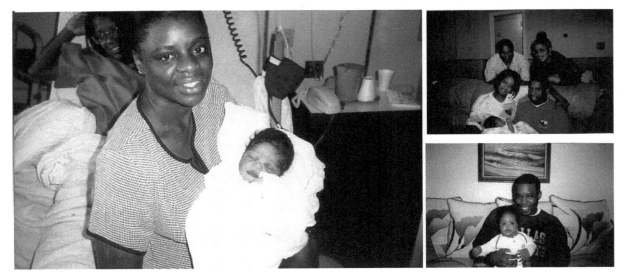

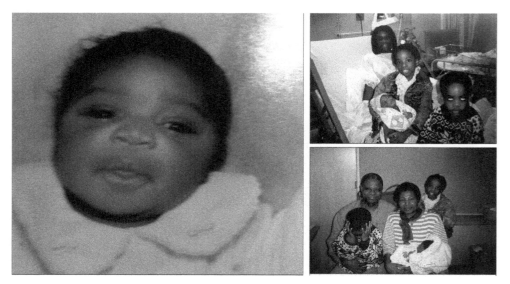

On December 22, 1997, another joyful event occurred in the extended Nsakala family when baby girl Constance Bena (Kosi) was born to Josée and Diampisa Bena at the University of Connecticut Health Center in Farmington. The left-hand photograph in this collage is a snapshot of Kosi at the health center. The top right photograph shows Kosi being held by big sister Luann while their proud mother is looking on in the background. Big brother Brian is looking stressed out, presumably because he's no longer the family's focal point. The lower right photograph shows Great-Aunt Luzibu holding Kosi during a visit to the UConn Health Center while Great-Uncle Nsakala and Luann are joyously sitting behind them, and Brian is still looking stressed.

By now it should be clear that Luzibu and Nsakala find family ties to be invaluable. When their daughter Lemvo's brother-in-law, Jonathan Mitchell, got married to Mikele Simkins in May 1998 in Winston-Salem, North Carolina, they flew down from Bradley International Airport with Mukiese;

Lemvo and Jay; and their son, James III. The collage on the previous page shows Janet Joiner, Jonathan's big sister, with their maternal uncles (top left); Alberta and Jim Mitchell, parents of the groom (bottom left); Mikele and Jonathan (top right); and Jay and Jonathan (bottom right).

Some of the wedding ceremony attendees are pictured in the next collage: Nsakala, Luzibu, Lemvo, J3, and Mukiese (top left); Alberta Mitchell with her two brothers, Cyril Walryn Lancaster on the left and Charlie Lancaster (bottom left); J3, Jay, and Lemvo (top right); and Nsakala, Luzibu, Janet, Kevin Joiner, and two unidentified persons (bottom right).

Early in 1998, the extended Nsakala family in greater Hartford decided to invite three relatives from the Democratic Republic of the Congo (DRC) to the United States. The "three amigos" (as they were affectionately called) are related to the family as follows:

- Kitomba kia Lwamazi is Josée Bena's father;

- Bena Nsakala Ndunga is Nsakala's brother and Diampisa's father; and

- Lubombolo lwa Nzambi is Luzibu Nsakala's brother.

The three amigos were taken to New York City by Diampisa and Nsakala for sightseeing. They visited such iconic places as the United Nations, Radio City Music Hall, and the World Trade Center.

The three amigos were also taken to Washington, DC, by Luzibu and Nsakala for sightseeing (see the next two collages). This collage shows them at the Lincoln Memorial; the White House, where they were serving a cake to visitors in commemoration of the 206th anniversary of the White House inauguration; and the US Capitol.

Here, they are shown visiting Arlington National Cemetery. They also visited other iconic places on the Washington, DC, Mall, including the Supreme Court, the Air and Space Museum, the African Museum of Natural History, and the Vietnam War Memorial.

Luzibu and Nsakala also took them to Groton, Connecticut, for a tour of the Naval Submarine Base New London, where they enjoyed entering an actual retired submarine and an anchored submarine parked outdoors.

In the top right photograph, the amigos are enjoying a nice stroll on the beach. In the bottom right photograph, they are enjoying a swim for the first time in the ocean water with other family members at Ocean Beach in New London, Connecticut. And the other two photographs on the left show the three amigos voluntarily doing household chores, such as mowing the yard and watering the vegetable garden.

The top photograph of the following collage shows Grace and Henry Ouma, who came for a visit from Piscataway, New Jersey, sharing a laugh with the amigos and Luzibu and Nsakala in the Nsakalas' South Windsor residence. In the lower left photograph, the three amigos are enjoying dinner with Barbara and Gary Tessier, who lived in Vernon, Connecticut. And the lower right photograph shows the amigos dining at Khadidiatou and Lamine Niang's home in Windsor. Both the Tessiers and Niangs are members of the Nsakalas' extended family.

The photographs in the collage below show the three amigos with others at Lemvo and Jay Mitchell Jr.'s family home in South Windsor. Sitting around a dinner table (right-hand photographs) with the three amigos are Karell Rose (Mukiese's fiancée), Mukiese, Luzibu, and Nsakala. Joining them for a snapshot in front of the house are Luzibu, Jay, and J3.

Toward the end of the three amigos' five-month visit to the United States, the family gathered at Olin Mills Studios in East Windsor for a picture with them.

And at the end of December 1998, the three amigos were ready to go back to their homeland, the Democratic Republic of the Congo. The photograph below shows them with some of the family members who accompanied them to John F. Kennedy International Airport shortly before they flew.

Surely, the extended family members and friends involved with the three amigos during their five-month stay in the United States had a ball with them. The amigos' visit was an experience of a lifetime; therefore, it felt bad to see them go back to the DRC. It should be remembered that King Solomon wrote clearly: "There is a time for everything, and a season for every activity under the heavens" (Ecclesiastes 3:1 New International Version).

In the spring of 1999, Nsakala attended a US Department of Energy–sponsored conference on environmental control from fossil fuels combustion sources in Washington, DC. Luzibu accompanied him. Luzibu and Nsakala spent a couple of days after the conference doing some sightseeing. They went around the famed Watergate complex (shown in the photographs on the left) and took a conducted tour of the humongous Pentagon complex. (Luzibu and Nsakala are shown in the lobby.) These and other iconic Washington, DC, places are historical sights to behold.

As mentioned earlier, the Ouma and Nsakala families kept in contact beyond their days together at Penn State University in the 1970s. It should be noted that seasons change, and time goes by, but true friendship remains. Some members of both families are shown in the next collage celebrating the graduation of Adhiambo Ouma from Rutgers University's Newark, New Jersey, campus in June 1999. Adhiambo is the oldest of the four Oumas' daughters; the right-hand photograph shows her flanked by sisters Atieno (left) and Akinyi.

In September 1999, Luzibu and Nsakala joined Nancy and Carroll Yoder and others in Wellman, Iowa, to attend the wedding reception of Chia Chi Chen (Judy) and Joel Yoder. Joel is the younger son of Nancy and Carroll Yoder. Carroll Yoder's parents hosted Luzibu when she first immigrated to the United States in September 1966. The lower left photograph shows Carroll, Judy's mother, and Nancy.

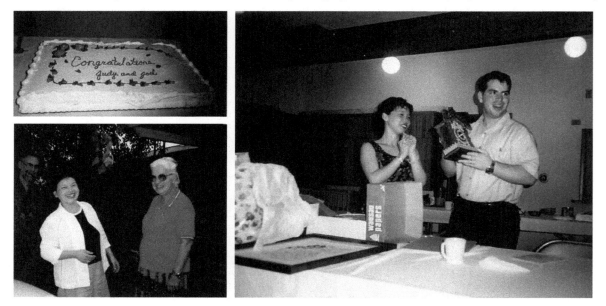

In late September 1999, Liliann Nzuzi Diangindula, a member of the extended family who lived in New York City, visited the Nsakala family in greater Hartford with a cousin of hers, Damas, from the Democratic Republic of the Congo, who lived in South Africa, where he worked as a medical doctor.

Picking apples and pumpkins from farms in greater Hartford is a big and exciting event, especially for children, in the month of October. On one Saturday morning, Luzibu and Nsakala crossed the Connecticut River on a ferry from Rocky Hill to Glastonbury with James A. Mitchell III and Luann and Brian Bena. As this collage shows, they are indeed having fun picking both apples and pumpkins. For the Nsakalas, quality family time is very important because it creates strong bonds, love, connections, and relationships.

Attending sporting events was also a well-loved activity of the Nsakalas. The University of Connecticut in Storrs has a juggernaut women's basketball team that has entertained the state and the nation over the years. This collage shows avid basketball fans boarding one of the many buses from Hartford to Piscataway, New Jersey, where UConn women played Rutgers University's women hoopsters. Luzibu is shown aboard a bus behind their friends Linda and Dick Borio (right-hand photograph). The University of Connecticut, Rutgers University, and the University of Tennessee are three long-standing rivals that popularized the National Collegiate Athletic Association's women's basketball league.

More family time was enjoyed when, in April 2000, Luzibu and Nsakala drove down to Piscataway, New Jersey, to spend the weekend with Grace and Henry Ouma. The visit was synchronized with Josephine Gurira's visit with Grace and Henry. Visiting from Zimbabwe, Josephine was staying with one of their daughters in the Washington, DC, area. The three majestic dames, Grace, Josephine, and Luzibu, are shown in the left-hand photograph in that order. The lower right photograph shows Josephine and Henry at the Metuchen, New Jersey, train station shortly before she embarked on her return trip to Washington, DC. Luzibu and Nsakala, frequent visitors of Grace and Henry, and vice versa, are shown in the top right photograph with the Oumas and other people from Kenya.

In June and July 2000, Luzibu and Nsakala went to Europe for a three-week vacation. While there, they visited with family and friends in Belgium and with friends in Switzerland and went sightseeing in Paris, France. In Belgium, Luzibu and Nsakala stayed with their friends Fortuna and Kanigula Mubagwa and their four children in Kumtich. At the time, the Mubagwas' eldest daughter,

Linda, was going to medical school at the University of Namur in Belgium. One day, Fortuna, Luzibu, Kani, and Nsakala went to fetch Linda from the university as it was the end of the academic year. The left-hand photograph shows all five of them posing with the Meuse River in the background. The photograph in the lower right of the collage shows Fortuna and three of her children (from left to right, Nsuli, Ndamuso, and Akonkwa) admiring some photographs Luzibu is showing them of the Nsakalas' extended family in the United States.

While in Belgium, Luzibu and Nsakala also spent some quality time with the family of their niece Claudine Munzenga Makinutewa in Wavre. Here, Luzibu and Nsakala are at the dinner table with Claudine; her husband, Bambi Gaby; and their three children (from left to right, Jonathan, Marie, and Allégresse).

After a few days in Belgium, Luzibu and Nsakala flew from Brussels Airport to Zurich, Switzerland. In Switzerland, they stayed with their friends Dora and Werner Schott and their children in Baden/Dättwil. The Schotts were Nsakala's landlords when he worked at ABB's Corporate Research Center Baden for six months in 1996. This collage shows Luzibu with Werner, Dora, and their children (from left to right, Gabriela and Pia), in the front yard of their home, enjoying a beautiful evening. Relationships are what bind people together in peace.

During this stay in Switzerland, Luzibu and Nsakala spent a day with their friends Monika and Jürgen Bittner in Lenzburg. Jürgen took them to Monte Generoso in Ticino Canton. Besides its imposing altitude of 5,581 feet (1,701 meters), Monte Generoso straddles both Switzerland and Italy. The panoramic view of Lake Lugano and the Alps from its summit is breathtaking. This collage shows their train ride to the summit of Monte Generoso.

Luzibu and Nsakala spent the last six days of their European vacation in Paris, France. They stayed in a hotel near the Saint Lazare train station, within walking distance of the famed Champs-Elysées. They walked along the Champs-Elysées from the Arc de Triomphe to the Louvre Museum, via the Jardin de Tuileries, and to many other places of interest. They took the Paris Métro to Château de Versailles, then to Cathédrale Notre Dame, and, finally, to Tour Eiffel, Quartier Latin, et cetera. This collage shows Luzibu standing with the Arc de Triomphe in the background, Nsakala standing at the foot of Tour Eiffel, and Luzibu and Nsakala standing in front of Cathédrale Notre Dame and the Louvre Museum.

The Nsakalas were in Paris when France defeated Italy in the Union of European Football Association's (UEFA's) Euro 2000 final match on July 2, 2000. The excitement of some Parisians throughout the night of July 2–3, 2000, resulted in the unfortunate looting of some storefronts on the Champs-Elysées and elsewhere.

There was so much to see in Paris that Luzibu and Nsakala were sorry they had not arranged to stay there longer beforehand. Anyhow, the whole European vacation was the experience of a lifetime.

In August 2000, the Nsakalas drove to Charlotte, North Carolina, with the Bena family to attend the wedding ceremony of Aimée Tuluenga and Paulin Minga. The top left photograph shows the Bena family at the ceremony. The bottom left photographs show the bride and groom at the altar. The right-hand photograph shows the Lusala family (Audrey, Brandon, Edward, and Marie). And Diampisa Bena is with his uncles (from left to right, Edward Lusala and Gaston Tuluenga), who are brothers.

The collage below features some of the other wedding ceremony revelers: Bwela Kiantandu with Josée Bena and Luzibu Nsakala; Liliann Nzuzi Diangindula with Nsakala, Luzibu, and Diampisa; Edward with Diampisa and Nsakala; and Luzibu with two of her former first-grade students from a Kibunzi primary school, Kali and Pauline.

In November 2000, the extended family welcomed a baby boy, Daniel Tuzolana, at New Britain Hospital, New Britain, Connecticut. In the top left and right photographs, respectively, Dan is shown lying in the hospital crib and being cuddled by Auntie Lutonadio Cady. In the bottom left and right photographs, he is being cuddled by his mom, Manzo Tuzolana, and his dad, Luvevo Nöel Kitomba.

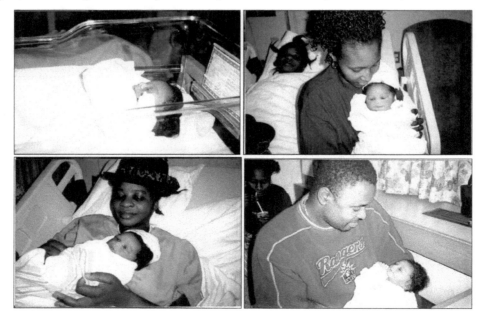

Below, Dan is pictured with other members of the extended family. In the left-hand photograph, he is being held/admired by Luann Bena. In the right-hand photograph, he is being held by Grand Auntie Luzibu Nsakala and surrounded by Luann, Brian Bena, Mom, Manzo, Kosi Bena, and James A. Mitchell III.

On January 21, 2001, Luzibu and Nsakala were again bursting with joy when their second grand-child, baby girl Zola Alana Mitchell, was born in Hartford Hospital to her proud parents, Lemvo and Jay Mitchell. (*Zola* means "love" in Kikongo.) The collage below shows Zola's picture, taken at the hospital; big brother James A. Mitchell III (J3) admiring her; and Zola with her happy family.

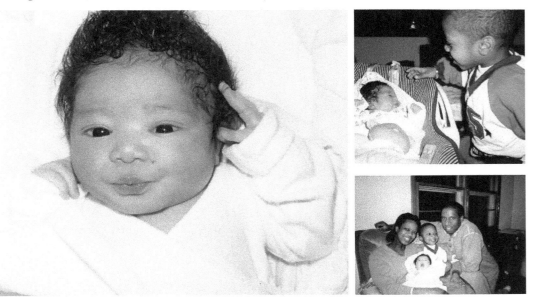

This collage shows Zola with joyous paternal grandparents Alberta and James A. Mitchell Sr. (top left photograph); maternal grandparents Luzibu and Nsakala, a.k.a. Yaya and Nkoko (bottom left photograph); and grandfathers, plus J3 (right-hand photograph).

The collage below shows Zola being dedicated at Crossroads Community Cathedral in East Hartford, Connecticut.

In another momentous event, Claudine Makinutewa, who lived in Wavre, Belgium, with her family, came to the United States with her daughter Allégresse and son Jonathan to visit the Bena family in West Hartford in 2001. The Benas brought them to South Windsor to visit with Auntie Luzibu and Uncle Nsakala. The left-hand photograph shows, from left to right, Allégresse, Luzibu, Kosi, Claudine, Luann, and Josée. Other family members are shown in the photographs on the right.

The left-hand photograph in the collage below shows Mukiese with his then-fiancée, Karell Rose, in the foreground, and, from left to right in the background, Zola, Jay, and Lemvo Mitchell; Anna Ogalo; Luzibu; J3; and Georgina Ogalo. Anna is Henry Ouma's sister, and she and her daughter were visiting the Ouma family in Piscataway, New Jersey, at the time. They took advantage of their time in the United States to also visit their friends, the Nsakala family, and other people in Connecticut. It is noteworthy that Anna was Lemvo and Mukiese's babysitter during their parents' Penn State University years.

165

This collage shows Luzibu and Nsakala with Josephine and Roger Gurira and the Mitchell Sr. and Jr. families in front of Crossroads Community Cathedral following a church service.

In October 2001, another momentous and joyful event took place: the celebration of Karell Rose and Mukiese Nsakala's wedding in Bolton, Connecticut. This collage shows Leslie Rose escorting his daughter Karell to the altar. In the bottom left photograph, Karell is being assisted by her friend and maid of honor, Tammy Wilson, and her sister Monique Rose. On the bottom right, Nsakala is escorting both Luzibu, Mukiese's mom, and Norma Rose, Karell's mom.

Here, the Reverend Hank Waltmeyer is officiating the ceremony (top right photograph), and Karell and Mukiese are saying their wedding vows (left-hand photograph). In the lower right photograph, Karell and Mukiese are shown cutting their wedding cake at the reception.

This collage shows the happy new couple, alone and with their wedding party. In the top right photograph Mukiese is with, from left to right, Luann Bena, Monique Rose, Tamika Wilson, Camille Rose, and Munlemvo Mitchell. And the lower right photograph shows Karell and Mukiese with James A. Mitchell III and Brian Bena in the foreground and Jay Mitchell, David Johnson, Steve Goodison, Patrick Antoine, Albert Avancena, and Kiley Sharpe in the background.

This photograph shows Karell and Mukiese with their parents, Norma and Leslie Rose and Luzibu and Nsakala, respectively.

This collage shows Karell's great-aunt Genrith Wilson (Auntie Jenny) sitting with her nephew Leslie Rose in the top photograph. The bottom left photograph shows the Bena family: Josée, Constance (Kosi), Luann, Diampisa, and Brian. The bottom right photograph shows Mukiese playing the violin while he waits for his bride to arrive at the altar.

The next two collages show wedding guests on the dance floor. A good time was had by all, as if to say, "Let them praise his name with dancing and make music to him with tambourine and harp" (Psalm 149:3 New International Version).

Finally, this photograph shows the reveling wedding attendees, who made themselves available for this and other snapshots. What a joyous day it was!

In December 2001, three members of the extended family visited the Nsakalas in greater Hartford. One of them, Luzolo Manikuna André, is shown in the left-hand photograph with Luzibu and Nsakala. The other two are shown in the top right photograph with Luzibu; in the middle is Liliann Nzuzi Diangindula, and on the left is Liliann's friend. Whereas Luzolo was visiting from Germany, the other two ladies were visiting from New York City. They all had come to join the family in a moment of sorrow: the passing of a young member of the extended family, Lutonadio Cady.

On April 12, 2002, Yaya Luzibu and Nkoko Nsakala were again bursting with joy when their third grandchild, baby girl Jianna Aimée Mitchell, was born in Hartford Hospital to her proud parents, Lemvo and Jay. Indeed, God's blessings continue! In the next two collages, Jianna is shown with her parents and siblings, Zola and James III, and both maternal and paternal grandparents.

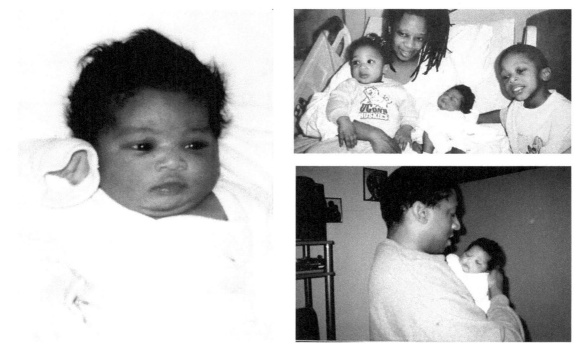

Here, Jianna is shown with Josée, Mukiese, and Diampisa, who are admiring the new member of the family.

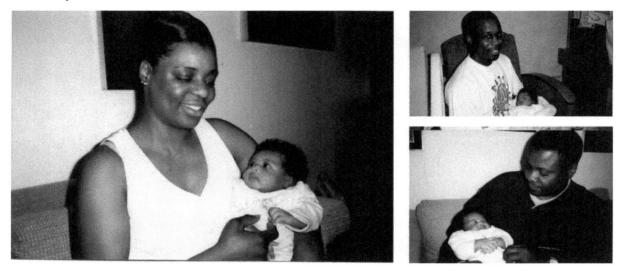

In May 2002, Luzibu and Nsakala traveled to Pine Hill, New Jersey, to attend the wedding ceremony of Mae and Antoine Nzima's daughter, Ayicha, and her husband. The top left and right photographs show the proud mother, Mae, with the bride and groom, and the proud father, Antoine, with the bride, the groom, and the officiating pastor.

One month later, in June 2002, Luzibu and Nsakala flew to Wellman, Iowa, to be with the Yoder family after the passing of Grandpa Lester Yoder. The photograph on the left in the collage below shows the Yoder clan. The photograph on the top right shows Carroll and Nancy Yoder with their two sons and their respective spouses (Karina and Eric on the left and Judy and Joel on the right) and their first granddaughter, Carrie.

In July 2002, Luzibu and Nsakala accompanied their son-in-law, Jay, and granddaughter Zola to New Rochelle, New York, to celebrate the ninety-fifth birthday of Jay's Great-Auntie Mattie. Zola, Jay, and Jim (Jay's father) are shown in the lower right photograph. And the guest of honor, Auntie Mattie, is shown in the top left photograph, wearing a white hat. Luzibu and Nsakala never forget the ties that bind them to the immediate—and extended—family.

Fostering that tradition, in July 2002, Luzibu and Nsakala flew to Florida to spend some time with Alberta and Jim Mitchell, Jay's parents, in Melbourne. The collage below shows, on the left, the foursome at Orlando International Airport. While in Melbourne, Jim and Alberta took Luzibu and Nsakala on sightseeing tours to Universal Studios (lower right photograph) and many other places. After about one week, they all drove up to Palm Coast, Florida, for a brief visit with Norma and Leslie Rose (top right photograph), Karell's parents, on their way to Columbia, South Carolina, where they attended a Richardson-Howell family reunion. Jim is part of the Richardson-Howell family. Following the reunion, Alberta and Jim took Luzibu and Nsakala to the airport in Myrtle Beach, South Carolina, to pick up a rental car. This rental car took Luzibu and Nsakala back to South Windsor after a brief visit with their friends Nancy and Carroll Yoder in Harrisonburg, Virginia.

In September 2002, Luzibu, Nsakala, Jay, Lemvo, and many more ADVO employees went to New York City on a bus to see a matinée showing of *The Lion King* on Broadway. Lemvo worked for ADVO (a direct mail marketing company) as a staff accountant. In the collage below, Lemvo, Jay, and Luzibu are enjoying themselves somewhere along Fifth Avenue. To illustrate that fact, Lemvo and Luzibu are posing for a photograph with a wax figure of Whoopi Goldberg.

In December 2002, Karell and Mukiese and Luzibu and Nsakala drove separately to Palm Coast, Florida, to celebrate Christmas with Karell's parents, Norma and Leslie Rose. The two collages below show family members enjoying Christmas Day dinner at the Rose family home. The first collage shows, clockwise, Nsakala, Leslie, and Norma; Howard Dryer and Auntie Genrith Wilson (Auntie Jenny); and Luzibu, Samuel (Sam), and Jean Rose.

This collage shows, clockwise, Leslie and Nsakala; Mukiese, Monique, and Karell; and Camille and Howard.

Here's a brief rundown of the Palm Coast family relationships: Auntie Jenny is Leslie's aunt; Camille, Monique, and Karell are Norma and Leslie's daughters; Howard is Camille's husband; Sam is Leslie's first cousin; and Jean is Sam's wife.

Leslie Rose, a real estate broker, took Luzibu and Nsakala around the city of Palm Coast in search of a property to potentially build a house on in the future. They settled on the property shown in the photo below. This is where Luzibu and Nsakala would eventually build their retirement home.

Back at home in Connecticut, at the beginning of 2003, niece Liliann Nzuzi Diangindula intro-duced Luzibu and Nsakala to a Congolese family from Kibunzi in the Democratic Republic of the Congo who lived in New York City. So, in April of the same year, Luzibu and Nsakala invited this multigenerational family to greater Hartford (see the collage below). The grandmother is Mama Be-tezi, the son is Nsiku, and his son's name escapes the authors. The mother of the child did not make the trip because of a prior commitment.

In terms of their own family, Luzibu and Nsakala made every effort to attend their grandchil-dren's sports events whenever possible. This collage shows James III playing T-ball in May 2003.

In the same month, Mukiese graduated from Rensselaer at Hartford with a master's degree in managing technology. The photograph below shows him with his wife, Karell Rose, and his parents.

The collage below shows the Nsakalas' extended family in greater Hartford, Connecticut. The photograph on the left shows Grace Ouma with Lemvo, Zola, and Jianna in the Nsakalas' home in South Windsor. The lower right photograph shows Nancy and Carroll Yoder with the Nsakalas during a visit to South Windsor. And the top right photograph shows Monique Rose with the other family women at Lemvo and Jay Mitchell's home. Whereas Grace and Henry Ouma were visiting from Piscataway, New Jersey, Nancy and Carroll Yoder were visiting from Harrisonburg, Virginia. Finally, Monique Rose was visiting from Boston, Massachusetts.

In February 2004, Nsakala was invited to present a technical paper ["Options for Controlling Carbon Dioxide (CO_2) Emissions: ALSTOM's Commitment"] at the international energy agency Asia-Pacific Economic Cooperation's conference on zero-emissions technologies in Gold Coast, Queensland, Australia. The top left photograph in this collage shows Nsakala during a stopover at Auckland, New Zealand. The bottom left photograph shows a panoramic view of the city of Gold Coast. The top right photograph shows Nsakala with a fellow chemical engineer, a Chinese gentleman, during a trip inside a rainforest. The visitors were also treated to a wine tasting at Mount Tamborine Winery & Homestead.

In late 2003, Luzibu and Nsakala signed a contract with ICI Homes of Daytona Beach to build them a home on their property in Palm Coast. Leslie Rose was instrumental in selecting ICI Homes. The builder broke ground in late February 2004. Luzibu and Nsakala provided Leslie Rose with the power of attorney to act on their be-

half throughout the construction phase. This collage shows the progression of work, culminating in Luzibu and Nsakala obtaining the certificate of occupancy at the beginning of September 2004.

In January 2005, Nsakala was invited to present a technical paper ("ALSTOM Circulating Fluidized Boilers Technology") at the Asia-Pacific Economic Cooperation's Clean Energy Technical Policy Seminar in Cebu, Philippines. Seminar attendees were given opportunities to tour various places on the island of Cebu. The photograph on the lower left of this collage shows attendees at a lignite-coal-fired power plant. The photograph on the top right is in sharp contrast with the maybe-four-star hotel across the street (not shown), where the seminar was being held.

In May 2005, Karell Rose graduated from Wesleyan University in Middletown, Connecticut, with a master's degree in social science. She is shown in this collage with her husband, Mukiese Nsakala; her sister Monique Rose; and her mother- and father-in-law, Luzibu and Nsakala.

At the end of June 2005, Nsakala flew to Europe. The first stop was Lisbon, Portugal, where he presented a technical paper at the Eighth Conference on Energy for a Clean Environment. The collage below shows Nsakala and some of the conferees at Cabo da Roca. This cape forms the westernmost extent of mainland Portugal, continental Europe, and the Eurasian landmass. It is a sight to behold!

From Lisbon, Nsakala flew to Zurich, Switzerland, for meetings/work with his colleagues at Corporate Research Center Baden/Dättwil. He took advantage of this trip to visit the usual family and friends in Belgium. Dr. and Mrs. Mubagwa (Kani and Fortuna) welcomed him to their home in Kumtich with open arms and hearts. This collage shows Kani with son Akonkwa and daughter Ndamuso (top left); Nsuli Mubagwa and Linda Mubagwa (second from the right) with their friends (top right); and Kani, Fortuna, and their friends (bottom two photographs).

Kani was also kind enough to shuttle Nsakala to and from Wavre, where his family lived. The left-hand photograph in the collage below shows Kani with Mama Biki Marie and Cécile Makinutewa with her children. The top right photograph shows Kani with Mama Biki, Cécile, and Claudine Makinutewa, and the lower right photograph shows Nsakala with Mama Biki, Cécile, and Cécile's daughter. It should be noted that Claudine and Cécile are Mama Biki's daughters.

The next collage shows Nsakala with Claudine Makinutewa and Bambi Gaby, Claudine's husband. Claudine and Cécile are Nsakala's nieces through marriage.

In July 2005, Luzibu and Nsakala drove from South Windsor to Piscataway, New Jersey, to visit with Grace and Henry Ouma. Dr. Emmanuel Hove, who taught chemistry at Rutgers University in New Brunswick, stopped by the Oumas' home to say hello to the Nsakalas. Hove, who is from Zimbabwe, studied at Penn State University contemporaneously with Henry and Nsakala.

In October 2005, Nsakala was again an invited guest speaker, this time at an international meeting sponsored by the Center for Coal in Sustainable Development in Brisbane, Australia. The collage below shows that the flight that Nsakala took to Brisbane from Los Angeles, California, made a stopover in Auckland, New Zealand. The other two photographs (from post cards) in the collage show the hotel where the week-long conference was held and the Brisbane harbor.

On the way back from Brisbane, Australia, Nsakala stopped by Honolulu, Hawaii, for two days to break up the long flight from Down Under. In Honolulu, Nsakala visited the USS Arizona Memorial, the resting place of 1,102 sailors and marines killed during the Japanese surprise attack on Pearl Harbor on December 7, 1941. It was actually the attack on Pearl Harbor and the Island of Oahu that led to the United States' direct involvement in World War II.

In February 2006, Nsakala was invited to present a technical paper ("Advances in Coal Combustion Power Technologies") at the Asia-Pacific Economic Cooperation's Clean Fossil Energy Technical Seminar in Lampang, Thailand. The conferees were treated to some awesome tours. The Buddhist temple Wat Phra That Lampang Luang was one of the places they visited.

They also toured what looked like a farm where elephants were raised and trained, as shown in the collage below.

The director of Nsakala's department (power plant research and development) at ALSTOM Power, Inc., was gracious enough to let him break up the otherwise-long Thailand-US trip. Hence, Nsakala spent three nights in Beijing, People's Republic of China. Nsakala toured the Forbidden City and Tiananmen Square on his own. Chairman Mao Zedong's pictures are prominently displayed everywhere on the square, as shown in the left-hand photograph of the collage below. Nsakala went inside the Great Hall of the People (top right), which holds Mao Zedong's mausoleum for daily viewing. His body appeared to have been encapsulated in glass or crystal. Featured in the square was a giant tableau (bottom right) advertising the Olympic Games that were to be held in the People's Republic of China in 2008.

The left-hand photograph in the collage below shows a typical scene on the streets of Beijing, with umpteen people riding their bicycles from here to there. He also toured the Great Wall at Badaling Pass (see the right two photographs). Nsakala walked on the wall for about an hour and a half (forty-five minutes each way).

In May 2006, Nsakala and his colleague Greg Liljedahl were set to go to Mannheim, Germany, then to Paris, France, on a business trip. They were asked by Dr. Allen Pfeffer, the power plant laboratory's director, to stop first in Barcelona, Spain, so that Nsakala could present a technical paper on his and Nancy Mohn's behalf ("The Potential of Clean Conventional Coal vs. Integrated Gasification Combined Cycle") at the American Society of Mechanical Engineers' Turbo Expo 06—Power for Land, Sea, and Air. The photograph on the left shows a panoramic view of beautiful Barcelona on the banks of the Mediterranean Sea. Greg and Nsakala took a bus tour of the city (top right) and walked around the perimeter of the unfinished Sagrada Familia (the Basilica and Expiatory Church of the Holy Family), designed by Antoni Gaudi in the 1880s.

After their business trip to Frankfurt-Mannheim, they flew to Paris to work for two days with their ALSTOM colleagues at Massey, with whom they were working on a joint project relating to the designs of advanced circulating fluidized bed power plants for carbon dioxide (CO_2) capture. On the third day, they traveled—via the Regional Express Network train (*Réseau Express Régional*), or RER, system—from Massey to Versailles, where they took a self-conducted tour of the Château de Versailles. This collage shows them enjoying the glory of Versailles. This place is truly awesome!

As a reminder, Mayiza Mvibudulu, one of Luzibu's brothers, had called in 2002 from Kinshasa, Democratic Republic of the Congo, to ask if Luzibu and Nsakala would consider inviting one of his children, Dieyatondulua Lutete (David), to the United States to further his education. David had just successfully completed his high school education and passed the state examination. Answering affirmatively to Mayiza's request, Luzibu and Nsakala decided to first pay for David's English-language study at Kinshasa Language Institute (Kali). They paid for all David's educational and living expenses in Kinshasa for five years. Makinutewa Félix, Nsakala's brother-in-law, served as the intermediary in all the financial transactions pertaining to David's education and living expenses. In his fifth school year, David took an English-language skills test, TOEFL (Test of English as a Foreign Language) at the US Consulate in Kinshasa and passed it. Given this success, Luzibu and Nsakala got David admitted to Essex County College (ECC) in Newark, New Jersey.

The collage below shows David arriving at John F. Kennedy International Airport (JFK) on Tuesday, January 9, 2007. Diampisa, Luzibu, and Nsakala were there to welcome him. It was a major event in the lives of the extended Nsakala family, as it represented the addition of yet another member to the family. David is the third child of Mayiza Mvibudulu and Mama Zola Betty (see Family Tree: Two Generations of Luzibu and Her Siblings in the appendix).

On Friday, January 12, 2007, Luzibu and Nsakala took David to Essex County College to start the registration process. After one or two semesters at ECC, David decided to switch his major from computer science to nursing. He would successfully complete his nursing education at this college. (See Part Three of this memoir.)

On February 17, 2007, Yaya Luzibu and Nkoko Nsakala were again bursting with joy when their fourth grandchild, baby boy Nkailu Manzambi Nsakala, was born in Manchester Hospital to his proud parents, Karell Rose and Mukiese Nsakala. *Nkailu Manzambi* means "gift of God" in Kikongo. Nkailu is shown in the collage below with his proud parents.

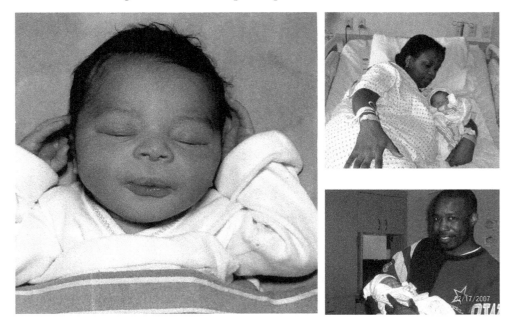

In the collage below, Nkailu is shown with, clockwise, Grandma Norma Rose and Yaya Luzibu Nsakala, Dad and paternal auntie Lemvo, and Grandpa Leslie Rose and Nkoko Nsakala. Everyone is beaming with joy.

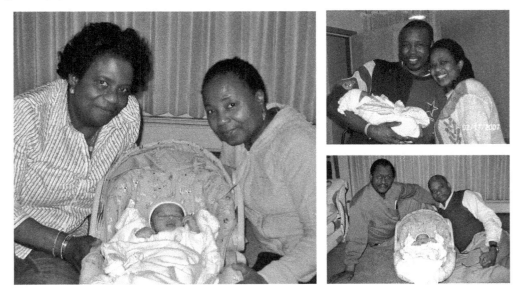

In the next collage, maternal auntie Monique Rose is all smiles while showing off her nephew Nkailu; Diampisa, Josée, and Kosi Bena join Nkailu's welcoming party to the world; and cousin David, who had arrived in the United States from the Democratic Republic of the Congo about one month earlier, strikes a pose with Nkailu.

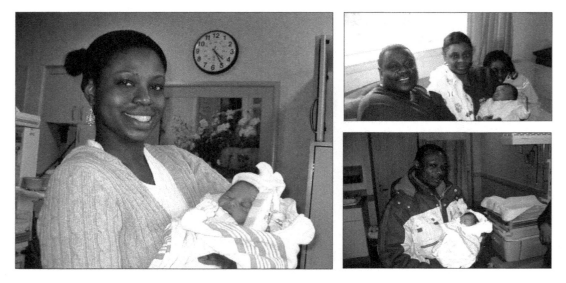

The collage below shows first-time dad Mukiese holding Nkailu with one hand while jumping with joy shortly after Nakilu's birth. A little later, his other maternal aunt, Camille Rose Dyer, is also visibly happy to be with her new nephew, Nkailu. And Mom holds Nkailu with an adoring expression, presumably whispering, "Son, I love you!"

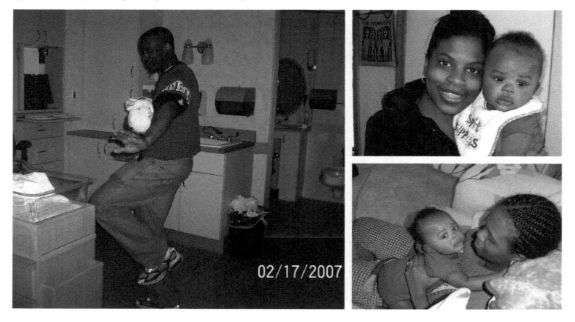

In March 2007, Nsakala accompanied John Marion, the Windsor, Connecticut, power plant laboratory director, to Baden, Switzerland, where they attended one of the many meetings at the ABB corporate headquarters. While there, Nsakala visited with Dora and Werner Schott (left-hand photograph). Two iconic places in Baden are shown on the right: Limmat River, which feeds into Lake Zurich down the road, and the tunnel, which is a gateway-like structure leading into the city of Baden. As mentioned previously, the Schotts, who were Nsakala's landlords in Dättwil in 1966, had become friends of his and Luzibu's.

Back on the home front, the Nsakalas' grandchildren were keeping active. The Mitchells' children were involved in such sports and activities as basketball, cross-country running, hockey, swimming, dancing, soccer, and T-ball. These extracurricular activities kept their parents very busy driving them from place to place. Whenever feasible, Yaya, Nkoko, or both would attend these events. This collage shows J3 posing with his hockey stick inside their home and playing (number 8 jersey) at the South Windsor Arena.

In June 2007, another family milestone was achieved. It concerned Luann Bena's graduation from Conard High School. Here, Luann is shown with her smiling and proud parents, Josée and Diampisa Bena, and the extended family.

In the fall of 2007, Zola and Jianna played on the same soccer team. The collage below features the team, Zola with the ball (top right), and Jianna with the ball (bottom right).

Ms. Joyce Draugelis babysat the Mitchell children (James III, Zola, and Jianna) at her home in South Windsor, Connecticut, for a number of years. She is shown in this photograph with the Mitchell children at Rye Street Park, South Windsor, where she joined the family to watch Zola and Jianna play soccer one day in the fall of 2007.

The Mitchell Jr. family has always participated in the live performance of *The Passion of the King* play at their church, Crossroads Community Cathedral in East Hartford. As the Bible teaches us: "Train a child in the way he should go, and when he is old, he will not turn from it" (Proverbs 22:6 New International Version). They are seen in the photographs in the collage below with family and friends after the performance on Good Friday, March 21, 2008.

The Mitchell children, Jianna, Zola, and J3, always hung out with Yaya and Nkoko. In this April 2008 collage, Yaya, James, Jianna, and Zola are preparing monkey bread for breakfast. The other two photographs show them enjoying the freshly baked monkey bread with Yaya and Nkoko.

In June 2008, Yaya Luzibu and Nkoko Nsakala joined the Mitchell Jr. family when Jay graduated from Rensselaer at Hartford with a master's degree in management.

From 1991 to 2003, Luzibu worked at Ames Department Stores Inc. in Rocky Hill, Connecticut, as a corporate staff accountant, with Bonnie Bunce, Alice Franco, Gisela Pano, and others. The four ladies kept in touch with each other even after Ames went bankrupt in 2003. In the summer of 2008, they organized a couple of luncheons/get-togethers with their husbands. In July, three of the four couples got together at Mill on the River in South Windsor. The top left photograph shows Gisela, Alice, and Luzibu. In the top right photograph, they are accompanied by their husbands, Nsakala, Geno, and John. The bottom left photograph features Alice, Luzibu, and Bonnie. In the bottom right photograph, Gisela, Bonnie, Alice, John, Geno, Luzibu, and Nsakala are shown.

In August 2008, a number of members of the extended family converged on Washington, DC, for a surprise birthday celebration for Alberta Mitchell, Jay Mitchell's mom. Present at this gathering were the families of Janet and Kevin Joiner, Lemvo and Jay Mitchell, Mikele Simkins and Jonathan Michell, and Luzibu and Nsakala, plus David. This collage shows Alberta and Jim Mitchell with all their grandchildren and some of the grandchildren in a hotel swimming pool. More of the party revelers are shown in the top right photograph. It should be noted that Alberta and Jim Mitchell are the parents of Jay, Janet, and Jonathan.

During the last week in August 2008, Josée and Diampisa hosted Diampisa's niece, Susanne Binga Kimpiatu, and her son, Mark Kimpiatu, who were vacationing in the United States from London. As usual, Diampisa took them to South Windsor to visit with the family elders, Luzibu and Nsakala. Here, the visitors are hanging out in the Nsakalas' home with other family members.

In September 2008, Luzibu and Nsakala flew to Belgium to participate in the wedding of Linda Mubagwa and Bosco Mpozi. Fortuna and Kani, the bride's parents, arranged for Luzibu and Nsakala to stay at the home of their friend Ms. Jo Mathieu, who lived in Landen (Walshoutem) with her daughter, Martine Laporte. The wedding ceremony took place in Saint Michel and Saint Gudula Cathedral in Brussels. This collage shows the wedding festivities. The top left photograph shows the newlywed couple with the bride's

parents. The bottom left photograph shows Luzibu signing the wedding documents as a witness. The top right photograph features the wedding party. And the bottom right photograph shows Luzibu, Nsakala, Martine Laporte, and Jo Mathieu sitting at the dinner table during the wedding reception at the Hotel Nivelles-Sud, Nivelles.

About one month later, in October 2008, Luzibu and Nsakala drove from South Windsor to Montréal, Canada, to participate in yet another wedding. It was the union of Ndandu Nzuzi Hornela and Kiasiswa Francis at the Première Eglise Évangélique Arménienne (First Armenian Evangelical Church), Montréal. Right after the wedding ceremony, the reception was held at Salle Le Parc. The top left photograph in the collage shows the newlywed couple with the parents of the bride, Mabetiteza Hélène and Ndandu Albert. The bottom right photograph shows Luzibu with Mabetiteza Hélène.

On Tuesday, November 6, 2008, the United States was host to a historical event that would reverberate all over the world. An African American man, Barack Obama, was elected the forty-fourth US president (Image[m]) by defeating Senator John McCain, as shown by the general election statistics in the top left photograph.

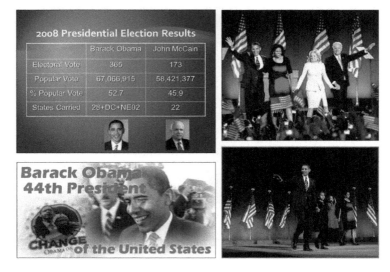

On Tuesday, January 20, 2009, President-elect Barack Obama was sworn in as the forty-fourth President of the United States (Image[n]). The top right photograph in the collage shows President Obama taking the oath of office from US Supreme Court Chief Justice John Roberts. The other photographs show a journal of President Obama's inauguration and the size of the crowds on the Washington Mall during the inauguration ceremony.

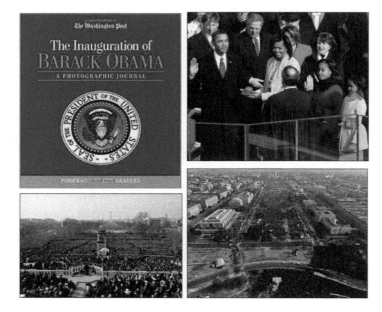

The election of President Obama brought tears of joy to Luzibu and Nsakala because it brought to their minds the Reverend Dr. Martin Luther King Jr.'s "I Have a Dream" speech, delivered on the steps of the Lincoln Memorial during the March on Washington for Jobs and Freedom on August 28, 1963. President Obama's election was, in a way, a partial fullfilment of Dr. King's dream that his "four children will one day live in a nation where they will not be judged by the color of their skin, but by the content of their character."

In May 2009, Luzibu and Nsakala vacationed at their home in Palm Coast, Florida. They asked their friends Nancy and Carroll Yoder to join them from Harrisonburg, Virginia, for one week. The four of them stayed inside the house because it rained almost constantly throughout the week. However, that did not dampen their spirits. In fact, as shown here, they are enjoying their fellowship over a glass of wine. The photograph on the left shows Nancy, Carroll, Luzibu, Leslie Rose, and Norma Rose. Nsakala is in the middle in the photograph on the right.

In June 2009, Mabetiteza Hélène and Ndandu Albert, who lived in Montréal, visited their chil-

dren in New Orleans, Louisiana, and Baltimore, Maryland. Luzibu and Nsakala took advantage of their stay in the United States to invite them to greater Hartford on their way back to Montréal. Hélène and Albert are shown with Luzibu and Nsakala at the Nsakalas' home in South Windsor. Luzibu and Hélène not only grew up together in Kibunzi but also graduated together from École Ménagère Kibunzi. Furthermore, Albert graduated from Kibunzi Primary School about two years after Nsakala.

On July 21, 2009, Yaya Luzibu and Nkoko Nsakala were once again rejoicing when their fifth grandchild, baby girl Nailah Anaïs Nsakala, was born in Hartford Hospital to her proud parents, Karell Rose and Mukiese Nsakala. In the collage below, Nailah is shown with her loving parents.

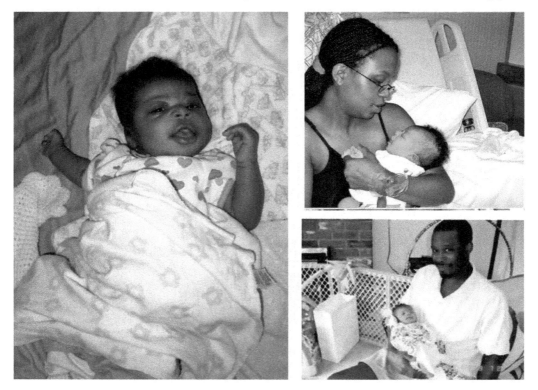

The next collage shows Nkailu lovingly admiring his baby sister while maternal grandparents Norma and Leslie Rose take turns holding Nailah tenderly.

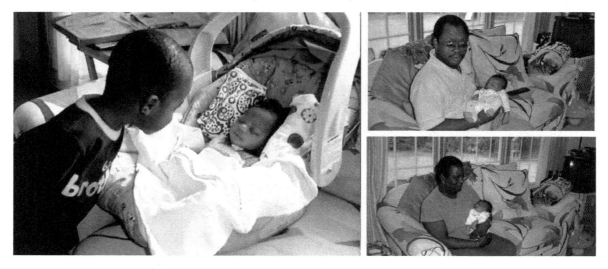

The collage below shows Dad smiling and holding Nailah gently while big brother Nkailu is bursting with joy; both sets of grandparents, Yaya Luzibu and Nkoko Nsakala and Grandma Norma and Grandpa Leslie Rose, are also visibly full of joy in the presence of their granddaughter Nailah. They continue to count their many blessings.

In September 2009, Luzibu and Nsakala vacationed yet again at their second home in Palm Coast, Florida. They had arranged beforehand for their friend Gary Tessier, who lived in Conway, South Carolina, to spend a weekend with them so he and Nsakala could install some ceiling fans in the house. Here, Gary and Nsakala are assembling one of the fans in the family room before mounting it on the ceiling. In total, they installed three ceiling fans. Yeah, good friends are forever!

In mid-September 2009, it was time for Dieyatondulua Lutete, or David, to start a new academic term at Essex County College in Newark, New Jersey. A contingent of four members of the extended family drove down to Newark with David to help him move into his apartment.

During the last week of September 2009, Nsakala flew out to Berlin, Germany, with colleague John Marion. From Berlin, John drove to Cottbus, Germany, to attend an international conference on carbon dioxide (CO_2) emissions control from fossil fuels combustion sources. The top right photograph shows the hotel where the conference took place in Cottbus. Interested conference attendees toured ALSTOM's thirty-megawatt thermal (MW_t) CO_2 capture pilot plant via oxygen-firing (oxyfuel) in Vattenfall, Germany. Nsakala is shown standing in front of the schematic of this facility, and the actual facility is pictured in the lower right photograph of the collage.

In October 2009, Luzibu and Nsakala watched a live performance of the play *Eclipsed* at Yale Repertory Theatre in New Haven, Connecticut. *Eclipsed* was written by playwright Danai Gurira, and it's the story of five Liberian women and their tale of survival near the end of the Second Liberian Civil War, which took place between 1999 and 2003. The top left photograph in the collage below shows Luzibu with the Guriras (Chiwoniso, Josephine, Roger, and Danai). Other cast members of the play are shown in the top right photograph.

March 2010 marked another milestone for the extended Nsakala family: baby Nailah Anaïs Nsakala was dedicated at Crossroads Community Cathedral (CCC). Pastor Shaun Wiles performed the dedication with the help of Mrs. Jennifer Capps, the wife of another CCC pastor, Donny Capps.

Soon after baby Nailah's dedication, Luzibu and Nsakala invited Josephine and Roger Gurira, who were living in the Washington, DC, area with their daughter Chiwoniso, to the March 2010 live presentation of the *Passion of the King* play at CCC in East Hartford. As always, the Mitchell family were cast members of the play. The collage below shows Josephine and Roger with the Nsakala's extended family at CCC following the play.

Remember what King Solomon wrote? "There is a time for everything, and a season for every activity under the heavens" (Ecclesiastes 3:1 New International Version). After over three decades—thirty-two and three quarter years, to be exact—of living and working in greater Hartford, Connecticut, it was time for Luzibu and Nsakala to retire from their respective jobs and move down to a place where the climate was warmer than in southern New England. Two United Van Lines movers loaded the moving truck, shown here on Thursday, May 27, 2010, with the Nsakalas' household belongings in South Windsor, for delivery to their retirement home in Palm Coast, Florida.

Even though Luzibu and Nsakala sold their South Windsor home in May 2010, they weren't scheduled to retire until the end of July. So they rented an apartment in the Homewood Suites by Hilton in Windsor Locks, Connecticut. They are shown at the Homewood Suites in July 2010, with Karell Rose, Mukiese Nsakala, and their children and Mabetiteza Hélène, who was visiting from Montréal.

It should be recalled that Makinutewa Félix is Diampisa Bena's maternal uncle. He and his wife, Biki Marie, lived in Wavre, Belgium. This family was, and continued to be, the glue that binds together the overall family in the Congo, Europe, and the United States. They facilitated virtually all transactions between the Nsakala family members in the diaspora and the Congo. Hence, early in 2010, the extended Nsakala family, including the Benas; the Lusalas from Bloomington, Illinois; and the Nsakalas, decided to invite them to the United States as an expression of their gratitude. That said, Makinutewa and Biki arrived in Connecticut at the beginning of July 2010. They are shown here (second from the left in the first row and second from the left in the back row) with the family in the atrium of the Crossroads Community Cathedral in East Hartford.

After visiting greater Hartford, Makinutewa and Biki spent two weeks in Bloomington, Illinois, visiting with the Lusalas. Subsequently, they went to Palm Coast to spend another two weeks with Luzibu and Nsakala, who had just retired there. Finally, they returned to greater Hartford to spend more time before returning to Belgium. All indications were that they enjoyed their stay in the United States with family and friends.

Back in Connecticut, Luzibu and Nsakala retired from their jobs on the last workday of July 2010. Nsakala's retirement party was held at the DoubleTree Hotel in Windsor Locks. The top left photograph shows John Marion, the director of products development and technology (PD&T) at ALSTOM Power, Inc., delivering some remarks about the footprint that Nsakala was leaving behind. In the bottom left photograph, Joe Quinn, one of the speakers at the party, is also making some remarks. Nsakala, top right, is making some remarks of his own, thanking everyone for everything. And on the bottom right, Nsakala is having a heart-to-heart talk with Carl Bozzuto, a mentor of his.

The rest of the party attendees are shown in this collage. Barbara Barberie, seen on the far right in the top left photograph, was the administrative assistant for PD&T's combustion technology department, where Nsakala worked. Shown in the bottom right photograph are the members of the Nsakala family who attended the party (from left to right, Diampisa Bena, Jay Mitchell, Nsakala, Luzibu holding Nailah, Mukiese Nsakala, Josée Bena, and Lemvo Mitchell).

Besides a monetary gift, Nsakala received a memorable photograph and a collage depicting some of his accomplishments at Combustion Engineering/ABB/ALSTOM Power.

In this photograph Nsakala is shown with some colleagues, from left to right, Julie Nicholson, Richard (Dick) Borio, John Marion, David Towle, and Armand Levasseur.

This collage depicts some of Nsakala's accomplishments throughout his tenure at Combustion Engineering/ABB/ALSTOM Power.

It turned out that RR Donnelly, where Luzibu was a staff accountant, and ALSTOM Power, where Nsakala worked, were located, at the time of their retirement, in the same building complex in Windsor, Connecticut. Luzibu's retirement party was strictly an internal affair. Well wishes for Luzibu from the RR Donnelly accounting group are expressed in the card shown here. One of her coworkers expressed his farewell like this:

"Dear Luzibu, You are my best work friend. I know that your even tempered, polite, and accepting ways have rubbed off on me, saving the lives of many of people I must deal with on a day to day basis. I have never worked with a better person or enjoyed it more. You have taught me that people from different cultures can be so much alike. I now know the content of a person goes beyond culture. You know I wish you the best and please keep in touch. You will be missed very much."

For years, Luzibu and Nsakala belonged to one of many small groups at the Crossroads Community Cathedral in East Hartford. Their group (in the left-hand photograph) consisted of Brenda Dimmock, Luzibu, Nsakala, Olga DeJesus, and Sheryl Dickon (seated) and Karen Lumpkin, Ron Lumpkin, Walter Dimmock, Jackie Smith, Isidor Smith, Edwin DeJesus, and Bob Dixon (standing). Additionally, Joy and David Fortt are shown sitting and standing at the far right of the right-hand photograph. The small group held a send-off party in mid-July 2010, for Luzibu and Nsakala at Sheryl and Bob Dickon's home in Manchester, Connecticut.

Before Luzibu and Nsakala moved to Florida, their greater Hartford family threw a send-off party for them at the Mitchell Jr. home in South Windsor.

The collage on the previous page shows the various family members enjoying their fellowship with each other. It was a bittersweet time for Luzibu and Nsakala; they were happy to move to a place with a warmer climate but sad to leave this loving and lovely family behind. In any case, "There is a time for everything, and a season for every activity under the heavens." The top left photograph shows Nsakala shaking hands with Diampisa while Luzibu and Josée look on. This was, symbolically, Nsakala passing the baton to Diampisa. The other three photographs show the party revelers posing for snapshots, mingling with each other, and just having fun together.

Here, Karell Rose and Mukiese Nsakala (top left photograph), Luvevo Noël Kitomba and Manzo Tuzolana (top right photograph), Luzibu and Nsakala (bottom right photograph), and Lukiantima (Josée) and Diampisa Bena (bottom left photograph) are chilling after the big meal.

Part Three

Life in the United States of America—The Joy of Retirement

Human beings all go through phases in life: they grow, they develop, they mature, and, if they are fortunate enough, they enjoy the retirement phase of life. As they continue to move on in life, they shift from one phase to the next. It was time for Luzibu and Nsakala to begin a new phase in their life together. What they desired was vitality, joy, and meaning in their lives, by God's grace and blessings.

9

The Joy of Retirement
in Florida

Chapter 9 treats various subjects of interest, namely:

- Being at home with family and friends;

- Domestic travel; and

- International travel.

At Home with Family and Friends

Palm Coast, Florida, is Luzibu and Nsakala's retirement home. This is where the events depicted in this section took place or originated from.

The United Van Lines truck is seen arriving from South Windsor, Connecticut, at the Nsakalas' home in Palm Coast, Florida, on Saturday, June 5, 2010, when two truck drivers delivered their belongings. Diampisa Bena and Nsakala were there to receive this delivery.

Remember Biki Marie and Makinutewa Félix contemporaneously visiting the family in greater Hartford from Belgium? By the time Luzibu and Nsakala left greater Hartford for Florida, Marie and Félix were on a two-week visit with Josephine Munlemvo and Edward Lusala in Bloomington, Illinois. Arriving from Bloomington on Wednesday, August 11, 2010, for a two-week visit, Marie and Félix were the Nsakalas' first visitors at their home in Palm Coast after their retirement.

Marie and Félix did a lot of things with Luzibu and Nsakala throughout their stay in the Sunshine State. Here, Félix and Nsakala are reading the news about the Democratic Republic of the Congo in French on the internet; then all of them are having breakfast (see the photograph on the previous page).

Here, they just came out of services, on two occasions, at the Palm Coast United Methodist Church.

The first thing they did almost every morning was to go to the many walking trails of Palm Coast and take a rather leisurely walk for thirty to forty-five minutes.

They also went to the beach on numerous occasions. Here they are enjoying themselves at Flagler Beach.

They also strolled on Daytona Beach. Luzibu and Nsakala took Marie and Félix into some gift shops and got them some Daytona Beach souvenirs.

At the end of their stay, Marie and Félix flew out of Orlando International Airport back to greater Hartford, where the Bena family was waiting for them. By their own account, their experience in Florida was a memorable one.

By this time, though, the extended family was going through difficult times, as one member, Leslie Rose, was ill and spending his last days on Earth. He passed away in mid-September. Hence, some extended family members from the greater Hartford area drove down to Palm Coast to attend his funeral services. In the collage below, Luzibu and Nsakala are shown in the left-hand photograph with Josée Bena, Luvevo Noël Kitomba, and Jay Mitchell. In the top right photograph, they are pictured with Diampisa Bena and Mohamed Lamine Niang.

The next photograph shows the visitors from greater Hartford preparing to leave for the Palm Coast United Methodist Church, where the going-to-the-Lord services for Leslie Rose were held. It is often said that a beautiful soul is never forgotten.

In January 2011, Josephine and Roger Gurira were spending their vacation with their daughter, Shingai Gurira, in Fort Lauderdale, Florida. They took advantage of their stay in Florida to spend time with Luzibu and Nsakala from Saturday, January 8, to Friday, January 14, 2011. The photographs in the collage below show Luzibu and Nsakala with Josephine, Roger, and Shingai Gurira.

During the Guriras' week-long stay in Palm Coast, the two families did a number of enjoyable things together. The first thing they did every morning was take a walk along one of the many Palm Coast walking trails. Here, for example, they are walking on the Saint Joe Walkway along the Intra-coastal Waterway.

Here, they are enjoying themselves at Bulow Creek State Park, which is home to huge oak trees and palm trees, among other flora species. This park offers an inescapable sense of serenity.

And here they are walking on the Flagler Beach Pier on one day and having breakfast at the Funky Pelican restaurant with some of Luzibu and Nsakala's friends on another day.

In June 2011, Luzibu and Nsakala had the pleasure of welcoming to their home their longtime friends Dora and Werner Schott from Switzerland for a few days. Here, the photos show Dora and Werner arriving in a rental car, Luzibu helping Werner with their suitcases, and Dora and Luzibu viewing a photo album together.

Luzibu and Nsakala took Dora and Werner to a variety of places in Florida. This collage shows them standing at the entrance of the "World's Most Famous Beach," Daytona Beach, and at Flagler Beach.

They also went sightseeing in Saint Augustine, where they took a city tour on the Old Town Trolley, visited the local alligator farm, and had lunch at the Santa Maria Restaurant, a favorite of Dora and Werner's.

In July 2011, the extended family celebrated the wedding of Camille Rose Dyer and Christopher McKenzie at the Hammock Beach Resorts in Palm Coast. The collage below shows, in the left-hand photograph, the bride and groom arriving at the wedding venue in a horse-drawn carriage. The top right photograph shows the mother of the bride, Norma Rose, making her entrance into the wedding ceremony room, followed by Samuel Rose, who gave his niece Camille away in marriage. The bottom right photograph shows the bride and groom saying their wedding vows.

The collage below shows, in the left-hand photograph, the bride and groom standing side by side in a room before or after the wedding ceremony. The top right photograph shows the bride and groom posing with the family matriarch, Genrith Wilson (Auntie Jenny). The bottom right photograph shows Camille and Chris with Camille's sisters, Monique Rose and Karell Rose, plus Karell's family: Mukiese (husband), Nkailu (son), and Nailah (daughter).

The snapshots below show Karell, Auntie Jenny, Luzibu, Nailah, and others during the wedding ceremony and Dieyatondulua/David with his Auntie Luzibu and Uncle Nsakala.

In December 2011, Luzibu and Nsakala welcomed members of the extended family visiting from Bloomington, Illinois: Josephine and Edward Lusala and Brandon Lusala, Edward's son. Here, they are shown with Luzibu and Nsakala at the entrance to Daytona Beach, posing with the ocean in the background, and with the Nsakala Jr. family (Mukiese, Karell, Nailah, and Nkailu), who were visiting from South Windsor, Connecticut, in front of Luzibu and Nsakala's swimming pool.

In January 2012, Luzibu and Nsakala welcomed longtime friends Nancy and Carroll Yoder, who were visiting from Harrisonburg, Virginia. This time, the monsoon-like rain of May 2009 did not happen. So the four of them were able to do some outdoor activities, such as walking along Flagler Beach and picking up oranges at Auntie Jenny's home, near where the Nsakalas live.

And the visitors kept coming. In March 2012, Luzibu and Nsakala welcomed David Towle, who had come from greater Hartford via Orlando for a one-day visit. David and Nsakala were colleagues at ALSTOM Power, Inc., in Windsor. Besides hanging out together at home, the three of them had lunch at the Golden Lion Café in Flagler Beach; they then strolled on the beach.

In June 2012, the Nsakalas had the pleasure of welcoming to their home Zenab and Iqbal Abdulally, who were visiting from greater Hartford. Iqbal and Nsakala had not only been colleagues working on the same projects at ALSTOM Power, Inc., in Windsor but were also good friends. Of course, Luzibu and Nsakala took Zenab and Iqbal around town. Here they are at the Flagler Beach Pier, enjoying the sunshine and admiring Mother Nature's beauty.

In August 2012, Luzibu and Nsakala welcomed to their home yet another couple, Olga and Edwin DeJesus, who were visiting from greater Hartford. The DeJesuses and Nsakalas forged their relationship when they belonged to a small group from Crossroads Community Cathedral in East Hartford. Here they are all enjoying a cup of tea/coffee together at the Nsakalas' home and reminiscing about their time in greater Hartford. They also visited Mrs. Norma Rose, Mukiese Nsakala's mother-in-law, who lives about 2 miles (3 km) from the Nsakalas' home in Palm Coast.

Here, Edwin and Nsakala are enjoying the warm water of the Nsakalas' backyard swimming pool, and the four of them are taking a walk along the Intracoastal Waterway in Palm Coast and frolicking in the Flagler Beach sand.

On Tuesday, November 6, 2012, US President Barack Obama won a deserved, outright reelection for a second four-year term in office. He defeated ex–Massachusetts governor Mitt Romney with a decisive 332 electoral votes versus 206 for Romney (270 electoral votes are required to win). The top right photograph shows the Obama family celebrating their victory with the family of Vice President Joe Biden on the stage of their election-returns-watching venue. The lower right photograph shows President Obama and Governor Romney either before or after one of their presidential debates on October 22, 2012, while the debate moderator Bob Schieffer looks on.

On Sunday, January 20, 2013, Barack Obama was sworn in to serve as president of the United States for another four-year term. These photographs show President Obama taking the oath of office from US Supreme Court Chief Justice John Roberts and speaking after taking the oath of office; the right-hand photograph shows the enormous size of the peaceful crowd on the Washington Mall during President Obama's inauguration (Image°).

President Obama's reelection proved that the United States was continuing to make giant strides toward the quest for racial equality, peace, and justice for all. Luzibu and Nsakala's hope was that this trend would continue.

In March 2013, Luzibu and Nsakala welcomed Mabetiteza Hélène for a three-week visit from Montréal. Hélène and Luzibu not only grew up together in Kibunzi but they also went to primary school together and graduated together from *École Ménagère Kibunzi*. Here, Hélène, Luzibu, and Nsakala are walking along the Intracoastal Waterway. They are shown posing for a photograph with Luzibu and Nsakala's friends after breakfast at the Funky Pelican Restaurant in Flagler Beach.

Luzibu and Nsakala also took Hélène sightseeing in Saint Augustine, Florida. The left-hand photograph shows them riding the Old Town Trolley, while the two right-hand photographs show them at the Saint Augustine Alligator Farm Zoological Park.

The photographs in this collage were snapped in March 2013 at the Palm Coast United Methodist Church's North Campus. The top left photograph shows on the far right the Reverend Dr. Kevin M. James Sr., senior pastor of the church, reading biblical verses to dedicate and celebrate the opening of "Buy a Brick Mural" for the church members. The bottom left photograph shows Luzibu on the far left, followed by Mabetiteza Hélène, plus other church congregants. The two right-hand photographs show more of the church members at the ceremony.

In June 2013, Luzibu and Nsakala welcomed to their home Josephine and Edward Lusala, who were visiting from Bloomington, Illinois, for a dual purpose: to visit with Luzibu and Nsakala and to check out, for the first time, the retirement home they had purchased earlier. Josephine and Edward had not seen this home because Luzibu and Nsakala had chosen it on their behalf with the assistance of a RE/MAX real estate agent. In this collage, they are shown standing in front of their Palm Coast home, and they are also shown visiting with Auntie Jenny and Mrs. Norma Rose.

Months of planning culminated in Luzibu and Nsakala welcoming the Bena part of the family from greater Hartford to their Florida home in early August 2013. The seven strong southern New Englanders—affectionately known as North Villagers—were to spend one week of fun in the Sunshine State. Going clockwise, Luzibu is shown with Josée Bena, Constance (Kosi) Bena, and Kitomba Lydia; Brian Bena is with ya Josée and sister Kosi; Lydia Kitomba (holding a tablet) is with Diampisa Bena and Germain Kitomba; and Lydia is with Diampisa, Guy Betamona, and Nsakala. To clarify, Lydia is Josée's sister, Guy is Lydia's brother-in-law, and Germain is Josée and Lydia's brother.

It goes without saying that dinner tastes better when the family eats together, and the fondest memories are made when gathered around a dinner table.

Who said that Ambassador Diampisa (as he is affectionately known by the extended family) could not swim? He and others are enjoying the warm 86° F (30° C) water of the pool. Guess what? The time spent with family was worth every second!

In the following collage, the family is having fun swimming at Flagler Beach. Everyone, it appears, is reveling in the majestic wonder of the Atlantic Ocean.

Never forgetting or taking for granted the ties that bind the family together, the group stopped by Mrs. Norma Rose's home (left-hand photograph), Auntie Genrith Wilson's home (top right photograph), and Jean and Sam Rose's home (bottom right photograph) as courtesy calls to check on the well-being of these members of the extended family, all of whom are Luzibu and Nsakala's neighbors in Palm Coast.

The following month, in September 2013, Luzibu and Nsakala's friends from Switzerland, Dora and Werner Schott, embarked on a tour of the United States with Judith, Dora's sister. To Luzibu and Nsakala's delight, they decided to spend four days with them in Palm Coast toward the end of their journey. The top two photographs show Judith, Dora, and Luzibu at breakfast in the Nsakalas' kitchen (top left) and Werner and Nsakala enjoying themselves in the Nsakalas' jacuzzi (top right). The two lower photographs show all of them walking on the Flagler Beach Pier.

As usual, Luzibu and Nsakala took their guests to Saint Augustine, where they all took a city tour on the Old Town Trolley and then had lunch at the Santa Maria Restaurant—as mentioned earlier, a favorite of Dora's and Werner's (top photographs). They also all went to frolic on the Daytona Beach sand (bottom photographs).

EF-1 Tornado Hits Palm Coast in December 2013

The Enhanced Fujita Scale (EF Scale) rates the intensity of tornadoes in some countries, including the United States and Canada, based on the damage they cause (Image[p]). This table shows the EF Scale with corresponding wind speeds and expected property damages.

EF Rating	Wind Speed	Expected Damage
EF-0	65-85 mph	**'Minor' damage:** shingles, gutters, tree branches.
EF-1	86-110 mph	**'Moderate' damage:** roof, broken windows, exterior doors, overturned mobile homes.
EF-2	111-135 mph	**'Considerable' damage:** roofs torn off, mobile homes destroyed, trees uprooted, cars tossed.
EF-3	136-165 mph	**'Severe' damage:** homes destroyed, buildings damaged, homes with weak foundations can be blown away.
EF-4	166-200 mph	**'Extreme' damage:** homes leveled, cars thrown, top story exterior walls of masonry buildings likely to collapse.
EF-5	>200 mph	**'Massive' damage:** homes swept away, high-rise buildings severely damaged, steel-reinforced concrete structures damaged, trees snapped.

On December 14, 2013, Palm Coast was hit by an EF-1 tornado. This clip from a local newspaper shows the amount of damage wrought by the tornado.

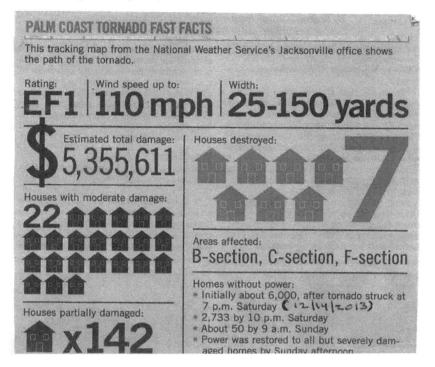

These photographs show the damage done by the EF-1 tornado to the Nsakalas' pool enclosure (right) and their neighbor's pool enclosure (bottom left).

With the tornado's destruction behind them, in mid-February 2014, Luzibu and Nsakala had the pleasure of welcoming Edna and Milford Yoder for a three-day visit from Wellman, Iowa, via Sarasota, Florida, where they had been visiting some family members. The next two collages show the four of them hanging out at Luzibu and Nsakala's home, walking along the Intracoastal Waterway, and standing on the Flagler Beach Pier. Milford is part of the Yoder family who hosted Luzibu in Wellman, Iowa, starting in September 1966. The bonds between the Nsakala and Yoder families continue to be strong.

On August 6, 2014, Khadidiatou and Lamine Niang, who had been visiting Orlando with their family, called Luzibu and Nsakala to see if they could stop by their home for a short visit the following day on their way back to greater Hartford. Of course, Luzibu and Nsakala said yes without hesitation. The following photographs show them enjoying dinner and, more importantly, fellowship with Luzibu and Nsakala. They continued their journey back to greater Hartford after dinner.

In mid-August 2014, Luzibu and Nsakala continued to welcome visitors to their home with open hearts and arms. This time, the visitors were none other than Poppy and Bene M'Poko. Bene, the ambassador of the Democratic Republic of the Congo to South Africa and dean of the diplomatic corps in Pretoria, and Poppy were dropping off their son at a college in Leesburg, Florida. To Luzibu and Nsakala's delight, they decided to visit with them for two days. By way of reminder, Bene and Nsakala came to the United States together on the US AID's ASPAU program in September 1965. These photographs show the four of them visiting with Norma Rose at her home and walking on the Flagler Beach Pier.

The following photographs show them hanging out with Poppy's nephew, who came to visit from Jacksonville, and having lunch in a restaurant along the Intracoastal Waterway in Marineland, Florida.

In December 2014, Luzibu and Nsakala had the great pleasure of welcoming Ndandu Nzuzi Hornela, Kiasisua Francis, and their four-year-old daughter Malia for a three-week visit from Edmonton, Canada. They went to Disney World in Orlando frequently throughout their stay, though they returned to Palm Coast each evening. Also visiting during the Christmas holiday from South Windsor were Karell Rose; Mukiese Nsakala (the authors' son); and their three children, Amias, Nailah, and Nkailu. This collage shows the family partaking in Christmas dinner together at the Nsakalas' home. What a blessing it was!

In the collage below, some family members, particularly the children, are enjoying the 95°F (35°C) jacuzzi water and harvesting oranges from the trees in the backyard.

Luzibu and Nsakala also took their visitors to Flagler Beach and Daytona Beach.

The next photograph shows Nzuzi, Malia, and Francis at Disney World, along with Santa Claus, during the Christmas season.

In late January 2015, Mary and Greg Liljedahl called to say that they were on vacation in South Florida and wondered if they could stop by their home for a quick visit. "Yes, of course," Luzibu and Nsakala responded. Hence, Mary and Greg arrived in Palm Coast on Wednesday, January 28, 2015. The four of them had fun throughout the two-day stay. They walked on the Flagler Beach Pier. They hung out together and reminisced about their time together in greater Hartford. The Liljedahls left for their drive back to their home in Tariffville, Connecticut, on Friday, January 30, 2015.

At the end of March 2015, Luzibu and Nsakala warmly welcomed to their home Judy and Joel Yoder and their daughters Carrie, Sofia, and Leah, plus Caleb (Judy's nephew) and Sam (a friend of the Yoders who was visiting the United States from Taiwan) for a three-day vacation from Harrisonburg, Virginia. Joel is Nancy and Carroll Yoder's son. To recap, Carroll facilitated Luzibu's immigration to the United States and had his parents host her at their home in Wellman, Iowa, in 1966. In this collage, the top photograph shows, from left to right, Joel, Sofia, Judith, Leah, and Carrie at breakfast in the Nsakalas' home. The bottom photographs show Luzibu posing with the visitors (right) in front of the house, and Nsakala posing for a photograph with the visitors and Auntie Jenny in her backyard (left).

These photographs show Nsakala and the visitors kayaking on the Intracoastal Waterway and Joel and Nsakala, with the children, enjoying the 95°F (35°C) jacuzzi water.

Luzibu and Nsakala also took their visitors walking along the Intracoastal Waterway and swimming at Flagler Beach.

Finally, they all went sightseeing in Saint Augustine, where they rode the Old Town Trolley, walked along Saint George Street, and toured Saint Augustine's Castillo de San Marcos.

Luzibu and Nsakala's grandchildren, Zola and James Mitchell III (J3), through their church, Crossroads Community Cathedral in East Hartford, Connecticut, won their respective contests to participate in the August 2015 Assembly of God/National Fine Arts Festival (AG/NFAF) in Orlando, Florida. Zola won the chance to sing "Beautiful Day" by Jamie Grace, and J3 won the chance to preach about the ability to "Love the Lord your God with all your heart and with all your soul and with all your strength" (Deuteronomy 6:5 New International Version).

The arrangement with Zola and J3's parents was as follows: since Luzibu was already in South Windsor during Jianna's hospitalization to surgically remove a benign brain tumor, and Jay and Lemvo were not able to accompany Zola and James to the AG/NFAF in Orlando, Yaya would fly with them to Orlando International Airport (OIA). Nkoko would pick them up from OIA, and he and Yaya would have them for six days, then accompany them to and stay with them at the AG/NFAF throughout their five-day program.

The photographs in this collage include a selfie of Yaya, James, Nkoko, and Zola on their way from OIA to Palm Coast; James preparing his sermon; Zola singing "Beautiful Day;" and James delivering his "Love your God" sermon. They both did a great job in their contests.

These photographs show Zola and James's relatives and various attendees of the festival, particularly from East Hartford's Crossroads Community Cathedral. The lower right photograph shows Jay Mitchell (Zola and James's father), Luzibu, Alberta and Jim Mitchell (Zola and James's paternal grandparents), Nsakala, James, and Zola.

This photograph shows the Mitchell Sr. and Nsakala families and perhaps most of the festival attendees from Crossroads Community Cathedral.

In May 2015, Didier Diyavanga informed Luzibu and Nsakala via email that he had been randomly selected for further processing for the Diversity Immigrant Visa Program by the US Consulate in Kinshasa, Democratic Republic of the Congo. One of the sine qua nons for further processing was the identification by a candidate of the name and address of a host or host family in the United States. Hence, Didier asked if Luzibu and Nsakala would be able to do it for him, his wife, and their two children. After some deliberation and consultation with Makinutewa Félix, who lived in Belgium with his wife, Biki Marie, Luzibu and Nsakala agreed to give them the chance of a lifetime. Fast-forwarding the tape, on the evening of Saturday, January 9, 2016, Didier Diyavanga; Nathalie Beyisa; their two-year-old daughter, Chloe; and their eight-month-old son, Rami, arrived at Orlando International Airport (OIA), where Luzibu and Nsakala picked them up. Additionally, Nathalie was expecting a child in mid-February 2016. The photographs on the previous page show Luzibu and Nsakala with the Diyavanga family at OIA (left-hand photograph), the Chevrolet Tahoe (top right photograph) rented by Luzibu and Nsakala to pick them up, and the Diyavangas' first family car (bottom right photograph) in the United States, a Kia Sorento station wagon.

On February 17, 2016, the family welcomed a baby girl, Dina, born to Nathalie and Didier at the Florida Hospital Memorial Medical Center in Daytona Beach. These photographs show Dina in her hospital crib; Luzibu, Nathalie, and the baby; and a crib with some gifts, supplied by Luzibu and Nsakala.

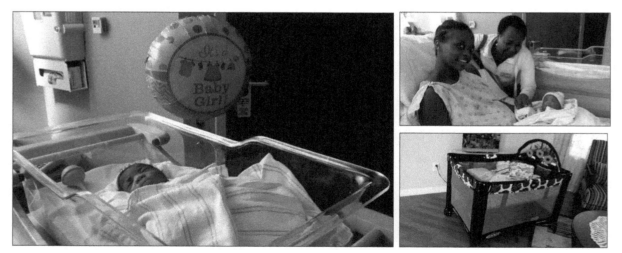

The top two photographs in this collage show the Diyavanga family with Luzibu, Nsakala, and Norma Rose; the bottom left photograph shows Lutete Dieyatondulua (David) and his then-fiancée, Shekinah Mulunda; the bottom right photograph shows David with Nsakala.

This photograph shows the Diyavanga family in front of the Nsakalas' porch right after a Sunday church service. In July 2016, they moved to an apartment in Jacksonville, Florida, as Didier had been working in Hastings, Florida, since the beginning of March 2016. Luzibu and Nsakala did more than just host the family. They took them in as if they were their own blood relatives. They oriented them to US life as much as possible and did for them what needed to be done. The experience was arduous but very rewarding, especially after the process reached a successful conclusion (i.e., when the family was on their own).

As shown in the collage below, Luzibu and Nsakala joined the Diyavanga family in Jacksonville to celebrate Chloe's third birthday on August 15, 2016.

At this writing, this family has moved on to Manassas, Virginia, where Didier is working at Amazon as an information technology engineer. OK, so what is the connection between the Nsakalas and this family, you might ask? Here is the answer in short: Luzibu and Nsakala met Didier in 2011 at Makinutewa Félix and Biki Marie's home in Kinshasa, DRC, where he was living at the time. Didier is Biki Marie's nephew, Biki Marie is Makinutewa Félix's wife, and Makinutewa Félix and Nsakala are brothers-in-law. Hence, in the Bakongo tribe's rather convoluted tradition, Nsakala is Didier's uncle. Bottom line? Luzibu and Nsakala are auntie and uncle to Nathalie and Didier and, for that matter, surrogate grandparents to their children.

The following month, the Nsakalas decided to make some updates and improvements to their home. These fifteen rooftop SunPower solar panels were designed by Power Production Management (PPM) of Gainesville, Florida. PPM subcontracted Florida Power Services (FPS) to install the five-kilowatt solar power system. FPS completed the installation on September 6, 2016.

This photograph shows how the solar power system (SPS) is connected to the Florida Power & Light's (FPL's) meter so that it operates in a "net metering" mode. Net metering simply means that any excess power produced by the solar power system is sold to FPL. FPL returns this power to the homeowner at night when the SPS is not operational.

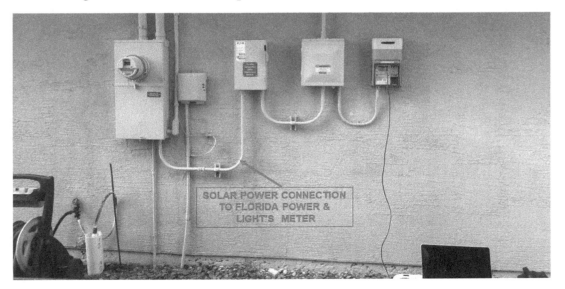

The environmental and financial benefits of solar energy are illustrated in the table below. The solar power system generated 16,189 kilowatt-hours from September 6, 2016, to April 3, 2019. There were 939 days during this time span. Hence, the solar system supplied, on average, 17 kilowatt-hours per day, or approximately 37 percent of the 46 kilowatt-hours per day needed by the household. The accompanying environmental savings were the equivalent of, for example, 12.3 tons of carbon dioxide (CO_2) emissions avoided and 8,821 pounds of garbage recycled (see additional benefits in the table).

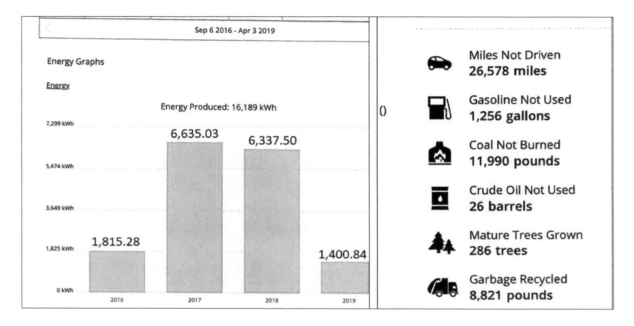

The bottom line is that the SunPower solar system has reduced the Nsakala household's monthly Florida Power & Light bill by about one third while at the same time helping take care of the environment.

Hurricane Matthew Hits Florida in October 2016

The Saffir-Simpson Hurricane Wind Scale (Image[q]) is a 1-to-5 rating based on a hurricane's sustained windspeed. This scale estimates corresponding potential property damages.

CATEGORY	WIND SPEED	DAMAGE
1	74-95 mph	Very dangerous winds will produce some damage
2	96-110 mph	Extremely dangerous winds will cause extensive damage
3	111-129 mph	Devastating damage will occur
4	130-156 mph	Catastrophic damage will occur
5	156+ mph	Catastrophic damage will occur

Atlantic Hurricane Matthew slammed Florida (see graphic below) as a Category 3 hurricane, with wind speeds in the 111 to 129 miles per hour (179–208 km/hour) range (Image[r]).

In anticipation of Hurricane Matthew landing on the Atlantic Ocean shores of Palm Coast on Friday, October 7, 2016, Palm Coast residents east of Interstate Highway-95 were required to evacuate on Thursday, October 6, 2016. Luzibu and Nsakala joined Norma Rose and Camille and Chris McKenzie at the Seventh-day Adventist's (SDA's) Camp Kulaqua in High Springs, Florida. They are all standing in front of the Live Oak Lodge, where they stayed for four days, right after the SDA sabbath service on Saturday, October 8, 2016.

Before leaving for Camp Kulaqua on Thursday, Luzibu and Nsakala protected their lanai in the pool area with hurricane shutters, as shown in the top left photograph. When they returned, they found devastating damage around town and in the area along the Intracoastal Waterway, as shown in the other two photographs.

For some happy news, on Sunday, March 5, 2017, the family celebrated the ninetieth birthday of Auntie Genrith Wilson (Auntie Jenny) at 5th Element Indian Cuisine, located in the European Village in Palm Coast. Truth be told, Auntie Jenny was so joyous that she acted like a kid in a candy store.

Celebrate the gift of life God has given you. Congratulations on your 90th Birthday!!
March 5, 2017

The following collage shows Auntie Jenny with two other nonagenarian ladies, Gloria Browne (left) and Albertine, in the left-hand photograph; with Luzibu and Nsakala in the top right photograph; and with Norma Rose and Camille McKenzie in the bottom right photograph.

The next collage shows Auntie Jenny and some of the party revelers.

Two months later, in May 2017, Luzibu and Nsakala took a Grand European River Cruise (see the International Travel section in Chapter 9), where they met several people, among them Karen and John Hovanec from Omaha, Nebraska. Karen and John were scheduled to attend a wedding ceremony in Orlando in early August. So they called Luzibu and Nsakala to see if they could stop by for a few hours during their stay in Orlando. Yes, was the answer, and on Friday, August 4, 2017, they visited for an overnight stay. The photograph on the left is a selfie of the four of them in the Nsakalas' swimming pool. The top right photograph was snapped on the deck of the Flagler Beach Pier.

Hurricane Irma Hits Florida in October 2017

In early October 2017, Atlantic Hurricane Irma first hit Florida's Gulf Coast as a Category 3 hurricane, though it was later downgraded to Category 1 status. The eye, trajectory, and typical impact of the hurricane are shown in these photographs (Image[s]).

Palm Coast experienced strong winds, and Luzibu and Nsakala lost power for seven days. So they used their propane gas grill to prepare home-cooked meals.

Several weeks later, life had returned to normal. Mae and Antoine Nzima of Flowery Branch, Georgia, were attending a conference in Orlando. A day before the end of the conference, they called Luzibu and Nsakala to see if they could stop by on their way back home. Of course, the answer was yes. So, on Saturday, December 9, 2017, they arrived in Palm Coast for a weekend visit. The four of them had fun together: they walked on the Flagler Beach Pier, went to services at Palm Coast United Methodist Church, and picked oranges in the backyard, among other activities.

At the end of January 2018, Luzibu and Nsakala had a good reason to be glad. Why? Gloria and Galen Yoder were planning to visit from Wellman, Iowa. Luzibu and Nsakala picked them up at Orlando Sanford Airport on Thursday, February 1, 2018, shortly after midnight. Here, the four of them are enjoying a leisurely time inside and outside the Nsakalas' home.

Below, the four of them are with the Nsakalas' friends with whom they go to breakfast on Friday mornings whenever possible. The left-hand photograph was snapped inside the Funky Pelican restaurant, located on the Flagler Beach Pier, and features from left to right, Galen, Gloria, Louise Delaere, Francine Smithson, Luzibu, Nsakala, and Ivor (Jack) Smithson. The two photographs on the right show the four of them on the pier.

Here, on the left, Galen is basically saying, "Move over, Arnold Palmer; there is a new kid in town—ha!" The top right photograph is a selfie of Galen and Nsakala at the beach off Jungle Hut Road in Palm Coast. While Galen and Nsakala were at the beach, Gloria and Luzibu were at a book-signing event sponsored by the University Women of Flagler (bottom right).

The four of them also went to EPCOT (Experimental Prototype Community of Tomorrow) Center in Orlando. This place is simply amazing, as depicted in this collage.

Linda Tamoulonis and Kerry Doherty and Karen and John Hovanec are the couples with whom Luzibu and Nsakala hung out during their May 2017 Grand European River Cruise (see the International Travel section).

In early March 2018, Linda and Kerry were planning to travel from their home in Dover, New Hampshire, to Florida to visit friends. They called the Nsakalas to see if they could stop by for a quick visit. The answer was yes. Hence, they arrived in Palm Coast on Monday, March 12, 2018, for a two-day visit. Luzibu and Nsakala took them to Saint Augustine for sightseeing. After taking a ride on the Old Town Trolley, they toured the Castillo de San Marcos. On the following page, the photograph on the left shows them posing on top of the castle. The other two photographs show them posing for some snapshots in the backyard of the Nsakalas' home.

In June 2018, Mabetiteza Hélène called Luzibu and Nsakala from Edmonton, Alberta, Canada, to say that she was planning to visit a friend in New Orleans, Louisiana, in early July 2018, and then she would visit with them in Palm Coast. Hélène spent one week with a friend of hers, Dr. Kuvibidila Solo Ruth, in Metairie, Louisiana, a suburb of New Orleans. Ruth drove Hélène to Palm Coast on Sunday, July 15, 2018, on her way to Washington, DC. One interesting fact is that the three ladies graduated together from École Ménagère Kibunzi in 1964.

While Ruth left on Tuesday, July 17, 2018, for her trip to our nation's capital city, Washington, DC, Hélène stayed behind to spend two weeks with Luzibu and Nsakala.

On one occasion, Luzibu and Nsakala took Hélène to Jacksonville to meet the Diyavanga family. Here, everyone is enjoying fellowship with the others inside the Diyavanga family's apartment.

On Thursday, July 26, 2018, Luzibu and Nsakala surprised Hélène with a visit to the Holy Land Experience in Orlando (Map[h]). The next photograph and the subsequent two collages depict various scenes that were enjoyed by all.

In the collage below, the photograph on the left shows Hélène with Norma Rose and Luzibu. The lower right photograph shows Hélène hanging out with some Palm Coast United Methodist Church people at a church picnic. The top right photograph shows Hélène and Luzibu at the breakfast table on Tuesday morning, July 31, 2018, before her trip back to Edmonton.

On February 17, 2019, Luzibu and Nsakala gladly welcomed members of the extended family, Josephine and Edward Lusala, to Palm Coast, where they came to retire from their jobs in Bloomington/Lexington, Illinois. They are shown in the left selfie between Luzibu and Nsakala. They are originally from the villages of Ntandu a Nzadi and Ndembolo, respectively, in the Democratic Republic of the Congo (see appropriate map in Chapter 2). The Lusalas and Nsakalas spent Memorial Day 2019 together, with Edward's grandchildren (Tony, Jordan, Brian, and Audrianna), shown here enjoying a swim in the Nsakalas' pool.

The photograph below shows Luzibu and Nsakala with their friends, from left to right, Susan Anderson, Mark Allaben, and Kenny and Debbie Peterson, strolling along the Intracoastal Waterway in March 2019. Debbie and Kenny were colleagues of Nsakala at ALSTOM Power, Inc. Susan and Mark, who also live in Palm Coast, are also friends of Kenny and Debbie.

Domestic Travel

In January 2012, Luzibu and Nsakala flew from Orlando International Airport to Newark, New Jersey, to attend the pinning ceremony of the nursing class of 2011 at Essex County College. Hooray! David (Dieyatondulua Lutete) was finishing his nursing studies. In the top left photograph, David and another student are with Luzibu, Mike Mathos, and Nsakala. Mathos, who lived in Newark with his family, was originally from Angola but had also lived in Congo-Kinshasa a few years before immigrating to the United States.

Below, Luzibu is shown with her nephew David. This was a particularly happy time because she and Nsakala had just fulfilled the promise they had made ten years earlier to her brother Mvibudulu Mayiza to take David under their wings and see to it that he received a good education.

In May 2012, Luzibu flew to greater Hartford. From there, she traveled to Newark with Josée and Diampisa Bena and Kitomba Germain to attend David's graduation ceremony. Clearly, Luzibu and Nsakala felt that a big financial burden had been lifted from their backs. Here, David and his auntie are filled with joy and pride for a job well done. By this time, David had already passed the necessary nursing license examinations in the states of New York and New Jersey and, hence, was officially a registered nurse (RN). Helping others achieve their dreams is very gratifying because, in return, you achieve yours. Praise be to God!

In August 2012, Luzibu and Nsakala joined their friends Francine and Jack Smithson and Elizabeth and Walter Fritz for a weeklong trip to Key West, via South Beach, Miami, Florida. These photographs depict their travel from South Beach to Key West. They made frequent stops along the way, such as at Bayside Marina & Boardwalk. They capped the night off with a nice dinner near their hotel in Key West: from left to right, Elizabeth and Walter Fritz, Francine and Ivor (Jack) Smithson, and Luzibu and Nsakala.

In Key West, all six of them participated in various activities, such as sightseeing, walking around town, and enjoying each other's company in restaurants. For example, while Elizabeth, Francine, and Luzibu went to the Butterfly and Nature Conservatory (bottom left) on Thursday, August 9, 2012, Walter, Jack, and Nsakala rented a boat for deep-sea fishing (top left). In fact, the professional boat operators on this fishing adventure went as far as 60 miles (about 100 km) from Havana, Cuba. A thrilling experience it was!

The following year, on Thursday, July 11, 2013, Luzibu and Nsakala arrived in Harrisonburg, Virginia, to visit with their friends the Yoders for two days on their way to greater Hartford, where they were going for a family visit. Come to find out, Karina and Eric Yoder's family and their friends were also visiting from Ohio. This collage shows many people hanging out at Judy and Joel Yoder's family home: brothers Eric and Joel; Luzibu and Nsakala; Karina's friend, Karina, and Luzibu; and the children of Karina and Eric and their friends.

This collage shows Nancy, Luzibu, Carroll, and Nsakala taking a morning walk, as they usually did whenever they were together, weather permitting, and other visitors hanging out in front of Nancy and Carroll's home and their neighbors' home. The Yoders' and Nsakalas' friendship ties are, for sure, closer than some blood ties!

Luzibu and Nsakala arrived in greater Hartford on Saturday, July 13, 2013. They stayed with the Mitchell Jr. family in South Windsor. On Sunday, July 21, 2013, the family in greater Hartford (or the North Village) convened at the Nsakala Jr. family home in South Windsor to celebrate Nailah Nsakala's fourth birthday. Norma Rose had also traveled from Palm Coast to celebrate Nailah's birthday. She is shown on the left of the bottom left photograph with the grown-up ladies of the "Nsakala tribe." The grown-up men and children are shown in the top and bottom left photographs, respectively.

On August 31, 2013, Yaya Luzibu and Nkoko Nsakala were again blessed and bursting with joy when their sixth grandchild, baby boy Amias Tayten Nsakala, was born in Hartford Hospital to his proud parents, Karell Rose and Mukiese Nsakala. What a blessing and precious gift!

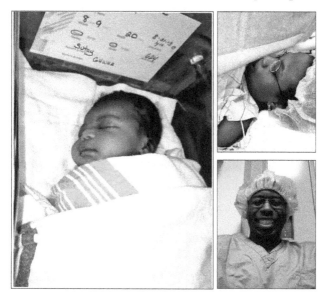

Amias is pictured with his mom, dad, and siblings. They all are joyous.

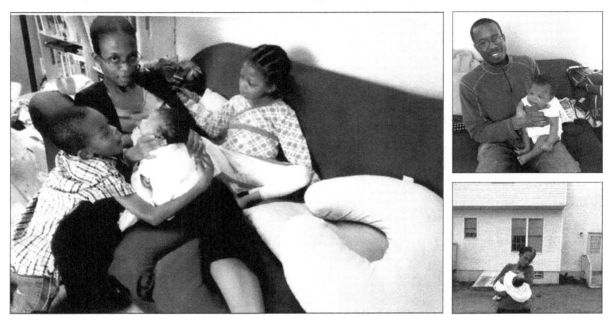

In the following collage, Nkailu (left-hand photograph) and Nailah are all smiles while holding their baby brother.

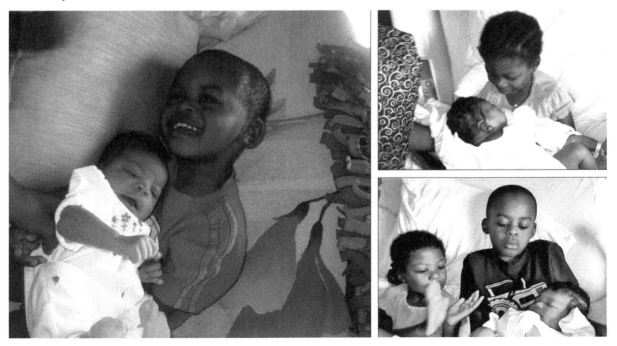

Ya Josée and aunties Lemvo and Monique are all smiles while holding and welcoming Amias in the family.

And, here, Grandma Norma Rose (lower right photograph), Yaya Luzibu (left-hand photograph), Nkoko Nsakala (top right photograph), and Nailah are enjoying their time with Amias.

On another trip to greater Hartford to attend the wedding ceremony of Luann Bena and Boris Chevannes in August 2014, Luzibu and Nsakala stopped by Harrisonburg, Virginia, to visit with the Yoder family for two days (August 22–24, 2014). Harrisonburg became a normal stopover for the Nsakalas on their way from Palm Coast to greater Hartford. The next two collages capture Luzibu and Nsakala's stay in Harrisonburg. The first collage shows, clockwise, Judy and Joel Yoder's family (Joel, Leah, Judy, Carrie, and Sofia), Luzibu, Nicole Yoder, Matt and Maria Swartzentruber, and Nsakala; and the lower left photograph shows Carroll and Nsakala in deep conversation. As a reminder, Nicole and Maria are Gloria and Galen Yoder's daughters.

This collage shows the family at dinner in Judy and Joel's home, celebrating Joel's birthday. Joel is cooking pizzas in his outdoor brick oven.

On Sunday, August 24, 2014, Luzibu and Nsakala arrived in the greater Hartford area. They would stay at the Homewood Suites in Windsor Locks until Sunday, September 7, 2014. Recall that in 1989, the extended Nsakala family welcomed their first third-generation child when baby girl Luann Bena was born to Josée and Diampisa Bena. Now, in 2014, the extended Nsakala family welcomed a son-in-law when Luann got married on Saturday, August 30, 2014, to Boris Chevannes. This collage shows people enjoying themselves at the prewedding (or traditional wedding) party held on Friday, August 29, 2014, at the Portuguese Club in Newington, Connecticut. In clockwise order, Luann's proud parents (in the yellow outfits); Josée and Diampisa Bena, leading the wedding party entrance into the ballroom; Luann and Auntie Cathy Kitomba Betamona following suit; the Reverend Donny Capp's family; and some party revelers dancing the night away.

Wedding guests came from abroad as well as various parts of the United States. Pictured, clockwise, are Luzibu, standing with Luzolo Manikuna's family from Germany and a lady from Belgium (fourth from the left); Suzanne Binga Kimpiatu from London, England, behind Luann and Boris; Noël Luvevo Kitomba with Paul Balenza and Hubert Betamona, both from the DRC; and Luzibu and Nsakala with Josephine and Edward Lusala from Bloomington, Illinois, and Biki Marie and Makinutewa Félix from Belgium.

Luann Bena and Boris Chevannes's wedding ceremony was held at Hope Christian Church in North Haven, Connecticut. Shown here are the groom's mother (Dawn Anderson in a pink dress) and the bride's mother (Josée Bena) lighting the unity candle, Luann and Boris saying their vows before the Reverend Donny Capp of the Crossroads Community Cathedral, and the newly wedded couple leaving the church altar.

The wedding reception was held at Cascade Fine Catering in Hamden, Connecticut. Some of the wedding reception attendees from Luann's side posed for photographs beforehand.

The next two collages feature the parents of the bride and some of the wedding reception attendees clearly enjoying themselves.

In June 2015, Yaya Luzibu and Nkoko Nsakala traveled to greater Hartford to attend the graduation ceremonies of their grandchildren: James III (from South Windsor High School) and Zola (from South Windsor Middle School). These snapshots show the family with James III in cap and gown at the UConn campus in Storrs and Zola holding her certificate at Timothy Edwards Middle School. Yes, life is a continuous learning process.

Yaya and Nkoko took advantage of their presence in greater Hartford to have a professional photographer take pictures of them with their six grandchildren:

- Front row: Nkailu Nsakala, Amias Nsakala, Yaya, James A. Mitchell III, and Nailah Nsakala; and
- Back row: Nkoko, Jianna Mitchell, and Zola Mitchell.

Luzibu and Nsakala's three-generation family tree, with them as grandparents, is shown below. In every conceivable way, the family is a link to our past and a bridge to our future.

- Generation 1: grandparents (Yaya Luzibu Nsakala and Nkoko Nsakala ya Nsakala);

- Generation 2: parents (daughter R. Munlemvo Mitchell and son Mukiese Nsakala with their spouses); and

- Generation 3: grandchildren (from Munlemvo and James: James III, Zola, and Jianna; from Karell and Mukiese: Nkailu, Nailah, and Amias).

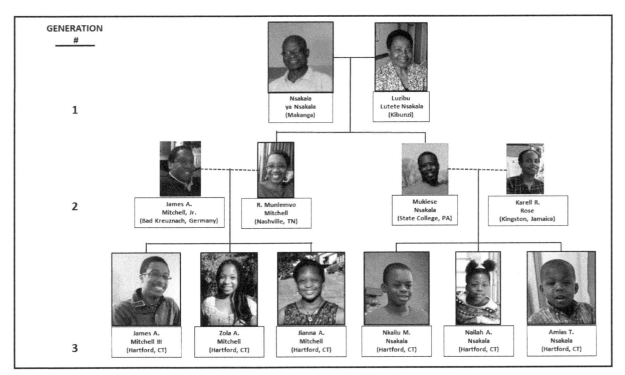

The Kikongo names for grandparents, parents, and grandchildren are given in the table below.

Generation #	English	Kikongo
1	grandparent (grandmother, grandfather)	yaya, nkaka/nkoko (gender neutral)
	grandparents (grandmothers, grandfathers)	bayaya, zinkaka/zinkoko (gender neutral)
2	parent (mother, father)	ngudi evo se (mama, tata)
	parents (mothers, fathers)	zingudi evo mase (bamama, batata)
3	sibling (sister, brother)	mpangi (ya nkento, ya bakala)
	siblings (sisters, brothers)	zimpangi (za bakento, za babakala)

On Friday, November 13, 2015, Luzibu and Nsakala flew out of the Jacksonville, Florida, airport to Logan International Airport, Boston, Massachusetts, to attend the wedding ceremony of Monique Rose and Nickolas (Nick) Moser on Saturday, November 14, 2015. The top left photograph shows Nick's sister reading a message during the wedding ceremony. The top right photograph features, respectively, the mothers of the bride and groom, Norma Rose (on the left) and Kate Moser (on the right). The two bottom photographs show Monique's side of the family during a visit on Sunday, November 15, 2015, at the house that Monique and Nick were renting in Boston. The left-hand photograph shows the three sisters (Camille, Monique, and Karell) with their spouses (Mukiese, Nick, and Chris). The right-hand photograph shows Auntie Genrith "Jenny" Wilson—the family matriarch—with other family members.

On Sunday, April 9, 2017, Luzibu and Nsakala headed to greater Hartford to celebrate Easter with family and friends up there. As usual, they took the opportunity to stop by Harrisonburg, Virginia, to visit with the family of Nancy and Carroll Yoder for two days. The Yoders' older son Eric and his family (top right) was also visiting, as was another couple from Pennsylvania. These photographs show them all hanging out together at Nancy and Carroll's home.

On Tuesday, April 11, 2017, Luzibu and Nsakala left Harrisonburg for greater Hartford, where they would stay with Karell Rose, Mukiese Nsakala, and family (the Nsakala Jr. family) in South Windsor. On Good Friday, some members of the extended family from greater Hartford (a.k.a. North Village) came to the Nsakala Jr. family home to break bread, partake in the Easter dinner together, and hang out. Allégresse Bambi from Belgium, who was doing an internship with a Hartford law firm and staying with the Bena family, joined the party. She is the young lady in the yellow dress.

In the evening, Luzibu and Nsakala joined other family members at Crossroads Community Cathedral to watch, live, the play *Passion of the King*. As these photographs show, the Mitchell Jr. family members were, as always, cast members of the show.

On Saturday, April 15, 2017, Luzibu and Nsakala joined the Ouma family at the Hyatt Regency Princeton in New Jersey for a surprise party for Grace and Henry Ouma from Kenya. The Oumas had come back to Piscataway, New Jersey, where they own a house, to visit their family and friends. The top left photograph shows Luzibu, Akinyi Ouma Lippencott (the Oumas' daughter), Grace and Henry Ouma, and Nsakala outside the hotel's ballroom where the party was held the night before. The top right photograph shows a few people around Grace and Henry during the party. And the two bottom photographs show Gracie Ouma-Cabezas (another daughter of the Oumas) and Akinyi Lippencott with their spouses. Not shown here are the Oumas' other two daughters, Atieno and Adhiambo.

In November 2017, Luzibu and Nsakala found themselves going to greater Hartford again, this time to celebrate Thanksgiving with the family in North Village. And, once again, they stopped by Harrisonburg, Virginia, to visit Nancy and Carroll Yoder and family for two days. While in Harrisonburg, Nancy, Carroll, Luzibu, and Nsakala went to a floral farm nearby, where they bought some poinsettias (seen in these photos).

Thanksgiving dinner was held at the Nsakala Jr. family home, where Yaya Luzibu and Nkoko Nsakala were staying. After a sumptuous meal, the family decided to snap some photographs, family by family and in groups. This collage features, clockwise from the top left, the Bena family, the Kitomba family, the Nsakala Jr. family, and the Mitchell Jr. family.

The next collage features the children of the North Village family and the original Nsakala Sr. family (Mukiese, Nsakala, Luzibu, and Lemvo).

The Yoder family was planning a family reunion in Wellman, Iowa, for June 30 through July 1, 2018. Not surprisingly, Luzibu and Nsakala were invited as part of the extended family. Hence, on Wednesday, June 27, 2018, Luzibu and Nsakala flew out of Daytona Beach International Airport to Cedar Rapids Airport for a week-long stay in Wellman. Gloria and Galen Yoder were their hosts. This collage shows them at the dinner table with Gloria and Galen and their eldest daughter, Rebecca. Mowers Plus is Galen's shop.

The two left-hand photographs show Luzibu, Carroll, and Nsakala with a fellow hosted by Carrie and Lester Yoder in the 1960s (left) and his wife (right) and Shirley Yoder, Carroll's sister-in-law. The right-hand photographs feature Edna and Milford Yoder's sons, Neil (top) and Doyle (bottom), with their families.

Group photographs were taken on the last day of the family reunion after a Mennonite church service and lunch at the Iowa Mennonite School in Kalona. This collage shows Luzibu and Nsakala with some of Lester Yoder's branch of the family tree.

In other family news, these photographs were snapped on the first school day of the 2018–2019 academic year for the South Windsor, Connecticut, school system: Nailah Nsakala goes into the fourth grade, Nkailu Nsakala into the sixth grade, Amias Nsakala into kindergarten, Zola Mitchell (on the left of the lower left photograph) and Jianna Mitchell go into the twelfth and eleventh grades, respectively. Yes, education is not only a ladder of opportunity but also an investment in one's future.

On Thursday, September 13, 2018, Luzibu and Nsakala drove from Palm Coast to Metairie, Louisiana, a suburb of New Orleans, to visit Dr. Solo Ruth Kuvibidila. This collage shows Ruth and Luzibu standing in front of Ruth's home, and Luzibu, Ruth, and Nsakala standing on the New Orleans River Walk with the majestic Mississippi River in the background. Luzibu and Nsakala obligatorily sampled the famous beignets and café au lait at the French Quarter in New Orleans.

Luzibu and Nsakala left Metairie on Sunday, September 16, 2018, for Montgomery, Alabama, where they toured the Legacy Museum and the National Memorial for Peace and Justice. These iconic civil rights monuments (Wikipedia[r,s]) provide a sacred space for truth-telling about the racial injustice in American history. The experience was, for the authors, a humbling and gut-wrenching one.

Shifting gears, on Friday, November 16, 2018, Luzibu and Nsakala drove from Palm Coast to Nashville, Tennessee, to attend, on the following day, the wedding ceremony of Liliann Nzuzi and Pastor Richard Davis, which was held at Mount Nebo Missionary Baptist Church.

Here, Edward Lusala is shown giving away his niece, Liliann, and Liliann and Richard are saying their vows.

This collage features elegantly dressed members of the wedding party: the maids of honor, the groomsmen, and the officiating pastors.

This collage shows Luzibu, Nsakala, and others with the newlywed couple during the wedding reception at the Radisson Hotel near the Nashville Airport.

On Sunday morning, November 18, 2018, Luzibu and Nsakala left Nashville for Harrisonburg, Virginia, to visit the Yoder family en route to greater Hartford, where they celebrated Thanksgiving with their family. On their way back to Palm Coast, Luzibu and Nsakala stopped overnight in Piscataway, New Jersey, where they visited with Grace and Henry Ouma. Grace and Henry, who live in Kendu Bay, Kenya, also own a home in Piscataway, where they go from time to time.

Two months later, in January 2019, Luzibu and Nsakala traveled again to greater Hartford to spend a week with family and friends. On one evening, they had dinner at the home of Josée and Diampisa Bena in West Hartford, as shown in the two left-hand and top right photographs. On most mornings, Luzibu (a.k.a. Yaya) accompanied grandson Amias Nsakala to the bus stop, as shown in the bottom right photograph.

In April 2019, Luzibu and Nsakala traveled yet again to greater Hartford to celebrate Easter with family and friends. Easter Sunday dinner was held at the Mitchell Jr. home in South Windsor. It's always a festival when the Nsakala clan gets together. It brings enjoyment and relaxation and offers the time needed to bond with each other. And it is also an occasion to give thanks to God for his bountiful provision. The food spread for this occasion is shown in the top left photograph. After dinner, family members hung out together (bottom right photograph), and Josée Bena is shown braiding Zola Mitchell's hair (top right).

This photograph shows Luzibu, Nsakala, and others right after the performance of *Passion of the King* at Crossroads Community Cathedral on Good Friday evening. J3, Zola, and Jianna Mitchell, who were cast members in the play, are shown still wearing their costumes.

International Travel

From their retirement in July 2010, through May 2019, Luzibu and Nsakala traveled internationally nine times: to Africa, the Caribbean Islands, Europe, and Central and South America as follows:

- Democratic Republic of the Congo in 2011;

- Europe (Switzerland and Italy) in 2012;

- Kenya in 2012;

- Eastern Caribbean cruise in 2012;

- Southern Africa Adventure (South Africa and Zimbabwe) in 2014;

- Panama Canal Grand Adventure cruise (Fort Lauderdale, Florida, to Los Angeles, California, through the Panama Canal) in 2016;

- Grand European Tour river cruise (Budapest, Hungary, to Amsterdam, Netherlands) in 2017;

- Cuba and Eastern Caribbean cruise in 2019; and

- Europe (Switzerland, Belgium, and the United Kingdom) in 2019.

Photographs of these trips are presented below.

Democratic Republic of the Congo (DRC) Trip in February–March 2011

One of the first things Luzibu and Nsakala decided to do after retirement was to go back to their country of origin, the Democratic Republic of the Congo, for a visit with family and friends. They arrived in the capital city of Kinshasa on Thursday, February 17, 2011, for a three-week stay, with the intention of going all the way to their villages of birth, Kibunzi for Luzibu and Makanga for Nsakala. They would quickly learn that the roads leading to those villages were in such a state of disrepair that it would not be wise or safe to go. Makinutewa Félix found them a hotel room at Centre Catholique Nganda (CCN), shown in the collage on the next page. CCN was a well-kept venue run by the local Catholic church. It had all the modern amenities: electricity, running water, and television, which, unfortunately, were all interrupted on a daily basis.

Luzibu, Nsakala, and Félix drew up the following schedule during their stay in Kinshasa:

- Félix would provide transportation with his car using his personal chauffeur.

- The Nsakalas would, for the most part, have meals at his family home.

- Félix would help schedule appointments with family members at CCN.

- Félix would be with Luzibu and Nsakala at many of the engagements, whenever possible.

This schedule worked well from the time it was drawn up to the time Félix dropped Luzibu and Nsakala off at Nd'jili International Airport on Tuesday, March 15, 2011, for their return flight to the United States. There just aren't words for Luzibu and Nsakala to convey to Félix and his family their gratefulness for all their help, forbearance, and love.

The next few collages show Luzibu and Nsakala with, for the most part, people from Luzibu's side of the family. In the picture on the next page, Luzibu is shown with her sole remaining younger brother, Lubambuka Malemba Oscar, at Centre Catholique Nganda.

The left-hand photograph shows Oscar with his wife, Mayamona Béatrice. The top right photograph shows sisters Mvibudulu Basala Espérance, Mvibudulu Mayiza Pauline, and Mayiza Mamita. Luzibu and Nsakala helped Oscar and Béatrice to travel from Kwilu-Ngongo, Kongo Central Province; they stayed at CCN while they visited. Mamita Mayiza traveled from the Port City of Matadi in Kongo Central. The three sisters made every effort to visit Luzibu and Nsakala at CCN, bringing along cooked food. It was an amazing display of affection and love by Luzibu's nieces (Mvibudulu Mayiza's daughters).

The next few photographs show Luzibu and Nsakala with many other members of Luzibu's side of the family. It is not possible to cite everybody's names; hence, only a selected few are named below. This collage shows Luzibu's brother Lubombolo's family. Top left photograph: Luzibu and Nsakala are standing in the back row with Lusambulu Philippe, Makiese Nelly, Tuzolana Marie, and Tekadiomona Pierre in the front row. Top right photograph: Lusambulu Philippe and Makiese Nelly in the front row; Tuzolana Marie, Pastor Lubombolo lwa Nzambi Kokolo, Luzibu, Mayavanga Albert, Tekadiomona, and Kokolo's wife in the back row. Bottom left photograph: Luzibu and Nsakala with Lubombolo lwa Nzambi's clan. Bottom right photograph: Luzibu with Tekadiomona and his family.

The following collage shows, clockwise, Luzibu with her cousin Tubombwa Oscar and his wife, Madeline (Mado); sitting in the front row, Mansiantima Flavine, Luzibu, Mayala Luzolo Nsezi, and in the back row, an unnamed person, Tubombwa, Mabungu Kiambote Dieudonné, and Mado. The bottom left photograph shows, from left to right, Lunimbu Nsezi, Mvwezolo Nsezi, Deka, Mabungu Kiambote Dieudonné, Baluengele Christine, Mansiantima Flavine, and Mayala Luzolo Nsezi. The bottom right photograph shows, from left to right, Mayala Luzolo Nsezi, Mvwezolo Nsezi, Mayiza Pauline, and Luzibu.

The third collage shows, in the top left photograph, Luzibu hugging her cousin Mantombulua Sophie; on the top right, Nsakala and Luzibu with Dimbani Gertrude and Sophie and Makinutewa Félix; on the bottom left, Luzibu with Dimbani Damiènne; and on the bottom right, Ady Lombume with her children. To clarify, Damiènne and Gertrude are Mantombulua Sophie's daughters, and Ady is Damiènne's daughter.

The fourth collage shows, in the photo on the left, Nsakala with Luzibu's cousin and her paternal aunt Kinkela Neli; and, on the right, Luzibu's other relatives, some of whom have already been identified.

Félix, Luzibu, and Nsakala also paid a visit to Mabetiteza Hélène's sister and niece in Ngalie-ma. In this collage, the top left photograph shows Luzibu with Febe Caroline (Hélène's sister) and Mpunani Pauline (Hélène's niece) at Caroline's home. The other three photographs in the collage were taken at Kivuila, Ngaliema, home of Makinutewa Félix and Biki Marie. They show Luzibu, Pauline, and Pauline's children; Luzibu having her hair braided by Mabetiteza Hudrice; and Félix and Luzibu with Bukutulu Aaron (Félix's cousin) and Mayambula Nzienda Arthur (Nsakala's nephew).

The next few collages show Luzibu and Nsakala with, for the most part, people from Nsakala's side of the family. Here, Nsakala is with his two remaining brothers, Bena Nsakala Ndunga (Bena) and Dessa Nsakala (Dessa) at Bena's family home in Kasa-Vubu.

In the collage below, the top left photograph shows Bena with his wife, Mama Kota Batunda Tusevo Esther, behind their home. The top right photograph shows Esther, Biki Marie (Makinutewa Félix's wife), Luzibu, and Félix; the bottom left photograph shows Félix with others; and the bottom right photograph shows Nsakala with additional relatives.

The collage above shows the family of Dessa Nsakala and Nkenda Makonko Pauline at their home in Ngaliema. The left-hand photograph shows Dessa and Pauline, plus their children and a grandchild as follows: Front row (from left to right): Madede Lessa Claudine, Diazola Herver, Batunda Arlette, and Mangiela Dessa (Claudine's daughter); back row (from left to right): Dessa Nsakala (Samy II), Metusala Nsakala (Samy I), Mantama Dessa Guylin, Dessa Nsakala (father), Nkenda Makonko Pauline (mother), Lutayi Dessa Lina, and Bwanga Nsakala Verlene; and right-hand photographs: Samy I and family (top), Samy II and wife (middle), and Tomba Dessa and children. Tomba, one of Dessa and Pauline's daughters, and her children arrived late on the scene.

This collage shows Nsakala with his nieces, nephews, and grandniece. Shown in the top two photographs, from left to right, are Mpitu Victorine, Komono Marceline, Komono Samy, Nsakala, and a grandniece. The bottom two photographs show Nsakala between Komono André and Batunda Esther Komono and Babeki Marie-Jeanne and Lutayi Rebecca, respectively. All are children and granddaughter of Komono Nsakala and Bankadila Nsimba Esther.

The top photograph of this collage shows Mayambula Mputi (Maya), Luyindula Nsakala Deling, Nsakala, Félix, and Mayambula Nzienda Arthur. Maya and Arthur are Nsakala's sister Mena Julienne's sons, and Deling is Nsakala's late sister Swamunu Makomba's son. Deling and Maya were sent to Kinshasa to meet Luzibu and Nsakala by Nsakala's sister, Mena, as she herself could not make the trip. The bottom left photograph shows Talu and his wife, Mandunda Bakembo Pascaline (Nsakala's niece), and Nsakala. The bottom right photograph shows Nsakala with his nieces Bena Bernadette and Bena Ndaya.

In keeping with the Bakongo tribe's customs, Luzibu and Nsakala were obliged to pay a visit to the family chief in Kinshasa, Ngizulu Simon, and his wife (right-hand photograph in this collage). They brought monetary and material gifts to the chief.

Luzibu, Félix, and Nsakala were invited by Damien and Sylvie Saila-Ngita for an afternoon get-together in Ngaliema. The hosts' guests included Joselyne (Papa Jean's wife), Félix, Saddam (Félix's driver), Luzibu, and Nsakala. It should be noted that the Saila-Ngitas also lived in West Hartford, Connecticut, at one point.

This collage shows the typical commercial activities of many residents of Kinshasa. The left-hand photograph features Binga Suzanne (Diampisa Bena's sister) in front of her kiosk, where she sells a variety of ready-to-consume products daily. The top right photograph shows local merchants at a market selling their cassava leaves, and the bottom right photograph shows a lady taking a bundle of fresh sugar canes to a local market.

Mbudi Nature is an attraction on the banks of the Congo River where people go to play, listen to a live band playing Congolese music, eat exquisitely prepared meals, watch Congo River water eddies swirling around, and admire the other side of the river, which is Congo-Brazzaville. Makinutewa Félix's family took Luzibu and Nsakala to Mbudi Nature for a Sunday afternoon of dinner and relaxation. *Libo-ke* was one of the very delicious dishes enjoyed by Luzibu, Nsakala and others at this venue. It consists of mildly spiced fresh fish or meat wrapped in banana leaves and cooked over a charcoal fire.

On another day, Félix and Bena took Luzibu and Nsakala to see Mama Lusavuvu Luzolo Bungiena in Bandalungwa. Also present were ya Maggie, Germain Kitomba's wife, and some of their children. Germain is Josée Bena's (of West Hartford, Connecticut) brother. Seeing each other again evoked tears of joy in some people.

This return trip to their homeland left Luzibu and Nsakala with mixed emotions. It was good to see some of their relatives and friends, many of whom they had not seen in decades or known beforehand. Nevertheless, it was disheartening to see some of them living in unthinkable misery brought about by the continued harsh economic conditions in the country.

European (Switzerland and Italy) Trip in April–May 2012

Luzibu and Nsakala spent two weeks (April 22–May 6, 2012) in Europe visiting friends in Baden/ Dättwil, Switzerland, and sightseeing in Rome, Italy. The left-hand photograph shows Luzibu and Nsakala at dinner at Dora and Werner Schott's home. Featured in the photograph, from left to right, are Giuliana, Luzibu, Nsakala, Alejandro's father, Alejandro, Gabriela, Pia, and Werner. To clarify, Gabriela and Pia are Dora and Werner Schott's daughters, Alejandro's father is Pia's husband, and Giuliana and Alejandro are Pia's children. Dora is shown with Luzibu, Nsakala, and Werner in the top right photograph, and the bottom right photograph shows Luzibu, Dora, Pia, and the children on the banks of Lake Zurich in Zurich, Switzerland.

Dora and Werner took Luzibu and Nsakala sightseeing in Switzerland, as evidenced by this collage. Luzibu and Nsakala are shown with a greeter at a glass manufacturing plant in Hergiswil (left); Dora, Werner, Luzibu, and Nsakala are shown in front of a flower garden on Mainau Island at Bodensee (Lake Constance) (top right); and Nsakala, Luzibu, Dora, and Werner are pictured at the Rheine Fall (Mini Niagara Falls, as Luzibu and Nsakala called them in jest) (bottom right).

Monika and Jürgen Bittner and their daughter Steffani took Luzibu and Nsakala sightseeing at Mines d'Asphalte in Neuchâtel, Switzerland, where they enjoyed the tour of the mine pit, followed by lunch at the Mines d'Asphalte Café.

On Monday, April 30, 2012, Luzibu and Nsakala boarded the Train Grande Vitesse in Zurich for an eight-and-a-half-hour ride to Rome via Zug, Lugano, Cuomo, and Milan.

Sightseeing in Rome was a thing of beauty. Luzibu and Nsakala climbed atop Saint Peter's Basilica after a conducted tour of the Vatican. The left-hand photograph shows a panoramic view of Rome, with Saint Peter's Square in the foreground. They also took a tour of the Colosseum (top right photograph) and a bus tour of the city of Rome.

Additionally, they visited the Spanish Steps (see collage below) and many other tourist venues in the heart of Rome (Campo de Fiori, Piazza Navona, the Pantheon, Parliament, Santa Maria del Popolo, et cetera).

This European tour gave Luzibu and Nsakala the opportunity not only to see their longtime friends in Switzerland but also to see, for the first time, some of the iconic places that Rome offers.

Kenyan Trip in July 2012

At the invitation of their friends Grace and Henry Ouma, Luzibu and Nsakala spent three weeks in Kenya in July 2012. They left Orlando for Nairobi on Thursday, July 5, 2012, arriving in the evening of the following day. They would spend most of their time in Kendu Bay, where the Oumas lived. Kendu Bay is located on the banks of the northeastern side of Lake Victoria, near the city of Kisumu. It is approximately 230 miles (370 km) northwest of Nairobi (see map).

In Nairobi, Henry took his guests to the Nairobi Animal Orphanage for a safari day. They saw all kinds of animals at this national park, including lions, giraffes, zebras, ostriches, and hippopotamuses.

In Kendu Bay, Luzibu and Nsakala received a warm welcome from Grace and Henry's relatives. This collage shows them at the dinner table with Henry's brother and cousins and their spouses. They received these clay pots from Uncle Shem Okombo (Henry's brother).

Grace and Henry Ouma are very entrepreneurial: they raise all sorts of crops, from millet, peanuts, and corn to butternut squash. They also raise herds of sheep, goats, cows, and chickens.

The Oumas' leadership in the community is quite admirable: they are involved in setting up a water-well pump for the community and, among other things, feeding some of the needy children of Alego Primary School and helping manage the Karachuonyo Constituency Development Fund.

Additionally, they help the community with fundraising for various causes. As shown in the collage below, they are holding a meeting to raise funds to supplement the cost of a dispensary being built nearby with money received from the Karachuonyo Constituency Development Fund. The man on the right in the top left photograph is Shem Okombo, Henry Ouma's older brother.

In this collage, the top left photograph shows a lady they called Nya Tan (from Tanzania), who lived with the Oumas, and JaKoredo, their chauffeur. The top right photograph shows Luzibu and Nsakala with Grace Ouma's father, Babba (father), during a visit to his home in Nyamweri. Luzibu and Nsakala are also shown with Grace (Henry's younger sister) in the lower left photograph and with Pennina (Henry's older sister) in the lower right photograph.

Grace and Henry also took Luzibu and Nsakala to Maseno, where they straddled the equator, then on to Kogelo Village, where they sat with Granny Sarah Obama (middle of lower right photograph), the step-grandmother of President Barack Obama. Around the corner from her home is the high school built by then-Senator Barack Obama.

In Nairobi, Grace, Henry, Luzibu, and Nsakala were invited to lunch at the China Plate Restaurant by Were Dibo Ogutu, Henry's maternal uncle, as shown in the top left photograph, before they left for Kendu Bay. Upon their return to Nairobi from Kendu Bay, they met with Winnie Mitoko for lunch in downtown Nairobi, as shown in the other two photographs. Luzibu and Nsakala knew Winnie through the Oumas during her days in the United States with then-husband Mika Mitoko and their children, when Mika attended Yale Medical School.

Then, on the evening of Wednesday, July 18, 2012, Grace, Henry, Luzibu, and Nsakala were invited to dinner by Anna and Charles Ogalo and their children. Anna is Henry's sister.

The Kenyan trip was refreshing in that it reminded Luzibu and Nsakala of their own beloved Democratic Republic of the Congo (DRC) in many ways. They were received by the Oumas' family and friends as they would have been by their own DRC family and friends. In other words, it affirmed to them that the African people's "welcoming spirit" is indeed pervasive.

Eastern Caribbean Cruise in November 2012

The seven-day Eastern Caribbean cruise on the *Norwegian Epic* was Luzibu and Nsakala's first cruise ever. It took place from Sunday to Sunday, November 17 through 24, 2012, as seen in the itinerary shown here. They were on the cruise with two other Palm Coast families, the Fritzes and the Delaeres.

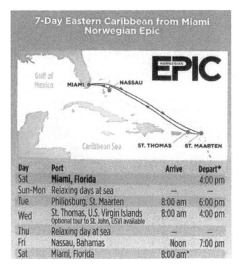

This collage shows Luzibu and Nsakala on the balcony of their stateroom while leaving Miami and heading out to sea.

These were the two Palm Coast families that Luzibu and Nsakala hung out with on the cruise. In the top left photograph are Louise Delaere (right) with her daughter Michelle. The top right photograph shows Michelle's sons Brent (left) and Evan, Jerry Delaere (Michelle's father), and Michael Fritz. The bottom left photograph shows, from left to right, Elizabeth Fritz, Luzibu, Nsakala, and Walter Fritz, and the bottom right photograph shows Walter, Elizabeth, Luzibu, Brent, Michael, and Nsakala enjoying lunch in Saint Maarten.

These photographs showing Luzibu and Nsakala all duded up were taken on one of two formal nights on the ship.

This collage shows Luzibu, Nsakala, and the Fritz family, plus Brent, in Nassau, Bahamas.

As stated before, this was the first cruise Luzibu and Nsakala had ever taken, and so they really didn't know exactly what to expect. Well, while they enjoyed their fellowship, especially with the two Palm Coast families on board, they thought that the size of the crowd on the *Norwegian Epic*, approaching four thousand people, was a bit overwhelming. Nevertheless, overall, the experience was enjoyable.

Southern Africa (South Africa and Zimbabwe) Adventure in November 2014

The fifteen-day Southern Africa adventure took place between Tuesday, October 21, 2014, and Saturday, November 8, 2014. The adventure was a grand tour of the country of South Africa and Victoria Falls in Zimbabwe. The map of South Africa is shown here (Map[j]).

They arrived in Johannesburg on Wednesday, October 21, 2014, where they spent their first night at the Protea Hotel Wanderers. The following day, they were driven to Kruger National Park, 280 miles (451 km) northeast of Johannesburg, by an employee of Thompsons Africa – a destination management compay that supplies full escorted and group series tours – for a two-day safari. The collage on the following page shows the hotel and their stopover (right-hand photograph) on their way to Kruger Park.

The top left photograph in the collage below shows a map of Kruger National Park. Luzibu is shown in the top right photograph with four ladies carrying their suitcases to the tented lodge (bottom right photograph) inside the Nkambeni Safari Camp (bottom left photograph), where Luzibu and Nsakala stayed for two nights.

James, also of Thompsons Africa (shown in the left-hand photograph in the collage below), was Luzibu and Nsakala's Kruger Park tour guide. Another Thompsons Africa tour guide is shown in the right-hand photograph in the collage with other tourists.

At the onset of the safari, James told Luzibu and Nsakala that the objective of the safari was to find the Big Five (Image[t]): buffalos, rhinoceroses, leopards, lions, and elephants. James succeeded in finding all of them, although the lions were the most difficult to locate because they sleep during the daytime and hunt at night.

The next two collages show a sampling of the animals that Luzibu and Nsakala encountered in the park, including rhinoceroses, elephants, buffaloes, giraffes, zebras, and kudus (large grayish-brown African antelopes).

This collage shows some of the people Luzibu and Nsakala met and rode with in the park in search of the Big Five and more (right-hand photographs). At the end of the safari on Saturday, October 25, 2014, this Thompsons Africa driver (left-hand photograph) took Luzibu and Nsakala to a local airport for their flight to Port Elizabeth, via Johannesburg.

After one night at the Paxon Hotel in Port Elizabeth (left-hand photograph), Luzibu and Nsakala were picked up on Sunday morning by a Thompsons Africa driver to start their four-day journey along the Garden Route in the van shown in the right-hand photograph. Aboard the van were five tourists from Great Britain and one from Sweden. The Garden Route (see the map of South Africa at the beginning of this section) lies along South Africa's southern coast, sometimes in proximity to the Indian Ocean, from Addo Elephant National Park near Port Elizabeth all the way to Cape Town. The splendor of the Garden Route is manifested by stunning scenery, as all the tourists aboard the minivan driven by the Thompsons Africa tour guide would discover.

Tsitsikamma National Park was the first stop along the Garden Route. The stunning beauty of the park is unmistakable; the suspension bridge and the view of the Indian Ocean were breathtaking. The fellow just behind the white sedan in the lower right photograph is the tour guide. Luzibu is the young lady in green jacket.

The next stop was Knysna, where the eight tourists plus their tour guide would spend two nights in the Knysna Hollow Country Resort (top left photograph). While there, they toured Featherbed (bottom right photograph), which is a nature preserve reachable only via a ferry crossing the Knysna lagoon. At the peak of Featherbed, one sees a spectacular panoramic view of both Knysna basin and the Indian Ocean. In the bottom left photograph, Luzibu and Nsakala are on top of Featherbed with the Indian Ocean in the background.

Luzibu, Nsakala, and some of the other tourists also went for a sunset whale-watching expedition off the Knysna coast. The tour guide was able to find a few colonies of humpback whales, as shown in the top left photograph. And the sunset was stunningly gorgeous.

On Tuesday morning, October 28, 2014, the tourists left Knysna for Oudtshoorn for more sightseeing and a night's stay at the Queens Hotel. In Oudtshoorn, the tourists had great adventures:

- A Cango Caves tour;

- An ostrich farm visit, followed by lunch featuring ostrich steaks as the main entrée; and

- A Cango wildlife tour.

Both Cango Caves and the ostrich safari are illustrated here: this collage shows tourists entering the caves, the silhouettes of Luzibu and Nsakala inside the caves, and the way the natives lived in the caves.

Oudtshoorn being the feather capital of South Africa made it attractive to tourists along the Garden Route. Luzibu, Nsakala, and the other six tourists from Great Britain and Sweden were taken on an ostrich safari, where they toured the farm and then had lunch, featuring ostrich steaks as the main entrée—yum! For entertainment, some brave souls took rides on ostriches!

On Wednesday, October 29, 2014, the tourists left the Queens Hotel in Oudtshoorn for Cape Town, via Hermanus, where they made a two-hour stop for lunch and whale watching. Luzibu and Nsakala arrived in Cape Town later in the day for a four-night stay at the Protea Hotel Sea Point. The first order of business on Wednesday night was to buy a SIM card for the cell phone that they had bought in Italy in 2012. This would enable them to communicate with family and friends in the United States and South Africa as well. Starting on Thursday morning, Thompsons Africa tour guides took them and other tourists on various sightseeing tours. They visited such iconic places as:

- Cape Point/the Cape of Good Hope;
- Kirstenbosch Botanical Gardens;
- The diamond district, city hall, the Castle of Good Hope, First National Bank Stadium (The Calabash), et cetera, as part of a city tour;
- Seals Island;
- A penguin colony;
- The wine country;
- Victor Verster Prison in Paarl; and
- Table Mountain.

Some of these places are shown in the photographs and collages presented below.

This photograph shows the Protea Hotel Sea Point, where Luzibu and Nsakala stayed. This hotel is strategically located in Cape Town's Sea Point area, only about one block from the Sea Point Promenade, which runs along the Atlantic coast. It also is just a few minutes by bus from such iconic places as the Victoria & Alfred Waterfront, the Cape Town Stadium, and Table Mountain.

The following day, their first tour was a ride around the city, including Cape Point, where they, with others on the tour, had lunch. They then went up to the lighthouse (bottom right photograph), from which they had a panoramic view of the oceans (lower left photograph). The bottom left pho-

tograph shows a clear line of demarcation which, the tour guide explained, was the meeting place of the Atlantic (top) and Indian (bottom) Oceans. The tour guide immediately said that his statement was for show only, because the official line of demarcation between the two oceans is at Cape Agulhas, which is about 155 miles (~249 km) southeast of Cape Point.

The day's tour culminated in a visit to the Cape of Good Hope. Seeing this geographical marvel was particularly momentous for Luzibu and Nsakala, as it was one of the world's iconic places that had been featured as *Cap de Bonne Espérance* in geography and history books during their high school days in Congo-Kinshasa.

Next up was a ride via a cable car to the top of the Table Mountain (1,085 meters or 3,560 feet in altitude) with other tourists. The 360° panoramic view of Cape Town and the Atlantic and Indian Oceans was breathtaking. From the top of Table Mountain, one could see clearly, for example, the Lion's Head mountain (lower right photograph) and Robben Island (lower left photograph), where Nelson Mandela served eighteen of his twenty-seven years of incarceration by the South Africa's apartheid regime.

Next up was a tour, taking Luzibu, Nsakala, and others to various parts of the city, including an Atlantic Ocean bay with the Twelve Disciples mountain range in the background (top left photograph on the following page) and the Kirstenbosch Botanical Gardens. The gardens house a huge collection of indigenous flora, such as heathery fynbos, flowering proteas (the South African national flower), and dramatically colored strelitzias (bird of paradise flowers).

The Seal Island cruise was next on the itinerary. The island is so named because of the Cape fur seals, numbering sixty-four thousand, that occupy five acres in the area. The water going to the island on a small boat was very choppy, and it appeared as if capsizing was not out of the question. Thank goodness, it did not happen. When one sees penguins, it is Antarctica that first comes to mind. So seeing them in Cape Town made it even more interesting. The Boulders penguin colony in Cape Town comprises some three thousand delightful African penguins. The colony, which has grown from just two breeding pairs in 1982, seems to be a big attraction for the tourists.

Saturday, November 1, 2014, was reserved for touring the wine country (see the next two collages). Luzibu, Nsakala, and others on the tour were treated to three wine-tasting venues. They could, if they so desired, taste up to fifteen different red, white, and rosé wines.

On their way back to Cape Town from the wine country, the tourists stopped by Victor Verster Prison in Paarl, where Nelson Mandela spent the last three years of his incarceration. It was there that, on Sunday, February 11, 1990, Nelson Mandela was freed at last. He came out with a clenched right fist (as shown in this photograph depicting his statue), shouting in the Xhosa language, "*Amandla!*" ("Power!"), to which the crowd responded, "*Awethu!*" ("To us!") Mandela and the crowd were repeating the African National Congress's age-old battle cry against the apartheid regime.

On Sunday, November 2, 2014, Luzibu and Nsakala flew out of Cape Town International Airport to Johannesburg, where they were met by a Congolese chauffeur who took them to the residence of Poppy and Bene M'Poko in Pretoria for, by prearrangement, a two-day respite from the tour with Thompsons Africa. As stated earlier, Bene M'Poko was the Democratic Republic of the Congo's ambassador to South Africa and dean of the diplomatic corps in Pretoria. This collage shows Luzibu and Bene's household chef and Nsakala and Bene inside and outside the M'Poko residence. Poppy M'Poko, Bene's wife, was in the United States visiting her family. In any case, Ambassador M'Poko offered his guests much-needed rest and calmness from the otherwise whirlwind nature of their Southern Africa adventure.

On Tuesday, November 4, 2014, Luzibu and Nsakala resumed their Southern Africa adventure by flying from Johannesburg International Airport to Victoria Falls Airport in Zimbabwe, where they would spend two nights cruising on the Zambezi River and touring Victoria Falls. This map shows Victoria Falls on the western side of Zimbabwe (Map[i]).

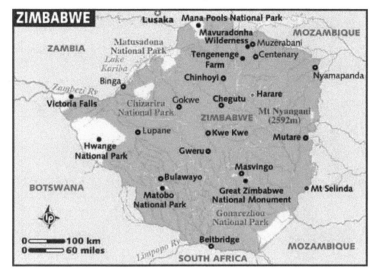

The photographs below show the British Airways airplane that took Luzibu, Nsakala, and other tourists from Johannesburg to Victoria Falls Airport. The lower left photograph features native dancers entertaining the arriving visitors.

After checking in to their hotel, Luzibu and Nsakala were taken to the Zambezi River for a sunset dinner cruise with other tourists.

The hippopotamuses and elephants were just a few feet away from the small boat carrying the tourists. There were also multiple sightings of crocodiles, and all sorts of birds were perched on tree branches on both sides of the river. The sights were spectacular.

On the next day, Wednesday, November 5, 2014 it was time for a two-hour walking tour along Victoria Falls. As can be seen in this collage, the view of the falls is spectacular.

At one end of the falls is a bridge that separates Zimbabwe from Zambia (top left photograph). Luzibu and Nsakala stayed in the hotel called Kingdom of Victoria Falls (lower left photograph). They also met two couples, one from Australia (top right photograph) and the other from Belgium (lower right photograph), that they hung out with.

On Thursday, November 6, 2014, Luzibu, Nsakala, and the other tourists flew back to Johannesburg on British Airways. Luzibu and Nsakala spent the last night of their Southern Africa adventure at the Protea Hotel Wanderers, where they had spent their first night.

On Friday, November 7, 2014, a Thompsons Africa tour guide picked them up from the hotel for their last tour, a tour of Johannesburg and Soweto (a township located southwest of Johannesburg). On this tour were also two couples from Belgium. Below is a list of some of the iconic places they visited.

- They passed by (1) the house where Nelson Mandela lived in Johannesburg at the time of his death in December 2013, (2) Winnie Mandela's house in Soweto, (3) Nelson and Evelyn Mandela's house, (4) Bishop Desmond Tutu's house, and (5) the Olympic Football Stadium.

- They toured (1) the Regina Mundi Catholic Church, and (2) the Hector Pieterson Memorial and Museum.

Here, Luzibu and Nsakala are posing under the sign welcoming visitors to Soweto (which is an abbreviation of South Western Townships).

Regina Mundi is the largest Roman Catholic church in South Africa, able to sit two thousand people, with standing room for five thousand. The church played a major role in the struggle for freedom. During the apartheid era, Regina Mundi opened its doors to anti-apartheid groups and provided shelter to anti-apartheid activists. The church logbook has Nelson Mandela's signature, along with those of other celebrities.

The next collage shows both the Nelson Mandela house and the Hector Pieterson Memorial and Museum.

- The Nelson Mandela House is where he and Evelyn lived with their children from 1946 to 1962. Mandela donated the house to the Soweto Heritage Trust in 1997. It is now a national museum.

- The Hector Pieterson Memorial and Museum commemorates the role of the country's high school student protests on Wednesday, June 16, 1976, against the substandard education in black schools in South Africa. A violent confrontation with the police ensued, igniting uprisings throughout South Africa in which hundreds of people died at the hands of the police. A twelve-year-old boy, Hector Pieterson, was shot and killed two blocks from where this museum is located.

Later in the day, a Thompsons Africa driver took the Nsakalas to Johannesburg International Airport for their flight back home to the United States.

The Southern Africa adventure was surely a memorable one. It appeared to Luzibu and Nsakala that everything was a highlight to behold. Every day was full of exciting events, and there never was a dull moment.

Panama Canal Grand Adventure in April–May 2016

Luzibu and Nsakala took their second ocean cruise aboard the *Island Princess*, leaving Fort Lauderdale, Florida, on Saturday, April 23, 2016, and arriving at San Pedro Pier 93 in Los Angeles, California on Sunday, May 8, 2016. The ports of call were:

- Aruba;

- Cartagena, Colombia;

- Panama Canal Transit;

- Puntarenas, Costa Rica;

- San Juan del Sur, Nicaragua; and

- Cabo San Lucas, Mexico.

The itinerary of this fifteen-day cruise is shown in this photograph taken aboard the *Island Princess* during one of two formal nights.

The *Island Princess* sailed from the Fort Lauderdale Pier on Saturday, April 23, 2016.

Luzibu and Nsakala hung out with four couples they met aboard the ship. They are shown here with two of the four couples. From the left of Luzibu, they are Van Huu and Tina from Sacramento, California (originally from Vietnam) and Aya and Sokan from Los Angeles (originally from Cambodia). Being with these couples helped Luzibu and Nsakala continue to hang on to their belief that people are more alike than they are different.

They were in Aruba for a few hours on Tuesday, April 26, 2016, as shown in these photographs.

Then on to Cartagena, Colombia, for a few hours on Wednesday, April 27, 2016.

They crossed the Panama Isthmus via the Panama Canal, from the Caribbean Sea to the Pacific

Ocean, all day Thursday, April 28, 2016. The three photographs on the right in this collage show the *Island Princess* going through one of three Panama Canal locks and a ship ahead of the *Island Princess* exiting a lock.

The system that lifts ships from the Atlantic Ocean up to 85 feet (26 m) to the main elevation of the Gatun Lake in three steps and down to the Pacific Ocean again is nothing short of an engineering marvel (Image[u]).

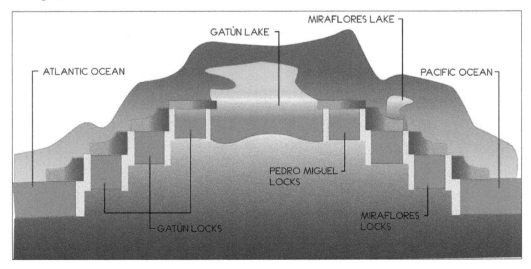

This collage shows that the Princess Cruises were celebrating their golden anniversary.

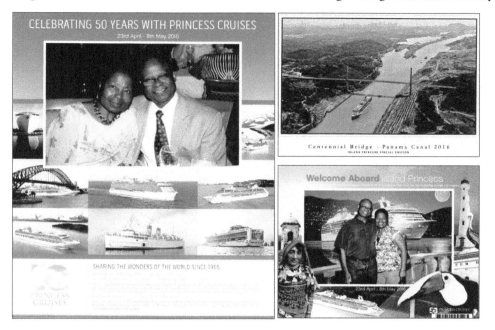

The Nsakalas experienced a formal night on Friday, April 29, 2016, while sailing from the Panama Canal to Puntarenas, Costa Rica. The left-hand photograph features Nsakala, Luzibu, Sokan, Aya, Tina, and Van Huu. The top right photograph shows, in the front row, Judy and Chalmers from Tallahassee, Alabama, and, in the back row, Nsakala; Luzibu; Joann and Kon from Vancouver, Canada; and Aya and Sokan. The lower right photograph shows Luzibu, Nsakala, and the two dining room waiters who served them on most nights. Sokan, Aya, Tina, and Van Huu were all from California.

On Saturday morning, April 30, 2016, the *Island Princess* arrived in Puntarenas, Costa Rica, for a few hours. Aya, Sokan, Luzibu, and Nsakala hired a local taxi driver (shown in the lower right photograph), who gave them a tour of Puntarenas after taking them out of town, all the way to Carara National Park.

On Thursday morning, May 5, 2016, the *Island Princess* arrived in Cabo San Lucas, Mexico, for a few hours. Here, Luzibu, Nsakala, and their usual friends took part in various sightseeing activities, including spending an hour on an iconic beach (top left photograph), strolling downtown (right-hand photograph), and enjoying lunch at a local restaurant while watching the Mariachi band play and entertain the crowd on this Cinco de Mayo (not shown).

On Sunday morning, May 8, 2016, Kon, Sokan, Nsakala, Van Huu, Tina, Luzibu, Aya, and Joann had their last breakfast together and said goodbye to each other.

This selfie was snapped while the *Island Princess* was in the process of docking on San Pedro Pier 93 in Los Angeles on the morning of Sunday, May 8, 2016.

These two photographs were taken outside San Pedro Pier 93, where Aya and Sokan's daughters came to pick them up and take them home.

Next, Luzibu and Nsakala would spend two nights at a hotel in Santa Monica, California. Here they are on the Santa Monica Pier on Sunday afternoon, May 8, 2016.

On Monday, May 9, 2016, Luzibu and Nsakala took a Beverly Hills/Hollywood city tour (the next two collages), which took them and other tourists on the bus to various places: Hollywood Boulevard, Melrose Avenue, the farmers market, Sunset Boulevard, Beverly Hills, Rodeo Drive, et cetera.

The Nsakalas' Panama Canal Grand Adventure was full of beautiful sightseeing venues. Traversing the 50-mile (80 km) Panama Canal through the three locks—which lift the ships from the Caribbean Sea a total of 85 feet (26 m) to the man-made Gatun Lake and then lower them down to the Pacific Ocean—was the highlight of the cruise for Luzibu and Nsakala.

Grand European Adventure (River Cruise) in May 2017

Luzibu and Nsakala flew from Daytona Beach on Friday, May 5, 2017, to Budapest, Hungary, via Atlanta, Georgia, and Amsterdam, Netherlands, arriving midmorning on Saturday, May 6, 2017. Their grand European adventure, on the ship *Viking Skadi*, went from Saturday to Saturday, May 6 through May 20, 2017. The fifteen-day itinerary of this adventure, from Budapest to Amsterdam, is shown in this photograph (Image[v]).

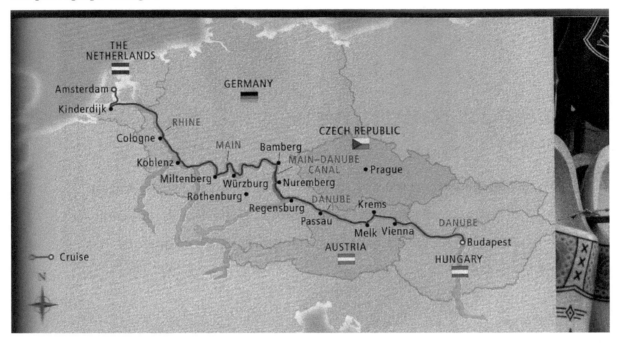

Their ship, the *Viking Skadi*, cruised through:

- Five countries: Hungary, Slovakia (no stop), Austria, Germany, and the Netherlands;

- Three rivers: the Danube, the Main, and the Rhine;

- One canal: the Main-Danube Canal; and

- Fifteen cities: Budapest, Hungary; Vienna and Melk in Austria; Passau, Regensburg, Nuremberg, Bamberg, Würzburg, Wertheim, Koblenz, and Cologne in Germany; and Kinderdijk and Amsterdam in the Netherlands.

Budapest, the capital city of Hungary, straddles the banks of the Danube River, with traditional hillside Buda on one side and modern Pest on the other. Walking and bus tours of Budapest were taken on Saturday afternoon and Sunday morning, May 6 and 7, 2017. This collage shows the cruise ship, the *Viking Skadi*, Luzibu and Nsakala on a bus tour, and the Hungarian Parliament Building on the banks of Danube River, lit up at night (lower right).

This collection of photographs shows some of Budapest's iconic places toured by Luzibu, Nsakala, and others on the cruise. The top left photograph features the Széchenyi Chain Bridge, which is the most famous of the seven bridges connecting the Buda and Pest sides of the city; it lights up the Budapest sky at night, as shown. Luzibu is sitting in front of the same bridge on the Buda side of the city. The lower left photograph shows the Roman Catholic Saint Stephen's Basilica, which was completed in neoclassical style in 1905. The lower right photograph shows the Heroes' Square, built in 1896 to mark the thousandth anniversary of Hungary. It is the largest and most impressive square in the city.

This collage features the tourists' visit to Matthias Church. The present building was built in the second half of the fourteenth century and was extensively restored in the late nineteenth century. The lower right photograph shows the church courtyard. The photograph of Luzibu and Nsakala (top right) was taken at the railing behind the courtyard, with the Danube River in the far background.

In the late afternoon of Sunday, May 7, 2017, the *Viking Skadi* sailed from Budapest for Amsterdam. The ship would go through sixty-eight river locks between Budapest and Amsterdam. The first one, located on the Danube River near Bratislava, Slovakia, is shown here just behind another ship, entering and leaving the lock (top and bottom photographs, respectively). The ship passed through without stopping. The view of Bratislavia on both sides of the Danube was breathtakingly beautiful.

The *Viking Skadi* arrived in Vienna, Austria, late in the afternoon on Monday, May 8, 2017, where sightseeing would take place until Tuesday evening. On Monday evening, Luzibu, Nsakala, and many other tourists took the optional excursion to a classical concert featuring the timeless music of two masters, Wolfgang Amadeus Mozart and Johann Strauss, as performed by the Vienna Residence Orchestra. It was all lovely.

The shore excursion on Tuesday, May 9, 2017, entailed a bus and walking tour of some of the iconic places in the city of Vienna.

- Ringstrasse (left-hand photograph): Reportedly the most beautiful boulevard in the world, this street is home to Vienna's best-known sights, such as the Imperial Palace, the Natural History Museum, the Parliament of Austria, and the Vienna State Opera.

- Hofburg Palace (top right): Serving today as the residence and workplace of the president of Austria, it was built in the thirteenth century and expanded several times afterward.

- Stadtpark or City Park (lower right): This gorgeous municipal park, spanning 16 acres (65,000 m²) in surface, is home to statues of several famous Viennese artists (Johann Strauss II, Franz Schubert, Emil Jacob Schindler, etc.). The tourists visited or passed by such other iconic places as Saint Stephen's Cathedral and Schönbrunn Palace.

The *Viking Skadi* sailed from Vienna late on the night of Tuesday/Wednesday, May 9–10, 2017, headed for Melk, Austria, the next port of call. The scenery on both sides of the Danube River in the Wachau Valley was truly a tapestry of rolling hills, vineyards, fortresses, and quaint fishing villages.

The *Viking Skadi* arrived in Melk midmorning on Wednesday, May 10, 2017. After lunch, most of the cruise guests took a tour of the Melk Abbey (top left photograph), a Benedictine abbey perched

on a rocky outcrop overlooking the Danube River, adjoining the Wachau Valley. Built in 1702, the abbey caught fire, for the second time, in 1974. It underwent restoration from 1978 to 1995. Luzibu and Nsakala are shown standing in the Prelate's courtyard. The lower left photograph shows Luzibu and Nsakala with the two couples they were hanging out with throughout the cruise. They are Karen and John Hovanec of Omaha, Nebraska, and Lin Tamoulonis and Kerry Doherty of Dover, New Hampshire. The bottom right photograph shows a panoramic view of Melk.

Continuing its journey, the *Viking Skadi* arrived in Passau, Bavaria, Germany, on Thursday morning, May 11, 2017. The Passau's claim to fame is that it is at the confluence of three European rivers: the Inn, the Danube, and the Ilz. Cruise guests were treated to a walking tour of a section of the city, which is characterized by narrow, cobblestone-covered streets. The Passau Glass Museum (top right photograph) is another iconic place they visited. Ultimately, they attended a marvelous organ concert at Saint Stephen's Cathedral (lower right photograph).

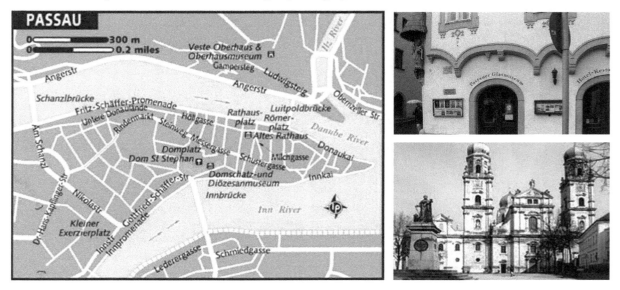

The *Viking Skadi* sailed from Passau at 5:15 p.m. for Regensburg, arriving there on Friday morning, May 12, 2017. This medieval city was untouched by World War II bombing. It is rich in architectural splendor with cobblestone streets. A walking tour took Luzibu, Nsakala, and others to such places as:

- Saint Peter's Cathedral (bottom right): This important Bavarian landmark epitomizes the intricate beauty of Gothic architecture.

- Emilie and Oskar Schindler's apartment (top right) following World War II: Oskar Schindler was a German industrialist who saved the lives of more than a thousand mostly Polish-Jewish refugees from the Holocaust by employing them in his factories during World War II. He was the subject of the 1993 drama film, *Schindler's List*, directed and coproduced by Steven Spielberg.

- The Rathskeller restaurant (bottom left): This is where Luzibu, Nsakala, and their friends (Kerry, Lin, John, and Karen) had lunch.

- The Regensburg Synagogue (left-hand photograph, Image[w]) and Jewish cemetery (top right): Lin and Kerry, plus an unidentified person, were photographed sitting at the cemetery site.

The *Viking Skadi* sailed from Regensburg at 4:15 p.m. for the Main-Danube Canal, on the way to Nuremberg. This collage shows the *Viking Skadi* in one of the locks of the canal.

The *Viking Skadi* arrived in Nuremberg at midday on Saturday, May 13, 2017. The bus and walking tour of this city offered a sobering experience because of the nature of the places visited: Nuremberg's International Military Tribunal (top left), where World War II criminals were tried; Adolf Hitler's rallying grounds (bottom left); and the Holocaust Memorial New Jewish Cemetery Nürenberg (right).

On the light side of things, the tourists also explored/visited various other pleasant places, such as the Market Square (shown here).

The *Viking Skadi* arrived in Bamberg, Germany, at 1:00 p.m. on Sunday, May 14, 2017, to drop off the guests who chose to go for a Bamberg city tour and those who opted for a Franconian country-side tour. The ship then proceeded to Zeil am Main, where all the tourists would rejoin the *Viking Skadi* by motor coaches. Luzibu and Nsakala were in the group of tourists who went for the Bamberg city tour, which included Bamberg City Hall, Bamberg Cathedral (left and top right), and the rose garden (lower right) at the New Residenz.

At the end of the guided excursion, Luzibu, Lin, Karen, John, Kerry, and Nsakala ventured into town on their own. They passed by a smoked beer (*Rauchbier*) brewery (top left), visited some gift shops, then sat at a restaurant next to the brewery to sample a variety of smoked beers (right-hand photographs). They then sat in front of a creamery in the town square and tasted their "spaghetti ice cream" (bottom left).

All tourists were back aboard the *Viking Skadi* by 6:00 p.m., which left soon thereafter for Markbreit/Würzburg. The *Viking Skadi* arrived in Würzburg, Bavaria, on Monday, May 15, 2017, at 12:45 p.m. The optional city tour centered on the Bishop's Residence (top and bottom left), whose main structure was inaugurated in 1744. The residence was almost completely destroyed in World War II. From 1945 to 1987, the building and interiors were reconstructed to their current state. The ceiling frescoes and other interior decorations are mind boggling. The gardens in the backyard (lower right photograph, for example) are beautiful. The Marienberg Fortress is seen perched on a hill overlooking the Main River (top right). The *Viking Skadi* sailed from Würzburg at 6:45 p.m. for Wertheim.

The *Viking Skadi* arrived in Wertheim on Tuesday, May 16, 2017, at 8:45 a.m. The guests were transferred by road trains (top middle photograph) from the parking lot where the ship was anchored to the edge of the town near the Leaning Tower of Wertheim, or Pointed Tower (top right), for a walking tour. The tour included City Hall, Market Square, and a glass-blowing shop (bottom right), where Luzibu, Nsakala, and others bought some souvenirs. Wertheim, which is located at the confluence of the Tauber and Main Rivers, is susceptible to flooding (bottom left). In fact, the Pointed Tower's noticeable lean is the result of over eight hundred years of flooding rather than any architectural defect. The ship sailed from Wertheim for Koblenz shortly after 12:45 p.m.

On the morning of Wednesday, May 17, 2017, the *Viking Skadi* dropped off the majority of the passengers in Marksburg, Germany, then proceeded to Koblenz. Luzibu, Nsakala, and the other passengers who had been dropped off in Marksburg took a tour of the seven-hundred-year-old Marksburg Castle. This castle was built in 1117 to protect the town of Braubach. It's perched on a hill overlooking the Rhine River. Many medieval castles were built to protect key roads and rivers, or, more accurately, the landowners extorted tolls from anyone passing by. The inside of this castle offers hints of the opulence of the old days, although today, it looks rugged, rough, and dilapidated.

At the end of the tour, a number of buses took the tourists to Koblenz, where they were reunited with others on the *Viking Skadi*, which was anchored by a gondola (shown in this photograph), which carried people from one side of the Rhine River to the other and back. The *Viking Skadi* sailed from Koblenz for Cologne, Germany, shortly after 3:00 p.m.

As the next two collages show, the Middle-Rhine region creates a stunning canvas of picturesque forests, vineyards, castles, and castle ruins.

The *Viking Skadi* arrived in Cologne at 9:00 a.m. on Thursday, May 18, 2017. A few words about Cologne: sustained bombing of this city by the Allied Forces from Great Britain, France, the Soviet Union, and the United States during the Second World War resulted in the destruction of 61 percent of its built-up area and a 95 percent reduction of its population of over 700,000 as a result of the massive evacuations of the people to rural areas.

Today, the rebuilt city of Cologne, shown here, is a bustling city of slightly more than one million inhabitants. Its skyline is dominated by the Cologne Cathedral, the seat of the archbishop of Cologne and of the administration of the archdiocese of Cologne.

The Cologne shore excursion entailed a bus tour of the city, followed by a walk to various iconic places, including the Cologne Cathedral (top left), the Roman-Germanic Museum (top right), Cologne City Hall, and Cologne Old Town (bottom left). The wedding party shown in the lower right photograph was headed to the city hall, the tourists were told, for the nuptial ceremony followed by a photographic session in front of the Old Town Monument, as seen behind the tour guide and two lady tourists in the lower left photograph.

The *Viking Skadi* departed Cologne for Kinderdijk, Netherlands, at 10:30 p.m., arriving on Friday, May 19, 2017, at 1:00 p.m. As seen in this graphic, Kinderdijk is situated in the Alblasserwaard polder (low-lying piece of land) at the confluence of the Lek and Noord Rivers.

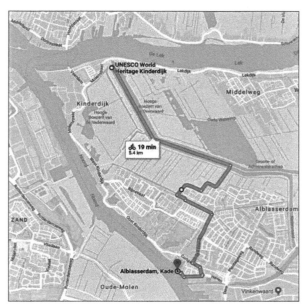

This village, with an altitude of only 3 feet (1 m) above sea level, is susceptible to flooding. A system of nineteen windmills, some of which were built around 1740, is used to drain the water from the Alblasserwaard polder into reservoirs. The optional shore excursion entailed touring the windmills of Kinderdijk. Some of them are shown in this collage, and Luzibu and Nsakala can be seen posing for a photograph across the canal from one of them (lower right).

The *Viking Skadi* sailed from Kinderdijk for Amsterdam shortly after 5:00 p.m. This being the last night of the cruise, the crew organized a farewell cocktail party, followed by a lavish dinner. The left and top right photographs in the previous collage show Luzibu, Nsakala, and others at dinner. The bottom right photograph shows the couple who entertained the guests every night of the cruise. Service throughout the cruise was impeccable. Staff members were gracious and friendly, and they treated everyone respectfully. It was a wonderful cruise experience.

The *Viking Skadi* arrived in Amsterdam on Saturday, May 20, 2017, at 6:45 a.m. A motor coach transferred Luzibu, Nsakala, and other guests to the Schiphol (Amsterdam) Airport (Image[x]), from which Luzibu and Nsakala flew back to the United States.

Viking's Grand European Tour river cruise differed from ocean cruises in that the shores on both sides of the river on which it was sailing at any given moment were constantly visible from the ship. And, unlike ocean cruises, the river cruise offered a port of call virtually every day, allowing the guests to take part in onshore activities. Additionally, the smaller ship (190 guests plus 50 staff members) offered a quainter atmosphere than that of large ocean cruise ships.

Cuba and Eastern Caribbean Cruise in January–February 2019

On Saturday, January 26, 2019, members of Luzibu and Nsakala's extended family, Josephine and Edward Lusala; Gertrude Luzolo; and her mom, Nsansi Mbondo, arrived at their house shortly after midnight from Bloomington/Lexington, Illinois. They came down for a few days' stay to check out the Lusalas' retirement home, which they were moving to in February 2019.

After breakfast with their guests from Illinois, Luzibu and Nsakala left in their Subaru Forester at 9:45 a.m. for Miami, en route to their Cuba and Eastern Caribbean cruise adventure, arriving at the Hampton Inn by Hilton Miami Airport East at 5:05 p.m.

A van full of hotel guests left the Hampton Inn on Sunday, January 27, 2019, at about 11:15 a.m. for Miami-Dade County Seaport, where, after going through security and Cuban visa processing, Luzibu and Nsakala embarked, around 12:45 p.m., on the Royal Caribbean *Empress of the Seas*. The itinerary of this seven-day cruise (Sunday through Sunday, January 27 through February 3, 2019) planned for ports of call at:

- Miami, Florida;

- Havana, Cuba;

- Nassau and CocoCay, Bahamas; and

- Miami, Florida, once again.

The *Empress of the Seas* left Miami Seaport at about 4:00 p.m., en route to Havana. This collage shows the ship leaving Miami while Luzibu and Nsakala were enjoying lunch.

The *Empress of the Seas* arrived in Havana on Monday, January 28, 2019, at about 7:00 a.m., after a rough night at sea. Havana had just suffered a severe tornado that killed three people. This was for a two-night port of call. At about 9:30 a.m., Luzibu and Nsakala joined many other guests on the Easy Panoramic Havana bus and walking tour. They visited such iconic places as:

- The Place de la Revolution (two left-hand photographs): This is where Fidel Castro used to give his four-to-six-hour uninterrupted speeches in front of one million plus people. Significantly, the face of Ernesto Che Guevara, Castro's revolutionary comrade, is displayed on the facade of one of the buildings on the Revolutionary Square (behind the tour guide, lower left photograph).

- Christ of Havana Sculpture: This iconic structure was inaugurated on Christmas Eve of 1958, fifteen days before Castro entered Havana on January 8, 1959, and overthrew the government of Fulgencio Batista. This sculpture represents Jesus of Nazareth on a hilltop overlooking the bay of Havana.

- Fusterlandia (top right photograph): This popular tourist stop is home to ceramic art created by artist José Fuster, known for his colorful, whimsical mosaics.

The tourists also visited/stopped by many other popular destinations in Havana, including Old Town Square, La Cabāna Fortress, Havana Cathedral, and Morro Castle. This collage shows a sampling of the classic cars that the tourists saw on the streets of Havana.

Luzibu, Nsakala, and other guests left by motor coach on Tuesday, January 29, 2019, at 7:30 a.m. for a tour of Rancho Vista Hermosa. This is a farm-to-table business with the following profile:

- 167-acre (68-hectare) farm;

- Thirty-five employees, twelve of whom are female;

- A hostess who is an agricultural engineer (top left photograph in the collage on the next page); and

- A large variety of farm products, including all sorts of vegetables and tropical fruits; a variety of animals; and an assortment of dairy products, beverages, and meats.

In this collage, Luzibu and Nsakala (lower left) are enjoying a drink prepared from a mixture of freshly squeezed sugar cane juice (top left) with Cuban rum (optional) and fresh mint (top right). The finished product is shown in the lower right photograph.

Lunch prepared from farm products (roasted pig, goat cheese, an assortment of vegetables, et cetera) was served while a local music group entertained the guests. The Rancho Vista Hermosa tour was the highlight of Luzibu and Nsakala's two-day stay in Cuba.

The *Empress of the Seas* sailed from Havana at about 5:00 p.m. on Tuesday, January 29, 2019, for Nassau, Bahamas. It arrived in Nassau on Thursday, January 31, 2019, at about 8:00 a.m. This collage shows Luzibu and Nsakala posing in front of their ship, two Bahamian street crossing guards (top right photograph), and the strawberry margaritas that Luzibu and Nsakala enjoyed at the Twisted Lime Sports Bar & Grill, near the pier where the *Empress of the Seas* was anchored.

At about 6:00 p.m., the *Empress of the Seas* sailed from Nassau for CocoCay, arriving on Saturday, February 2, 2019, at about 7:00 a.m., after a full day of cruising the Caribbean Sea. The *Empress of the Seas* is shown in the top left photograph, anchored offshore. Thus, the guests went ashore and back to the ship through a tendering process: i.e., via a transfer in relatively small boats. CocoCay is a small island, less than one mile wide. Royal Caribbean Cruises Ltd., which owns Royal Caribbean International, among other cruise lines, holds the lease on the island, where they take their guests for a few hours of optional swimming, kayaking, snorkeling, scuba diving, or just relaxing on the beach. The *Empress of the Seas* left CocoCay for Miami at about 5:00 p.m.

One of the things that set the Cuban and Eastern Caribbean cruise apart from other cruises that Luzibu and Nsakala had taken before was that Cuba reminded them of their lives in the Democratic Republic of the Congo (DRC). Cuba seems like a third-world country. It also reminded the authors of some other things about the DRC: fresh-squeezed sugar cane beverages, ways of fresh-food preparation, and the sounds of music. As the result of a nearly five-decade-long blockade and embargo imposed by the United States, Cuba is a country stuck back in time. However, Cuba has one of the highest literacy rates in the world, as 99 percent of the Cuban population can read and write. Additionally, education and medical care are provided free by the government.

European (Switzerland, Belgium, and Great Britain) Trip in May 2019

Luzibu and Nsakala spent two weeks (May 11–24, 2019) in Europe visiting friends in Baden/Dättwil, Switzerland, and friends and family in Belgium and London.

Pictured in the collage below, Dr. Jürgen Bittner (top right) is one of the people Nsakala worked with at Asea Brown Boveri's (ABB's) Corporate Research Center in Baden/Dättwil, Switzerland, in the 1990s. Since then, Luzibu and Nsakala have forged an enduring friendship with Jürgen; his wife, Monika (top left); and their daughter, Steffani (top right). So, each time Luzibu and Nsakala went to Switzerland, they would get together with the Bittners. On Sunday, May 11, 2019, they were invited for a raclette dinner (raclette is a typical Swiss dish) at the Bittners' home in Lenzburg. A raclette dinner consists of various chesses, boiled potatoes, tomatoes, mushrooms, onions, bell peppers, cured meat, bacon, and much more. These photographs show everyone enjoying this delicious meal.

Dora and Werner Schott were Luzibu and Nsakala's hosts in Switzerland. As has been said before, the Schotts and Nsakalas have been closely knit friends since 1996, when Nsakala lived in an apartment rented from them by ABB. They have visited each other multiple times. Here, the foursome is enjoying dinner at the Schotts' home in Baden/Dättwil.

Dora and Werner took Luzibu and Nsakala to several venues for sightseeing (Interlaken, the Abbey Library of Saint Gallen, the chocolate factory in Buchs, et cetera) during their four-day stay. This collage shows all four of them during their visit to Interlaken on Monday, May 13, 2019. The scenery—including snow-capped peaks—while cruising on Lake Brienz on the Jungfrau ship, was breathtaking.

Luzibu and Nsakala flew from Zurich International Airport to Brussels on Tuesday, May 16, 2019, where their friend, Dr. Kanigula Mubagwa (Kani), was waiting for them. Kani and his wife, Fortuna, put Luzibu and Nsakala up in an Airbnb in Zoutleeuw village, which is located about ten minutes by car from their own home in the village of Wange (Landen).

On Wednesday, May 17, 2019, Kani took his guests to Kortrijk, Belgium, where they had lunch. They then went to Lille, France (top left), for a drink and sightseeing around the beautiful "City Centre," where the streets are cobblestone. The Atonium is a landmark building in Brussels (top right), originally constructed for the 1958 World's Fair. Fortuna and Kani took Luzibu and Nsakala to the Atonium, where they met Akonkwa Mubagwa. They all went to the top for a panoramic view of Brussels. Absolutely stunning! Subsequently, they drove to Grand-Place of Brussels (bottom left), where they enjoyed lunch (bottom right).

Additionally, Fortuna and Kani took Luzibu and Nsakala to Tervuren for a tour of the Royal Museum for Central Africa (not shown). The DRC is a focal point of this museum. The large array of Congolese artifacts there is mind boggling.

When Fortuna and Kani Mubagwa's daughter, Linda, got married to Bosco Mpozi in September 2008, Luzibu and Nsakala traveled from the United States to Belgium to attend the event. The Mubagwas arranged for them to stay with Ms. Jo Mathieu in Landen (Walshoutem). On Monday evening, May 20, 2019, Jo invited Fortuna, Kani, Luzibu, and Nsakala to her home for a multiple-course dinner. It was wonderful to see Jo again after an eleven-year hiatus, and the evening couldn't have gone better!

On Saturday, May 18, 2019, Nsakala's niece, Claudine Makinutewa (top left), picked Luzibu and Nsakala up from the Airbnb in Zoutleeuw around 11:00 a.m. to take them to the apartment of her parents, Biki Marie and Makinutewa Félix, in Fleurus, Belgium. On their way to Fleurus, they stopped by the campus of Louvain-la-Neuve University to say hello to Claudine's daughter, Alégresse Bambi (top right), who was studying for her final exams. Luzibu and Nsakala hung out in Fleurus with Biki Marie and Makinutewa Félix (bottom right) and their daughter Cécile Makinutewa and her five children (bottom left).

On Tuesday, May 21, 2019, Fortuna and Kani took Luzibu and Nsakala to the train station at Brussels Midi for their two-hour ride on the Eurostar to London Saint Pancras. The point of this trip segment was for Luzibu and Nsakala to go from continental Europe to Great Britain via the Chunnel, or Channel Tunnel, which is beneath the English Channel, connecting France to Great Britain. Meanwhile, Claudine Makinutewa contacted her cousin, Susan Kimpiatu, who lives in London with her family. Hence, the stay in London became part sightseeing, part hanging out with family. That said, on Tuesday evening, Mark Kimpiatu, Susan's son, picked Luzibu and Nsakala up from their hotel, Hampton by Hilton London Waterloo Hotel, and took them to their flat for dinner. The top left selfie shows Luzibu and Nsakala with Susan Kimpiatu; her husband, David Tange; and Mark. Davina, the Kimpiatu's daughter, is not shown in the selfie. On Wednesday, May 22, 2019, Susan took Luzibu and Nsakala to Nando's Restaurant near the Hampton Hotel for dinner (right-hand photographs). Susan's brother, Chris Sita, and his fiancée, Nadege Le Den (bottom left), also visited Luzibu and Nsakala on the following evening.

Wednesday and Thursday were devoted to sightseeing of some of London's iconic sites. They used Golden Tours' "Hop-On Hop-Off" service for going from place to place. They, for example:

- Toured the Westminster Abbey (top left, next page);

- Went to the gate of Buckingham Palace (top right);

- Crossed London Bridge on foot;

- Cruised the River Thames from London Bridge to Tower Bridge (bottom left and right); and

- Stood in front of Big Ben, which was undergoing an extensive renovation.

On Friday, May 24, 2019, Luzibu and Nsakala flew back from London Heathrow to Orlando International Airport via Newark Liberty International Airport.

This European trip was fulfilling for Luzibu and Nsakala because it afforded them the opportunity to reconnect with family and friends in continental Europe. Furthermore, they had the opportunity to tour some of the iconic places in London together for the first time.

Part Four

Life in the United States of America—Other Things

10

Recreation, Hobbies, and Giving Back to the Community

Recreation and Hobbies

Luzibu and Nsakala like to stay active. Below is a list of some of their favorite pastimes.

- Common activities: walking, working out at a health club.

- Luzibu's activities: gardening, sewing, cooking, reading, knitting, learning to play piano, et cetera.

- Nsakala's activities: golfing, reading, fishing, learning to play guitar, et cetera.

Common Activities

Whether in retirement in Palm Coast, Florida, or during their working days in greater Hartford, Connecticut, Luzibu and Nsakala have always incorporated physical activities into their lives. When they're not working out at a health club, they can be found walking along the local streets or trails. In 2012, Luzibu and Nsakala compiled a three-year diary—"A 1,095-Day Diary"—spanning the years 2009 through 2011, to compare their lifestyles while working throughout the year in 2009, working part of the year and being retired the other part of the year in 2010, and being fully retired in 2011. Not surprisingly to them, their levels of physical activity did not change significantly. Today, they alternate between working out at a local health club and walking along the Intracoastal Waterway, the local beach (as shown in the following collage), and the many beautiful walking trails of Palm Coast.

Luzibu's Activities

To plant a garden of flowers or vegetables is to believe in tomorrow, because where the flowers bloom, so does hope. Luzibu enjoys a lot of activities, such as gardening, sewing, cooking, and reading novels in conjunction with a book club. Why does Luzibu enjoy gardening? Because she loves and enjoys everything about being outdoors. Gardening relaxes her, and she admires how the seeds grow from nothing to beautiful flowers or bountiful vegetables and sees how God's miracles manifest themselves. Luzibu is passionate about nature's collective world: plants, animals, the landscape, and other features and products of the earth. There is a breathtaking beauty in nature. Gardening can provide much more than adding beauty to the yard; it acts as therapy in the form of exercise, stress relief, and getting in contact with nature. More importantly, gardening allows one to be aware of the five senses: hearing, touching, smelling, seeing, and tasting. The following saying always comes to Luzibu's mind: "A heart without love is like a garden without flowers."

In this collage, the members of the Bling Book Club of Palm Coast, Florida, are shown. Shown in the top and bottom left photographs are Louise Delaere and Rhonda Stapleford. In the right-hand photograph, from left to right, are Elizabeth Fritz, Francine Smithson, and Luzibu. Luzibu and her book club have read seventy-seven novels since 2011. The books range from fiction to nonfiction genres. What a learning experience that is!

Luzibu also enjoys sewing and cooking. She is very creative and imaginative. Some of her creations are, for example, shown in this collage.

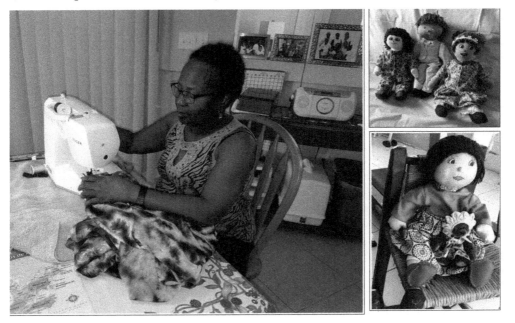

Nsakala's Activities

Nsakala enjoys reading tremendously. While his book reading tends to happen in spurts, he constantly reads newspapers, magazines, and internet news in French about, for the most part, the Democratic Republic of the Congo. He also has been teaching himself to play guitar. In addition to these activities, he enjoys playing golf for pleasure and charitable causes. In this collage, Nsakala is playing in charity golf events with the Eagles Golf Club of Palm Coast for the African American Cultural Society of Palm Coast at the Cypress Golf Course in 2016 and 2017. In the 2016 photograph (top), Nsakala is with, from left to right, Henry Douglas, John Reid, and Frank Phillips. In the 2017 photograph (bottom), he is with, from left to right, Doug Brown, Frank Phillips, and Roy Lorentz.

In the top left photograph, Nsakala is competing for fun with other people on the top deck of the *Island Princess* during the 2016 Panama Canal cruise. In the top right photograph, he is playing solo on the top deck of the *Viking Skadi* during the 2017 Grand European river cruise. Back home, the two bottom photographs show Nsakala playing golf for fun with his friends: in the lower right photograph, from left to right, Patrick Miller, Mark Allaben, and Ivor (Jack) Smithson at the Palm Harbor Golf Course in Palm Coast in 2018. This foursome tries to play nine holes of golf once a week whenever possible.

Giving Back to the Community

"Everyone to whom much is given, of him will be much required" is a direct quote from the Bible (Luke 12:48 Revised Standard Version). "Much is given" refers to resources such as finances, talents, intellectual abilities, spiritual gifts, et cetera. Luzibu and Nsakala adhere to this principle and think of it as giving back to the community. Throughout their careers, Luzibu and Nsakala each made sure to contribute, through payroll deductions for the most part, to a variety of causes, including the Sickle Cell Disease Association of America Inc. and United Way General Fund. The following eight collages illustrate some of what they have done for their communities over the years.

Affordable Housing

While living in West Hartford, Luzibu and Nsakala belonged to an organization, West Hartford Interfaith Coalition (WHIC), that built new housing and rehabilitated old housing in the community, with funding from the government and other charitable entities, for people who otherwise could not afford it. The first collage shows two of the many families who benefited from WHIC's endeavors, and the second collage shows typical housing developments by WHIC.

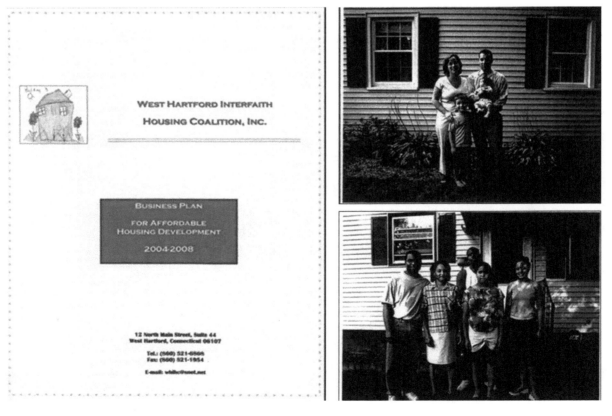

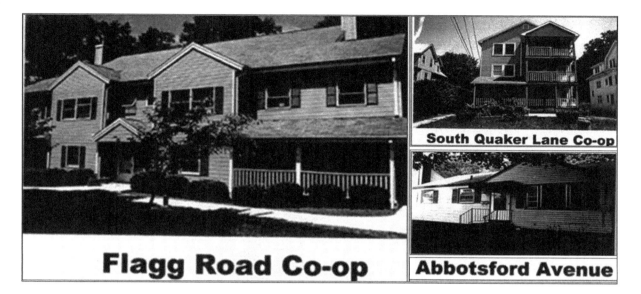

Flagg Road Co-op

South Quaker Lane Co-op

Abbotsford Avenue

Since their retirement in Palm Coast in 2010, Luzibu and Nsakala have worked with other congregants from the Palm Coast United Methodist Church to help with some of Flagler County's Habitat for Humanity endeavors in Bunnell, Florida, as shown in the following collage.

Resource Vegetables Gardening

Palm Coast United Methodist Church (PCUMC) proudly sponsors Boy Scout Troop 402, among other youth-related organizations in the community. In 2012, the PCUMC Garden Ministry asked the Boy Scout troop to construct a fenced-in garden with nine four-foot-by-eight-foot raised planter boxes (as shown here) at the North Campus on Belle Terre Parkway. The purpose of this garden was to grow fresh vegetables that would be donated entirely to Flagler County's food bank, also known as the Resource Center, in Bunnell.

In 2013, Leslie Thornton, then PCUMC's manager of the North Campus, asked if Mamie Godfrey and Luzibu would work the gar-

den for the church. They said yes, and both their spouses, William and Nsakala, agreed to join them in this endeavor. After a very fruitful harvest season, in the spring of 2014, Joe Codie, the new North Campus manager, obtained some funds and worked with the Godfreys and the Nsakalas to expand the garden size and add three more raised box planters, bringing the total to twelve. William, Mamie, Luzibu, and Nsakala are shown in the left-hand photograph below. Joe Codie is shown with William and Luzibu during the construction of the additional three four-foot-by-eight-foot planter boxes.

At planting times, there were always other PCUMC members who helped, as this collage attests to. The late Genetta Rodriguez (standing, top right), for example, helped with her expertise in gardening. And Michele Seyfert (left, bottom right photograph) was always there to help upon request.

This collage shows Luzibu, William, Mamie, and Nsakala at one of many harvest times, and it also shows some of the vegetables grown, including yellow squash and eggplant on the vine.

Mamie and Luzibu are shown bundling freshly picked vegetables before delivery to the food bank in Bunnell.

As the harvested vegetables were delivered to the food bank and when the clients were being served, one of Mother Teresa's statements came to Luzibu's mind: "If you can't feed a hundred people, then feed just one."

The Empowerment of Women

Luzibu is involved in a nonprofit organization called University Women of Flagler (UWF) that is dedicated to advancing educational opportunities for the women and girls of Flagler County to help them achieve their full potential. UWF has awarded scholarships to some Flagler County high school graduates who are continuing their education in four-year colleges and universities. The scholarships are funded through donations, fundraising events, and sponsorships. The purpose of this organization is to unite graduates of accredited educational institutions in order to promote equality, education, intellectual growth, individual worth, cultural interests, and the development of opportunities for women and girls in the Flagler County area.

University Women of Flagler

Luzibu Nsakala

Membership since 2012-2013

Educational History:

Bachelor's Degree from Central Connecticut State University

Occupation(s):

Company staff accountant

Positions Held in UWF

Corresponding Secretary   50-50

Marching for Causes

Over the years, in both greater Hartford, Connecticut, and Palm Coast, Florida, Luzibu has marched with others to help raise funds for a variety of causes. She has participated in such charity events as the March of Dimes, the Susan G. Komen Race for the Cure, and the March Against Hunger. This collage shows Luzibu delivering the money that she personally raised as an advocate through the Palm Coast United Methodist Church for the Walk to End Alzheimer's Disease. This particular event was held by people from both Flagler and Saint Johns' counties at the River to Sea Preserve in Palm Coast on September 29, 2018. Through their actions, they were saying, in effect, "Take a stand and walk to end Alzheimer's disease; together, we can end Alzheimer's disease."

Authors' Note

At this point, the authors wish to answer three questions geared toward explaining, briefly, why and how they wrote this memoir and what lessons they drew from it.

Question 1: Why does writing this photographic memoir matter?

Answer: The answer can be summarized as follows:

- As the readers know, the title of this memoir is *Humble Beginnings: A Photographic Memoir*. In keeping with the English-language adage "A picture is worth a thousand words," Luzibu and Nsakala decided to subtitle their work *A Photographic Memoir*. They feel that the visual part of this memoir can elicit any number of interesting comments/interpretations/thoughts from the readers, independent of their original intents.

- The idea of writing a memoir has been on the minds of Luzibu and Nsakala for quite some time, as stated in the introduction. The story they wanted to tell is that of their humble beginnings and how they succeeded against all odds.

- Their purpose was to leave a legacy behind for their family, friends, and other readers who could benefit from their experience from humble beginnings in the Democratic Republic of the Congo (DRC) to the United States.

- This memoir shows that with hard work, persistence, support from family and friends, and God's grace, one can achieve a high degree of success irrespective of his or her first station in life.

Question 2: How did you go about putting this memoir together?

Answer: Research, which is an ongoing process, has been an important pillar of this project. The major steps taken were as follows:

- Luzibu and Nsakala consulted with their family in the DRC and the United States over the years on matters pertaining to their ancestry and their extended family's connections, relationships, and whereabouts. They used this information, along with their own knowledge, to put together the "Growing Up in Kibunzi and Makanga-Kibunzi Villages" section in Chapter 2 and the family trees presented in the memoir.

- Luzibu and Nsakala collected over four thousand photographs from their own physical and electronic albums, from family members, and from friends. They digitized potentially good storytelling photographs and classified all the photographs systematically. The final prioritization resulted in more than 638 photographs and collages, which are included in this memoir. Some of the photographs that Luzibu and Nsakala would have liked to include in this memoir but, regrettably, did not have a possession of are 1) Luzibu's father, Lutete David Duele; 2) Luzibu's mother, Madede Lessa, with Munlemvo and Mukiese (Luzibu and Nsakala's children); 3) Nsakala's mother, Lutayi Rebecca; and 4) Nsakala's father, Metusala Nsakala, with Munlemvo and Mukiese.

- Luzibu and Nsakala studied the architecture of some photographic memoirs and various books with a considerable number of photographs (Gates, 1999; Mann, 2015; Souza, 2017).

- Luzibu and Nsakala conducted an extensive literature survey on the history of the DRC from the Scramble for Africa in the 1880s through 2019, among other things. Their sources of information were a variety of books, articles published in scientific and engineering journals, and the World Wide Web (see bibliography).

- Luzibu and Nsakala created a dynamic road map based on the available information and consulted with family and friends on a continual basis. That information was used to write and update this memoir.

Question 3: What lessons can you draw from the experience of writing this memoir?

Answer: Coauthoring anything (a book, an article for publication in a journal or for presentation to a public audience, a musical score, or anything else) requires that the coauthors be, ideally, on the same page throughout the product development. To this end, Luzibu and Nsakala implemented the following lessons, which serve them well daily, to put together this memoir:

- Patiently and carefully listen to your coauthor's viewpoints before reacting;

- Ask questions to make sure that you understand what you are hearing;

- Express your own viewpoints clearly and without hesitation, whether or not they are in accordance with those of your coauthor; and

- Communicate with each other constantly to reinforce each other's viewpoints and/or achieve common ground in the event of any divergence of thoughts.

Luzibu and Nsakala's final hope is that this memoir explains their ancestry and how proud they are to be in a position to write it for posterity to read and treasure, knowing that they worked and lived their lives to become the people they are today.

Appendix

Family Tree: Two Generations of Luzibu and Her Siblings

This family tree shows Luzibu, her siblings (yellow background), their spouses, and their children.

TWO GENERATIONS OF LUZIBU AND HER SIBLINGS

1. Lubombolo lua Nzambi [M]
- Mbiyavanga Madede [F]
- Tekadiomoka Pierre [M]
- Manzambi Lubombolo [M]
- Tuzolana Marie [F]
- Makiese Bayikumana Nelly [F]
- Lusambulu Mawazola Philippe [M]

Matondo [F]

2. Basilwa Mvutudulu Mattieux [M]
- Basilwa Belinda [F]
- Basilwa Jonathan [M]
- Basilwa Tutala [F]
- Basilwa Héritier [M]

Mavinga [F]

3. Mayiza Mvibudulu [M]
- Luzibu Mayiza Chantal* [F]
- Mvibudulu Basala Espérance [F]
- Mvibudulu Mayiza Pauline [F]
- Dieyatondulua Duele David [M]
- Mayiza Mamita [F]
- Mayiza Batoma [M]

* Different Mother

Zola Betty [F]

Nsakala ya Nsakala [M]
- R. Munlemvo Mitchell [F]
- Mukiese Nsakala [M]

4. Luzibu Lutete Nsakala [F]

5. Kiambote Duele [M]
- Kiambote Duele Trésor [M]
- Mabungu Kiambote Dieudonné [M]
- Tukibanzila Mumpasi Thèrese [F]

Nkembi Mabungu Hélène [F]

6. Lubambuka Malemba Oscar [M]
- Mambueni Mireille [F]
- Lubambuka Luzolo Ganelon [M]
- Lutiaku Lubambuka Gyvano [M]
- Lutete Mala Octave [M]
- Malemba Zola [M]
- Basilwa Vuvu Mocrano [M]
- Mayala Lubambuka [M]
- Bavedila Mwanda Mermance [M]

Mayamona Béatrice [F]

387

Family Tree: Two Generations of Nsakala and His Siblings

This family tree shows Nsakala, his siblings (yellow background), their spouses, and their children.

TWO GENERATIONS OF NSAKALA AND HIS SIBLINGS

1. Bena Nsakala Ndunga	M

1. Nsakala Joseph	M
2. Binga Souzane	F
3. Bena Diampisa	M
4. Bena Bernadette	F
5. Bena Constance	F
6. Bena Claude	M
7. Bena Jeannette	F
8. Bena Ndaya	F
9. Bena Nzuzi	F
10. Bena Ali	M
11. Bena Marie*	F
12. Swamunu Bena*	F
* Different Mother	

Batunda Tusevo Esther	F

2. Komono Nsakala André	M

1. Lutayi Komono (Mamy)	F
2. Babeki Marie-Jeanne	F
3. Komono André	M
4. Mpitu Victorine	F
5. Komono Samy	M
6. Komono Marceline	F
7. Komono Bena	F
8. Komono Papy	M
9. Batunda Esther Komono	F

Bankadila Nsimba Esther	F

Bakembo	M

1. Lutayi Elisa	F
2. Mandunda Bakembo Pascaline	F
3. Bakembo Chantal	F
4. Bakembo Augustine	F
5. Batunda Esther	F
6. Bakembo Dany	M
7. Kinkela Charles*	M
*Different Father	

3. Munlenvo Luvisa Lessa	F

Mayambula Mputi	M

1. Dianzenza Nsakala*	M
2. Mayambula Nzienda Arthur	M
3. Lutayi Mayambula	F
4. Mayambula Mputi (Maya)	M
5. Bena Mayambula	M
*Different Father	

4. Mena Julienne	F

5. Dessa Nsakala Ngonde	M

1. Metusala Nsakala Samy I	M
2. Dessa Nsakala Samy II	M
3. Lutayi Dessa Lina	F
4. Mantama Dessa Guylin	M
5. Tomba Dessa Sylvie	F
6. Madede Dessa Claudine	F
7. Komono Nsakala Trésor	M
8. Batunda Nsakala Arlette	F
9. Buanga Nsakala Verlene	F

Nkenda Makonko Pauline	F

6. Nsakala ya Nsakala	M

1. R. Munlemvo Mitchell	F
2. Mukiese Nsakala	M

Luzibu Lutete Nsakala	F

Mavambu Nsembani	M

1. Luyindula Nsakala Delings	M
2. Makiadi Bena	M
3. Tunuana André	M
4. Mfukusu Mavambu	F
5. Lusilulu Mavambu	M
6. Pauline Mavambu	F
7. Bilongo Mavambu	M
8. Malayi Mavambu	F
9. Nlandu Mavambu	M
10. Nsenga Mavambu	M

7. Swamunu Makomba	F

Family Tree: Five Generations of Luzibu's and Nsakala's Combined Families

This family tree comprises a combined five-generation representation of Luzibu's and Nsakala's relationships.

The direct-lineage, five-generation combined family tree, in which Luzibu and Nsakala are generation 3, is shown below, and the corresponding English-Kikongo words are provided in the table that follows. The place of birth of each person in the tree is given in parenthesis.

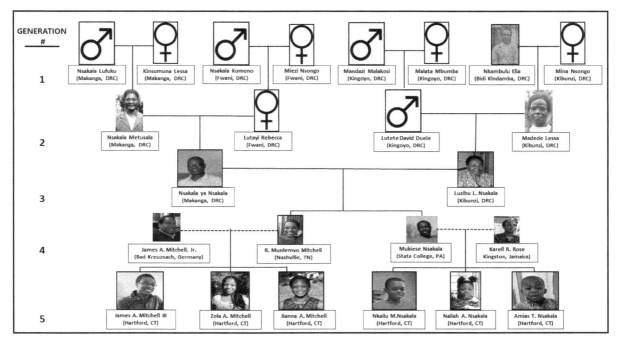

The table below provides a glossary of the terms in English and Kikongo for the five-generation family tree, in which Luzibu and Nsakala are generation 3.

Generation #	English	Kikongo
1	grandparent (grandmother, grandfather)	nkaka/nkoko, yaya (gender neutral)
	grandparents (grandmothers, grandfathers)	zinkaka, bayaya (gender neutral)
2	parent (mother, father)	ngudi evo se (mama, tata)
	parents (mothers, fathers)	zingudi evo mase (bamama, batata)
3	sibling (sister, brother)	mpangi
	siblings (sisters, brothers)	zimpangi
4	child (daughter, son)	mwana (wankento, wabakala)
	children (daughters, sons)	bana (bankento, babakala)
5	grandchild (daughter, son)	ntekolo (wankento, wabakala)
	grandchildren (daughters, sons)	batekolo (babakento, babakala)

Family Correspondence Samples

Communication in the Nsakala family, whether at home or outside the home, is extremely important because it enables each family member to express his or her needs, wants, concerns, and opinions openly and honestly. The following letters and postcards illustrate how Mukiese, Lemvo, and their parents communicated with each other when they were apart. And this modus operandi continues today.

Lemvo wrote this postcard from Newark, Delaware, where she was attending a conference in 1991.

Here, Mukiese is writing to his parents while he was at Rutgers University in Piscataway, New Jersey, in 1993.

1993

Hey Kids,
How goes it? Here's the Claim form and receipt from the Health center. Attach receipt to the form and I'm sure you know what to do with it. Enough of this business... How's Uncle Bena doing? Say hi to everyone for me. Talk to yo soon.

Luzibu wrote this letter to Nsakala from West Hartford while Nsakala was on a business trip in Baden, Switzerland, in 1994.

> 2/9/94
>
> My Love,
>
> I miss my brown "Muffin". When is my Muffin coming home? I'm counting down, two more wks? To be exact 17 dys. Who is counting?
>
> Everyone is fine, besides the frigid weather we are still having. Yesterdi (ay) 2/8/94, we had about 3" and todi (ay) we are expecting 3-4" more snow, plus the freezing rain. By the time it is all over Thursday, we would have had from 6" to 12" in the Hartford area. We wish Mother Nature would lighten up and take it easy on us. The snow plower is working on a OK, so don't worry.
>
> Good news! WHIC prevails over zoning for the project on Flagg Rd. Read the clipping.
>
> I'm glad that you have talked to Claudine and that the folks in Zaire are all doing fine and were happy for their wedding gifts. How about the Mutaguas & Mama Barbu, have you made contact yet?
>
> Well, Muffin, I'm eating well and getting fat ☺, so don't you worry. Just take care of yourself and I will take care of myself.
>
> Anyway Pumpkin, Ich bine cranke nihit. Ich liebe dich zere. Ha! ha! Can you take that?
>
> Take care!
> Peace!
>
> Love,
> Luzibu

Nsakala wrote this postcard to Luzibu while he was on a business trip in Baden in 1994.

> 2/25/94
> Schloss Schartenfels, Baden (Schweiz)
>
> My Love,
> I'm writing this card after packing. Hey! I'll be afloat in less then 24 hrs. I'm just as excited as a kid in a candy store. This is the longest we have been apart since God united us together. Baby, you have no idea how much I missed y'a. Tomorrow... back together - I can't wait. See y'a before this arrives. So.... love
> N y N
>
> LUFTPOST
> PAR AVION VIA AEREA
>
> Ms. Luzibu Nsakala
> 169 Hollywood Ave.
> West Hartford
> CT 06110
> U. S. A.

Addendum

This addendum summarizes Luzibu and Nsakala's achievements, expressed as **curriculum vitae.**

Curriculum Vitae of Luzibu L. Nsakala

Background

Hard working, dedicated, and detail-oriented accounting professional with a broad range of experience in general accounting and fixed assets accounting. Solid background in month-end close process. Ability to meet tight deadlines in fast-paced environment. Team player with excellent work ethic. Computer proficient. Eager to take on new challenges and learn new skills.

Employment

Moore Wallace, Windsor, CT

Staff Accountant   *4/2003–7/2010*

- Prepare accounting related entries to numerous registers, journals, and logs

- Conduct monthly and quarterly account reconciliations to ensure accurate reporting and ledger maintenance

- Analyze financial statements for discrepancies

- Reconcile balance sheet accounts

- Assist in preparation of budgeting process

Ames Department Stores, Rocky Hill, CT

Senior Staff Accountant   *8/95–4/2003*

- Perform general ledger and fixed assets month-end close functions

- Prepare fixed assets mass additions, maintain changes/deletions of retired fixed assets and run monthly depreciation

- Prepare and post journal entries

- Reconcile balance sheet and income statement accounts and provide monthly analysis to senior management

- Assist in preparation of property accounting departmental budgets

Achievements

- Key participant in implementation of Oracle Financials System at Ames Department Stores, Inc. (1999)

- Received Star Performer award for promoting communication among various departments, which resulted in gaining commitments to meet goals at Ames Department Stores, Inc. in 2000

Staff Accountant   *03/93–08/95*

- Assisted in month-end closing process

- Analyzed monthly budget variances

- Provided general accounting service for retail store chain

- Analyzed balance sheet and income statement accounts and troubleshooted store management profit & loss variance inquiries

Account Representative   *02/91–03/93*

- Reviewed and processed pre-petition bankruptcy Claims

- Researched disputes and discrepancies in claims using online database

- Interacted heavily with vendors by telephone and in writing

- Negotiated final settlements for payments and issued reports

The Travelers Insurance Companies, Hartford, CT

Accounting Technician/Accounting Specialist   *03/80–09/87*

- Researched and corrected written premiums errors reported by states

- Researched and reviewed automobile re-insurance policies

- Assisted in preparations of various financial and statistical reports

- Computer Skills

- Microsoft Office (Excel, Word, Access, and Power Point)

- Oracle Financial Systems

- Education

- BS, Accounting, Central Connecticut State University, New Britain, CT, 1990

- Certificate, Accounting, Morse School of Business, Hartford, CT, 1980

Curriculum Vitae of Dr. Nsakala ya Nsakala

Nsakala ya Nsakala: Principal Consulting Engineer, Boiler Combustion Systems, ALSTOM Power, Inc. [2], Windsor, Connecticut, USA

Summary of Qualifications:

Dr. Nsakala has an extensive background in the chemistry and physics of solid fuels combustion and gasification. Building on his doctoral work at Pennsylvania State University, he developed at Combustion Engineering, Inc. (C-E) in-house bench-scale test facilities—drop tube furnace systems 1 and 2, and four-inch fluidized bed combustor—and related methodologies for deriving fundamental kinetic information from solid fuels. Based on this information, Dr. Nsakala led work on the development of tools for predicting the performance of C-E's tangentially fired (T-fired) boilers from the standpoints of unburned carbon and oxides of nitrogen (NOx) emissions.

After C-E was acquired by Asea Brown Boveri (ABB), Dr. Nsakala provided technical support in the development and performance prediction of an ABB/C-E wall-fired burner and led investigations into air toxics emissions from burning coals and refuse-derived fuels in bench-scale, pilot-scale, and commercial-scale furnaces and boilers. Dr. Nsakala spent six months in Baden/Dättwil, Switzerland, in 1996, under the auspices of ABB's Corporate Research Center, to support work on naphtha combustion for ABB gas turbines application. Also, Dr. Nsakala led the T-fired Performance Predictions and Coal Combustion Fundamentals programs, which were multi-year, core-technology efforts focused on the development of analytical and predictive tools to support NOx emissions and carbon loss performance predictions. Results were geared toward helping reduce the financial risks associated with ABB's boiler performance guarantees to its customers.

In the past ten years of his career, Dr. Nsakala devoted much of his time and energy as a team leader on the development of oxy-combustion (i.e., oxygen-fired) technology for the mitigation of greenhouse gas emissions, principally CO_2, from fossil fuel-fired power plants. Dr. Nsakala coauthored numerous technical papers and publications on fuels combustion technology and oxy-combustion technology development for CO_2 capture and storage. He is a coauthor of three inventions on CO_2 capture systems, which were granted by the US Patent Office in 2012 and 2014.

Professional Activities:

- Participant in US Department of Energy (DOE) University Peer Review Meeting at Bethesda, MD, August 21–23, 1990

---

2   Combustion Engineering, Inc. (C-E), which hired Dr. Nsakala in December 1977, was acquired by Asea Brown Boveri (ABB) in November 1989. ABB and ALSTOM formed a fifty-fifty joint-power generation venture in March 1999. In March 2000, ALSTOM acquired all shares of ABB's shares. Hence, at his retirement in July 2010, Dr. Nsakala was an employee of ALSTOM Power, Inc.

- Session cochairman at the Fourth Annual Pittsburgh Coal Conference, September 28–October 2, 1987

- Participant in DOE University Peer Review Meeting in Pittsburgh, PA, April 17–18, 1985

- Session cochairman at the First Pittsburgh Coal Conference and Exhibition, Sept. 17–21, 1984

- Participant in numerous domestic and international conferences on fossil fuels' combustion science and technology, where he was an attendee, an invited speaker, and/or a technical paper presenter

Technical Publications:

- Over twenty publications in various international and domestic journals and proceedings dealing with "Combustion Science and Technology," vis-à-vis fossil fuels combustion fundamentals, and CO_2 capture from fossil-fueled combustion systems

Personal Background:

- Doctor of Philosophy in Fuel Science, Pennsylvania State University, University Park, PA, 1976

- Master of Science in Fuel Science, Pennsylvania State University, University Park, PA, 1973

- Bachelor of Arts in Chemistry, Cum Laude, Fisk University, Nashville, TN, 1969.

Awards:

- Named Distinguished Engineer of the Year in 1995 by the American Society of Mechanical Engineers (ASME), Hartford, Connecticut, section

- Coauthor of two award-winning technical papers:

  - "An Advanced Methodology for Prediction of Carbon Loss in Commercial Pulverized Coal-Fired Boilers," which received a Best Paper Award at the 1986 ASME/IEEE (Institute of Electrical and Electronic Engineers) Joint Power Generation Conference, Fuels and Combustion Technologies Division, Portland, OR, USA.

  - "Controlling Power Plant CO_2 Emissions: A Long-Range View," which received the "Innovation Award" at Power-Gen Europe, Track 3, Brussels, Belgium, 2001

- Coauthor of three patents:

  - Patent No. US 8,230,796 B2, "Air-Fired CO_2 Capture Ready Circulating Fluidized Bed Heat Generation with a Reactor Subsystem." Coinventors: Herbert E. Andrus, Gregory N. Liljedahl, and Nsakala ya Nsakala. June 12, 2012

  - Patent No. US 8,196,532 B2, "Air-Fired CO_2 Capture Ready Circulating Steam Generators." Coinventors: Herbert E. Andrus, Gregory N. Liljedahl, and Nsakala ya Nsakala. July 31, 2012

  - Patent No. US 8,695,514 B2, "Gas Leakage Prediction System." Coinventors: Glen D. Jukkola, Gregory N. Liljedahl, Nsakala ya Nsakala, and Mark Palkes. April 15, 2014

Professional Affiliations:

- Member of American Chemical Society, Division of Fuel Chemistry

- Member of American Society of Mechanical Engineers

Glossary

English-to-Kikongo Glossary

English	Kikongo
aunt, aunts	tata nkento, ba tata nkento
avocado, avocados	voka, mavoka
baptize	botika
bless	sakumuna
break	tolula
brother, brothers	mpangi ya bakala, zimpangi za babakala
canoe, canoes	nlungu, minlungu
cassava, cassavas	yaka, mayaka
child, children	mwana, bana
clay pot, clay pots	nkudu, minkudu
corn, corns	sangu, masangu
daughter, daughters	mwana wa nkento, bana ba bakento
dowry	nkanka
father, fathers	tata, batata; se, mase
fishing net	konde
follow	landa
go	kwenda
God	Nzambi
God Dwells Here	Nzambi Ukundanga Mwamu
grandchild, grandchildren	ntekolo, batekolo
granddaughter, granddaughters	ntekolo wa nkento, batekolo babakento
grandmother, grandmothers; grandfather, grandfathers	yaya, bayaya; nkaka, zinkaka
grandparent, grandparents	nkayi, zinkayi
grandson, grandsons	ntekolo wa bakala, mintekolo mia babakala
hoe, hoes	nsengo, zinsengo
Holy Spirit	Mpeve ya Nlongo
hymn, song	nkunga
hymns, songs	minkunga
jump	dumuka
king, kings	ntinu, mintinu
layperson, laypersons	nkengi, minkengi
mother, mothers	mama, bamama ; ngudi, zingudi
name, names	nkumbu, zinkumbu
paddle, paddles	nkafi, zinkafi
papaya, papayas	kimandi, bimandi
parent, parents	ngudi, zingudi; se, mase
pastor, pastors	mvungi, mimvungi
patience	mvibudulu
sibling, siblings	mpangi, zimpangi
sister, sisters	busi, bibusi
son, sons	mwana wa bakala; bana ba bakala
step	diata
stump, stumps	sinza, bisinza
teacher, teachers	nlongi, minlongi
together, togetherness	kintwadi
twin, first born; twins, first born	nsimba, zi Nsimba
twin, second born; twins, second born	nzuzi
uncle, uncles	ngw'a nkazi, ngudi za nkazi
village, villages	bwala, mabwala

English-to-French Glossary

English	French
big	grand
church	eglise
commission	commission
Course	cours
democracy	démocratie
electoral	lectoral
fruit	fruit
majority	majorité
party	partie
pastor	pasteur
people	peuple
presidential	présidentiel
progress	progrès
reconstruction	réconstruction
refresher	perfectionnement
school	école
social	social
teacher	maître, instituteur
union	syndicat

Bibliography

Anonymous. Nkunga mia Kintwadi. Falköping, Sweden: Imprimé à Gummessons Boktryckeri AB, 1963.

CitizenPath. s.v. "Immigration Forms Made Simple." Accessed December 23, 2018. https://citizenpath.com/immigration-quotes-great-americans.

Cornevin, Robert. *Histoire du Congo (Léopoldville)*. Paris: Editions Berger-Levrault, 1963.

Diyavanga, Didier. "République du Congo, Kongo Central Province." Private Communication, 2018.

Gates, Henry Louis Jr. *Wonders of the African World*. New York: Alfred A. Knopf, 1999.

Google Maps. s.v. "List of natural resource reserves in the DRC today." Accessed December 23, 2018. https://www.google.com/maps/d/viewer?mid=1W34lX4hLPH blDHpb9_FkJ3CTw8c&vpsrc=6&ctz=180&ie=UTF8&msa=0&t=p&ll=2.062911870265734%2C24.300098580766416&spn=19.668423%2C29.838867&z=5&source=embed.

Hochschild, Adam. *King Leopold's Ghost: A History of Greed, Terror, and Hero ism in Colonial Africa*. Boston and New York: Houghton Mifflin Company, 1998.

Image.[b] s.v. "African Farming." Accessed December 24, 2018. https://www.google.com/search?q=african%20farming

Image.[x] s.v. "Amsterdam Schiphol Airport." Accessed May 20, 2017. https://images.app.goo.gl/eKunEmEtKdhGwBfR8

Image.[h] s.v. "Corn Plants." Accessed December 24, 2018. https://images.app.goo.gl/b5PB77Rip fy1p89b9

Image.[p] s.v. "Enhanced Fujita Scale." Accessed December 30, 2018.https://images.app.goo.gl/ZJ9Edw9mwERtJLYb8

Image.[k] s.v. "Empire State Building." Accessed December 30, 2018. https://images.app.goo.gl/hc t4EZRRSPuYXnyj8

Image.[a] s.v. "Fishing_with_cast-net_from_a_boat_near_Kozhikode_Beach." Accessed December 24, 2018. https://images.app.goo.gl/UHWmzqzLEu33pMxp6

Image.[s] s.v. "Hurricane Irma." Accessed March 27, 2020. https://images.app.goo.gl/3ihKxxUoqvzK mawk8

Image.[r] s.v. "Hurricane Matthew Official Track." Accessed December 30, 2018. https://images.app.goo.gl/UU1cpFokesyVuN-Vn9

Image.[e] s.v. "Mangoes." Accessed December 24, 2018. https://media5.picsearch.com/is?pl5zTRp 8FUxbkV7UIvX6uzSGB-UHrQlUVMMn5aLueBg&height=255

Image.[m] s.v. "Obama 2008 Election Night." Accessed December 25, 2018.https://images.app.goo.gl/K7uxSk4GNbkWPccd8

Image.[n] s.v. "Obama 2009 First Inauguration. Accessed December 25, 2018 https://images.app.goo.gl/8rLCi7tDJLZJBCJH8

Image.[o] s.v. "Obama Second inauguration." Accessed March 27, 2020. https://images.app.goo.gl/8c7A7ZalJdb4uNYx9

Image.[u] s.v. "Panama Canal Locks." Accessed March 1, 2020. https://images.app.goo.gl/xuxLnyvim CyixMtY6

Image.[f] s.v. "Papayas." Accessed December 24, 2018. https://images.app.goo.gl/zVnnZmDJWYLdC yLTA

Image.[c] s.v. "Peanuts." Accessed December 24, 2018. https://images.app.goo.gl/i1BXg8Gq3sePD

5PZ7

Image.[q] s.v. "Saffir-Simpson Hurricane Wind Scale." Accessed December 30, 2018. https://images.app.goo.gl/sJ8uPyEjYx-wqq9pH6

Image.[d] s.v. "Safus." Accessed December 24, 2018. https://images.app.goo.gl/e6Y58F3HjbP3sReg7

Image.[j] s.v. "Statue of Liberty." Accessed December 30, 2018. https://images.app.goo.gl/otXkoXSFfMmtVEu47

Image[t]. "Tinker, Andy and Lorrain. "Kruger Park Map." Published by ATP Publishing, 2012. Accessed October 23, 2014.

Image.[i] s.v. "Tudor Hotel." Accessed December 30, 2018. https://images.app.goo.gl/LCA2fyxgH9My hU4t8

Image.[l] s.v. "UN Building New York City." https://images.app.goo.gl/SYdnDPWXiU5v1Qb88

Image.[v] "Viking Skadi Cruise Itinerary (May 6-20, 2017)." Accessed May 6, 2017.

Image.[w] "Viking Skadi Cruise: The Regensburg, Germany, Synagogue." Accessed May 12, 2017.

Image.[g] s.v. "Yucca: The Root Crop That Keeps Giving." Accessed December 24, 2018. https://images.app.goo.gl/EhHigpJAQM6rPQtG7

Independence of the Congo (1959–1960). Accessed December 23, 2018. www.globalblackhistory.com/2016/10/independence-congo-1959-1960.html.

Kloser, Christine. *Get Your Book Done*, 2013. Accessed October 19, 2018. www.GetYourBookDone.com/ebook-discount.

Mann, Sally. *Hold Still: A Memoir with Photographs*. New York, Boston, and London: Little, Brown and Company, 2015.

Map.[d] s.v. "A History of Africa, Chapter 7, Part 2." Accessed December 22, 2018. https://images.app.goo.gl/W4pWVCAWxH-7pqUrg9

Map.[f] s.v. "BelgianCongoProvinces-1933-60.svg." Accessed December 22, 2018. https://images.app.goo.gl/X4Q7qR3iDQ97va-qN7

Map.[c] s.v. "Kimpa Vita Kingdom of the Kongo | Kongo Kingdom map | Kingdom of . . .

pinterest.cl." Accessed December 22, 2018. https://images.app.goo.gl/GWGQ8fdC5sjzweRbA

Map.[g] s.v. "Provinces of the Democratic Republic of the Congo." Accessed December 22, 2018. https://images.app.goo.gl/2G-2JM2LxPRVTA3797

Map.[h] s.v. "The Holy Land Experience." Accessed December 30, 2018. https://images.app.goo.gl/PJ5JphSwmlQjC7HS9

Map.[j] s.v. "South Africa Map," Accessed April 30, 2020 https://images.app.goo.gl/hbAp1cQKdm wSUB7t8

Map.[b] s.v. "Thesis-statement-for-the-history-of-the-republic-on-congo-721975." Accessed December 22, 2018. https://images.app.goo.gl/idjcq95otpezhvvM9

Map.[a] s.v. "US States East of Missippi River." Accessed March 27, 2020. https://images.app.goo.gl/86CfKredD9RMmY3d6

Map.[e] s.v. "Why was the African independence delayed?" Accessed December 22, 2018. https://images.app.goo.gl/4b1w54WLnNafse6K7

Map.[i] s.v. "Zimbabwe." Accessed December 31, 2018. https://images.app.goo.gl/KcQnHBN4zmTZ PVNv6

McKenzie, Camille. *Long Journey to Freedom*. North Charleston, SC: CreateSpace, 2015.

Meredith, Martin. *The Fate of Africa: A History of Fifty Years of Independence*. New York: BBS Public Affairs, 2005.

Nsakala, Luzibu L., and Nsakala ya Nsakala. "A 1,095-Day Diary." Private Communication, 2012.

Nsakala, Nsakala. "An Experimental Study of the Effects of an Electric Filed on Methane/Nitrogen/Oxygen and Methane/Argon/Oxygen Opposed/Jet Diffusion Flames." Master's thesis, Pennsylvania State University, 1973.

Nsakala, Nsakala. "Characteristics of Chars Produced by Pyrolysis Following Rapid Heating of Pulverized Coal." PhD thesis, Pennsylvania State University, 1976.

Palmer, Georg, and Oscar Stenström. *Mavanga Ma Nzambi Mu Kongo: Nsamu wa S.M.F.–M.E.S. 1881–1956*. Brazzaville, the Congo: E.E.M.M. Matadi–E.C.C., 1961.

Sartre, Jean-Paul. *La Pensée Politique de Patrice Lumumba*. Paris: Éditions Présence Africaine, 1963.

Bibliography

Souza, Pete. *Obama: An Intimate Portrait*. New York: Little, Brown and Company, 2017.

The United Methodist Hymnal. Nashville, TN: The United Methodist Publishing House, 1989.

Wikipedia.[j] s.v. "Alliance of Democratic Forces for the Liberation of Congo." Accessed December 26, 2018. https://en.Wikipedia.org/wiki/Alliance_of_Democratic_Forces_for_the_Liberation_of_Congo.

Wikipedia.[d] s.v. "Belin Conference." Accessed December 22, 2018. https://en.Wikipedia.org/wiki/Berlin_Conference.

Wikipedia.[p] s.v. "Boma, Democratic Republic of the Congo." Accessed December 30, 2018. https://en.Wikipedia.org/wiki/Boma,_Democratic_Republic_of_the_Congo.

Wikipedia.[e] s.v. "Decolonisation of Africa." Accessed December 21, 2018. https://en.Wikipedia.org/wiki/Decolonisation_of_Africa.

Wikipedia.[a] s.v. "Democratic Republic of the Congo." Accessed December 23, 2018. https://en.Wikipedia.org/wiki/Democratic_Republic_of_the_Congo.

Wikipedia.[q] s.v. "Inga Dams." Accessed December 31, 2018. https://en.Wikipedia.org/wiki/Inga_dams.

Wikipedia.[i] s.v. "Joseph Kabila." Accessed December 26, 2018. https://en.Wikipedia.org/wiki/Joseph_Kabila.

Wikipedia.[k] s.v. "Laurent-Désiré Kabila." Accessed December 26, 2018. https://en.Wikipedia.org/wiki/Laurent-D%C3%A9sir%C3%A9_Kabila.

Wikipedia.[g] s.v. "Kasa-Vubu." Accessed December 25, 2018. https://en.Wikipedia.org/wiki/Joseph_Kasa-Vubu.

Wikipedia.[n] s.v. "Kongo Central." Accessed June 3, 2018, https://en.Wikipedia.org/wiki/Kongo_Central.

Wikipedia.[b] s.v. "List of Counties and Dependencies by Area." Accessed September 7, 2018. https://en.Wikipedia.org/wiki/List_of_countries_and_dependecies_by_area.

Wikipedia.[c] s.v. "List of Countries by Population (United Nations)." Accessed September 7, 2018. https://en.Wikipedia.org/wiki/List_of_countries_by_population_(United_Nations).

Wikipedia.[o] s.v. "List of Provinces of the Democratic Republic of the Congo." Accessed December 29, 2018. https://en.Wikipedia.org/wiki/List_of_provinces_of_the_Democratic_Republic_of_the_Congo.

Wikipedia.[f] s.v. "Patrice Lumumba." Accessed December 26, 2018. https://en.Wikipedia.org/wiki/Patrice_Lumumba.

Wikipedia.[i] s.v. "Mobutu Sese Seko." Accessed December 25, 2018. https://en.Wikipedia.org/wiki/Mobutu_Sese_Seko.

Wikipedia.[r] s.v. "The Legacy Museum." Accessed October 1, 2018, https://en.Wikipedia.org/wiki/The_Legacy_Museum.

Wikipedia.[s] s.v. "The National Memorial for Peace and Justice." Accessed October 1, 2018. https://en.Wikipedia.org/wiki/The_National_Memorial_for_Peace_and_Justice.

Wikipedia.[m] s.v. "Félix Tshisekedi." Accessed February 22, 2019. https://en.Wikipedia.org/wiki/Joseph_Kabila.

Wikipedia.[h] s.v. "Moïse Tshombe." Accessed December 24, 2018. https://en.Wikipedia.org/wiki/Mo%C3%AFse_Tshombe.

Yahoo. s.v. "Kongo Kingdom." Accessed December 23, 2018. https://images.search.yahoo.com/yhs/search;_ylt=AwrCmnRfuyNcNyAAwNsPxQt.;_ylu=X3oDMTB0N2Noc2llBGNvbG8DYmYxBHB vcwMxB.

About the Authors

Luzibu Nsakala, born on June 13, 1948, was the fourth of six siblings born to Madede Lessa and Lutete David Duele in Kibunzi, a village located in the southwestern part of Congo-Kinshasa. She went to primary school and the post primary École Ménagère in Kibunzi, after which she taught kindergarten in Kibunzi in 1964–1966. In 1964, Luzibu met Nsakala, whom she married in 1966. She immigrated to USA in 1966 to join Nsakala, who was studying at Fisk University in Nashville, Tennessee. Luzibu and Nsakala had their first child, a daughter, R. Munlemvo Nsakala, born in 1967 in Nashville, and their second child, a son, Mukiese Nsakala, born in 1972 at Penn State University, Pennsylvania, where Nsakala was pursuing PhD studies. In 1977, the family moved to Greater Hartford, Connecticut, where Nsakala started work at Combustion Engineering, Inc. in Windsor, Connecticut. In 1980, Luzibu graduated from Morse School of Business, then started work at Travelers Insurance. She would later matriculate full time at Central Connecticut State University, graduating in 1990 with a BS degree in accounting. Luzibu then started work at Ames Department Stores in Rocky Hill, Connecticut as a staff accountant. In 2003, she started work at RR Donnelley Company in Windsor, Connecticut as a staff accountant/cost analyst. Luzibu retired from RR Donnelley in 2010 and moved with her husband to Palm Coast, Florida, where they now live.

Nsakala ya Nsakala, born on November 30, 1941, was the sixth of seven siblings born to Lutayi Rebecca and Nsakala Metusala in Makanga village, near Kibunzi. Nsakala graduated from Kibunzi primary school in 1958, and from Kimpese secondary school in 1964. He taught at Sundi-Lutete High School in 1964–1965. In 1964, Nsakala met Luzibu, whom he married in 1966. He immigrated to the USA in 1965 to study at Fisk University in Nashville, Tennessee, under the auspices of the African Scholarship Program of American Universities (ASPAU), after a three-month intensive study of English and American culture at the School for International Training in Brattleboro, Vermont. Luzibu and Nsakala had their first child, a daughter, R. Munlemvo Nsakala, in 1967, and, in 1969, he graduated from Fisk University with a BA degree in chemistry. In 1969, the family moved to Pennsylvania State University, where their son, Mukiese, was born in 1972. Nsakala graduated from Penn State in 1973 with an MS degree in fuel science and in 1976 with a PhD degree in fuel science. In 1977, the family moved to Greater Hartford, Connecticut, where Nsakala started work at Combustion Engineering, Inc. Nsakala worked with teams that developed innovative solutions for burning fossil fuels efficiently and cleanly for power generation. Nsakala was widely published in prestigious journals and made numerous presentations at science and engineering conferences all over the world. He won numerous awards and coauthored three patents. In 2010, he and his wife retired in Palm Coast, Florida, where they now live.

CPSIA information can be obtained
at www.ICGtesting.com
Printed in the USA
JSHW052041300421
14209JS00001B/1